Economic News

This book tells the story of how the news media can help the inattentive members of the public become better educated and knowledgeable "economic citizens." The authors argue that changes in the economy, journalism, and consumer culture have made economic news more visible, more mainstream, and more accessible. They show how economic news not only affects economic perceptions, but also interest in the economy, knowledge about the economy, and economic voting. Relying on statistical analyses, the book provides a comprehensive and systematic study of the effects of economic news.

Arjen van Dalen is a Professor with Special Responsibilities at the Centre for Journalism at the University of Southern Denmark. He wrote his PhD dissertation on Political Journalism in Comparative Perspective. His research interests are in comparative communication research, in particular the relations between journalists and politicians, as well as economic news. He has published about these topics with Cambridge University Press and in journals such as *Political Communication, International Journal of Press/Politics, Journalism*, and *Public Opinion Quarterly*.

Helle Svensson has a PhD degree in Journalism from the University of Southern Denmark. She wrote her PhD dissertation on the effects of economic news and the role of emotions. Her work is published in journals such as the *European Journal of Communication* and the *International Journal of Communication*. She currently works as Senior Analyst at LEGO.

Antonis Kalogeropoulos is a Postdoctoral Research Fellow at the Reuters Institute for the Study of Journalism, University of Oxford. He has a PhD in Journalism and is the co-author of the Reuters Institute Digital New Report 2017. His work is published in journals such as *Journalism Studies, International Journal of Public Opinion Research*, and *Mass Communication and Society*.

Erik Albæk is a Professor at the Centre for Journalism at the University of Southern Denmark. Professor Albæk has been visiting professor at MIT, Harvard University, Vilnius University (Lithuania), Potsdam University (Germany), and the University of Amsterdam. He has been the chairman of the Danish Social Science Research Council and the Nordic Political Science Association. He has published articles in journals such as *Journalism and Mass Communication Quarterly, Political Communication, Journal of Communication*, and *Party Politics*.

Claes H. de Vreese is a Professor and Chair of Political Communication at the Amsterdam School of Communications Research ASCoR, University of Amsterdam. He has published dozens of articles in international journals on political communication, journalism, media effects, and electoral behaviour and European integration.

Routledge Research in Journalism

Economic News
Informing the Inattentive Audience

Arjen van Dalen
Helle Svensson
Antonis Kalogeropoulos
Erik Albæk
Claes H. de Vreese

Routledge
Taylor & Francis Group

NEW YORK AND LONDON

First published 2019
by Routledge
52 Vanderbilt Avenue, New York, NY 10017

and by Routledge
2 Park Square, Milton Park, Abingdon, Oxon OX14 4RN

First issued in paperback 2020

Routledge is an imprint of the Taylor and Francis Group, an informa business

© 2019 Taylor and Francis

The right of Arjen van Dalen, Helle Svensson, Antonis Kalogeropoulos, Erik Albæk, and Claes H. de Vreese to be identified as authors of this work has been asserted by them in accordance with sections 77 and 78 of the Copyright, Designs and Patents Act 1988.

Library of Congress Cataloging-in-Publication Data
Names: Van Dalen, Arjen, 1980– author. | Svensson, Helle (Helle Mølgård), author. | Kalogeropoulos, Antonis, author. | Albæk, Erik, author. | Vreese, C. H. de (Claes Holger), 1974– author.
Title: Economic news : informing the inattentive audience / Arjen van Dalen, Helle Svensson, Antonis Kalogeropoulos, Erik Albæk, Claes H. de Vreese.
Description: London ; New York : Routledge, 2018. | Series: Routledge research in journalism ; 23 | Includes bibliographical references and index.
Identifiers: LCCN 2018036941 (print) | LCCN 2018044589 (ebook) | ISBN 9780429427558 (ebook master) | ISBN 9781138356429 (hardback : alk. paper) | ISBN 9780429427558 (ebk)
Subjects: LCSH: Economics—Press coverage. | Economics—Public opinion. | Economics—Research. | Mass media—Economic aspects. | Journalism—Economic aspects.
Classification: LCC HB74.2 (ebook) | LCC HB74.2 .V36 2018 (print) | DDC 070.4/4933—dc23
LC record available at https://lccn.loc.gov/2018036941

ISBN 13: 978-0-367-58366-8 (pbk)
ISBN 13: 978-1-138-35642-9 (hbk)

Typeset in Sabon
by Apex CoVantage, LLC

Contents

Illustrations

Figures

Tables

Appendix Tables

Boxes

Preface

How citizens and consumers form impressions of the economy, and the implications of this process, are real issues in today's world. The economic voting literature is huge but pays relatively little attention to how the media report the economy and the media's effects on citizens. Do the media cater to a small elite? Do they help or confuse citizens? And who benefits the most? We believe that these should be core questions for communication scientists, journalism scholars, political scientists, sociologists, economists, and public opinion researchers in today's "economized society."

With these considerations in the back of our minds, Erik Albæk and Claes de Vreese applied to the VELUX Foundation for a grant. We thank VELUX for offering generous support to form a team, collect unique longitudinal data, and thoroughly investigate these questions. We were blessed to have a team of excellent and energetic scholars with complementary skills and interests. Helle Svensson and Antonis Kalogeropoulos completed their PhD dissertations within the project, Arjen van Dalen was a postdoc, and Erik and Claes were principal investigators. The project was marked by a truly collaborative spirit that spun across data collection, PhD dissertations, and articles.

This book presents a novel take on media and the economy. It presents a comprehensive set of arguments and evidence on how the media affect citizens. Specific elements of evidence have been presented at various conferences and workshops, as well as in journals such as *Journalism, International Journal of Communication, European Journal of Communication, International Journal of Public Opinion Research*, and *Public Opinion Quarterly*. In none of these highly specific and specialized venues, however, were we able to articulate the surprising finding of how mainstream media help the inattentive citizen in an economized world. We address that question in the book, which we see not as the end of a research agenda but hopefully as an important step towards a comparative research agenda. We highly value all the input from conference participants, reviewers, editors, and colleagues.

We want to express our gratitude to several persons and institutions who each in their own way made a valuable contribution to the research project in general, and this book in particular. We want to thank TNS Gallup for the good collaboration in the design and data collection of our panel study. We are also grateful to the publishers of *Journalism Studies, International Journal of Communication, European Journal of Communication, International Journal of Public Opinion Research,* and *Public Opinion Quarterly* for granting us permission to draw on our earlier work that is published in their journals: van Dalen, Arjen, de Vreese, Claes, and Albæk, Erik. (2017). Economic news through the magnifying glass. *Journalism Studies,* 18(7): 890–909; Svensson, Helle M., Albæk, Erik, van Dalen, Arjen, and de Vreese, Claes. (2017). Good news in bad news: How negativity enhances economic efficacy. *International Journal of Communication,* 11(17): 1431–1447; Kalogeropoulos, Antonis, Albæk, Erik, de Vreese, Claes, and van Dalen, Arjen. (2015). The predictors of economic sophistication: Media, interpersonal communication and negative economic experiences. *European Journal of Communication,* 30(4): 385–403; Kalogeropoulos, Antonis, de Vreese, Claes, Albæk, Erik, and van Dalen, Arjen. (2017). News priming and the changing economy. *International Journal of Public Opinion Research,* 29(2): 269–290; van Dalen, Arjen, de Vreese, Claes and Albæk, Erik (2017). Mediated uncertainty: The negative impact of uncertainty in economic news on consumer confidence. *Public Opinion Quarterly,* 81(1): 111–130.

Without the help of the following student assistants and coders, this project would not have been possible: Adam Engel, Casper Hougaard Pedersen, Emilie Holkmann Olsen, Erik Jessen, Esben Snoer Iversen, Inaam Nabil Abou-Khadra, Jesper Englund Hansen, Katrine Bisgaard, Katrine Lund-Hansen, Kim Andersen, Kristoffer Havn Clasen, Lea Lyngby Petersen, Louise Matthiesen, Lærke Bonnesen, Mie Foged Filtenborg, Morten Falk, Peter R. Damgaard, Rikke Søholm, Sebastien Blakskjær Vlamynck, Sophie Smitt Sindrup, Søren Olivarius, and Teodor Rørbech.

We wish to thank our colleagues at the Center for Journalism at the University of Southern Denmark and the Amsterdam School of Communication Research, as well as other colleagues who contributed to the project as reviewers or discussants, or in other ways. At the University of Southern Denmark, we want to thank, in particular, Bert Bakker, Jonas Blom, Peter Bro, Erik Gahner Larsen, David Hopmann, Morten Skovsgaard, Christian Elmelund-Præstekær, Jakob Ohme, Kim Andersen, and Camilla Bjarnøe Jensen. The automated content analysis would not have been possible without the help of Zoltán Fazekas. Peter Kjær, Paul Marx and Hajo Boomgaarden gave valuable input at the start of the research project. At later stages Regula Hänggli, Sophie Lecheler, Jörg Matthes, Kasper Møller Hansen, Stuart Soroka, and Mark Boukes provided insightful comments and suggestions. We furthermore want to thank the numerous panel members and discussants with whom we discussed preliminary findings at conferences, and whose discussions and input helped shape the content of this book—in particular, Adam Shehata, Rens Vliegenthart, Alyt Damstra, Claudia Seifert,

Poul Thøis Madsen, and Vaclav Stetka. We likewise thank the anonymous reviewers for their insightful comments on this book manuscript.

We thank Anette Schmidt for her support in managing the grant. Annette Andersen and Tina Guldbrandt Jakobsen provided valuable help in proofreading several chapters of this book. We thank Alicja Kozlowska for carefully copyediting the first draft of this manuscript. Any errors are obviously solely our own responsibility.

On a personal note, Arjen would like to thank Cathrine Kier, Jan Kleinnijenhuis, and Nikki Usher. Their input, comments, and suggestions helped to shape the argument in the book. In addition, Arjen is grateful to the Amsterdam School of Communication Research for hosting him as a visiting scholar in the fall of 2013 and to the Center for Advanced Studies of the Ludwig-Maximilians-Universität in Munich for hosting him as a Visiting Fellow in the summer of 2015. In Munich, Thomas Hanitzsch and his research group, as well as Rasmus Kleis Nielsen and Lars Willnat, provided helpful comments on the early ideas for this book. Finally, Arjen would like to thank Ania, Joke, Jan, Lies, Thijs, Charlotte, and Ania's family in Poznań for their support during the whole period of this project.

This book is accompanied by an online appendix which presents the numbers on which the figures in the book are based, as well as a number of supplementary analyses. The online appendix is available here: https://doi.org/10.5281/zenodo.1435692.

1 Introduction

The economy is extremely complex and endlessly changing. For these reasons, it can be hard for citizens to grasp. Different economic indicators may simultaneously signal that the economy is both improving and worsening. In one day stock markets may boom and employment figures decline. At the same time, national economies are highly co-dependent and reliant on transnational developments and markets. The economy's various dimensions and developments, often pointing in opposing directions, leave citizens with multiple interpretations. In addition, in periods of economic crisis, developments are rapid and characterized by a high degree of uncertainty. In such contexts, even economic experts may have difficulties understanding the causes and consequences of economic booms and bursts (Helleiner, 2011). If the experts themselves struggle to comprehend, explain, and predict the invisible hand's influence over markets and trends in a nation's economy, where does this leave ordinary citizens and their ability to navigate their economic surroundings? In this book we focus on how *economic news* helps citizens to understand the economy and shape their economic perceptions.

We argue that citizens are deeply dependent on information provided by the media to make sense of the economy. Despite criticism that journalists are ill-prepared to cover the economy in all its complexity, that economic news makes people overly pessimistic, and that it does not provide the public with the information it needs (e.g., Hetsroni, Sheaffer, Ben Zion, and Rosenboim, 2014; Starkman, 2014), we show that economic news plays a vital role in making the audience both learn about economic developments and generate accurate economic perceptions. We also show that the audience who benefit the most from exposure to economic news—by having their attention to, and knowledge about, the economy enhanced—are those citizens who are neither intrinsically interested in the economy nor motivated to follow economic news. We call this group "the inattentive audience" (Baum, 2003). We further argue that economic news has increased its capacity to inform and engage citizens because it has become more mainstream; in other words, economic journalists today increasingly use the news values that are used in ordinary journalism—such as identification and domestication—to select, frame, and present news. We show that these content characteristics have surprisingly positive consequences.

Why is it important that citizens learn about economic developments and generate accurate economic perceptions, and why is it important to know how news helps them to achieve these goals? First of all, economic perceptions have a strong influence on economic developments. Economic perceptions predict future spending (Dunn and Mirzaie, 2006; Nguyen and Claus, 2013; Van Oest and Franses, 2008). For more than half a century, we have known that citizens change their economic perceptions simultaneously, which causes recessions or booms in the economy (Katona, 1960). Second, knowledge about economic developments and the state of the national economy are essential for democratic citizenship. Economic perceptions affect attribution of political responsibility and trust in political institutions. They strongly influence citizens' evaluations of politicians (MacKuen, Erikson, and Stimson, 1992), and they affect election outcomes. Since the end of the Cold War world, economic performance, according to some, has gained an even stronger role in national politics (Hetherington, 1996, p. 392). Along with conversations with friends and colleagues as well as personal experiences, media coverage of the economy is the prime source of information for economic perceptions and knowledge. When it comes to perceptions of the national economic climate, the media are the most important source of influence (Mutz, 1998). A vast number of studies have established links between economic news reporting and various outcomes in politics, economic evaluations, and everyday decisions and behaviour (Hester and Gibson, 2003; Sanders and Gavin, 2004). We advance the literature on this topic by studying how the specific content—rather than mere news exposure—affects economic perceptions.

How Economic News Became Mainstream

Over the last decades, economic news has become more readily available, more mainstream, and more accessible.[1] We live in an era where economic news is an almost ubiquitous part of our daily news diet. And because it has become more available, mainstream, and accessible, economic news, just like political news, is increasingly subjected to media news values such as identification and negativity (Kjær and Langer, 2005). In 1973, the assistant managing editor of the *Washington Post*, Richard Harwood, acknowledged that business and economics received less space in his newspaper than sports: "I guess it is because we think sports is more interesting to readers than business and economics. I know it is to me" (Welles, 1973). His words illustrate how economic news was covered for a long time: confined to the specialized pages in the back of the newspaper and primarily aimed at an elite audience of people with a professional interest in economics and business.

Over time, economic news has changed significantly. Roush (2006) argues that economic news began to prosper as early as the 1950s. Over the years more and more space has been allocated to the media's business sections. At the same time, and especially since the 1980s, journalists started to pay more attention to how a mainstream audience can be reached with economic information and how broad economic trends can best be made understandable to the general audience by explaining how developments affect their everyday lives. In 2006, Roush (2006, p. 144) observed that "putting economic trends and analysis into context for the average reader is one of the hardest tasks for business journalists to perform, but it is one that has occurred with increasing frequency over the last 15 years." Thus, Harwood may have been right in observing that sports was more interesting to readers than business and economics. But part of the reason may have been that the media back then were less able to convey business and economics to their audience in an interesting manner.

The mainstreaming of economic coverage dovetails with the mediatization of politics and changes in political news over the same period of time (Brants and Van Praag, 2006; Strömbäck, 2008). Until the 1960s, political news, particularly in the democratic corporatist countries of northern Europe, was covered according to a political logic: politicians set the agenda and journalists covered what politicians had to say in a respectful and sacerdotal tone. Over time, coverage of political news changed as the media became more and more professional and autonomous. Now, political coverage followed a media logic: decisions on what to cover and how to cover it were based on news values, and audience interest was catered to. Adherence to media logic affected the way political news was covered, which included more critical reporting, more human-interest framing, and more strategy framing.

What explains the mainstreaming of economic news—that is, that the media today provide economic news to a broad audience in regular news sections rather than address a specialized audience in special news sections, and that journalists nowadays apply ordinary news values when covering the economy? Broadly, three sources of change can be identified. First, journalism has changed. Over time, journalism has become more autonomous and professional, which is evident from journalists' increasing levels of education, the rise of professional journalism schools, the implementation of journalistic codes, and the development of strong journalistic professional cultures. This trend took off in the 1970s and was largely inspired by American developments, most noticeably the Watergate scandal. Kjær and Langer (2005, p. 215) argue that this trend could also be observed in business coverage, in which journalists likewise took a more autonomous stance. Since then, economic coverage has increasingly been produced by specialist reporters rather than generalists. Moreover, the increasing commercialization of the media business has also affected the shift in economic news. One strategic response to growing competition on the news market and declining readership numbers has been to produce economic news that attracts a broad audience.

Second, the economy has become more important. Its increasing importance is observable in two ways. First, corporations have become ever larger. Indeed, in the globalized economy they have at times become as important or powerful as the states that they are dealing with. Now, extremely powerful economic actors operate worldwide, some with larger economies of scale than whole countries, ranging from Royal Dutch Shell to Toyota and Microsoft. Second, economic logic has spread through news domains. Blumler and Kavanagh (1999, p. 210) speak of *economization*, defined as the "increasing influence of economic factors and values on the political agenda and other areas of society, including culture, arts and sports." Economic considerations have become fundamental to all aspects of life. Consequently, previously autonomous sectors, like education and health care, are increasingly managed on the basis of economic criteria, monetary incentives, and business logic.

Third, the audience has changed, and the market for economic news has grown. The increasing centrality of the economy in human lives, partly due to ever-increasing household incomes, has meant that information on housing markets, pensions, stock markets, and pension schemes has become relevant to an expanding proportion of the audience. Furthermore, as noted by several scholars, previous distinctions between private, public, and commercial spheres are becoming blurred (Bauman, 2000). For example, consumption patterns can be a way of expressing both citizenship and political preferences. Eide and Knight (1999) also observed these changes in journalism. In line with the blurring of previously distinct spheres, newspapers and other journalistic genres have developed and become more mixed and inclusive—for instance, by offering more information that is immediately relevant and useful to the audience in their everyday lives—and view service journalism as part of this trend. For example, journalists may advise the audience on how to deal with money problems or what to consider when buying a house.

Since the 1970s, these forces have gradually led to a change in the style of economic news. The Great Recession of the late 2000s and early 2010s (Kriesi and Pappas, 2015), which affected economies worldwide, has further sped up the mainstreaming of economic news. Media business has come under increased pressure from decreasing profit margins and advertising income. These constraints have forced journalists to cater more to the tastes and preferences of the mass audience. In addition, the journalistic profession has been heavily criticized for taking the perspective of business insiders and for being too close to the economic experts and professionals that journalists are supposed to cover critically. This criticism has led to a wave of self-reflection within the journalistic profession about how best to serve the public (Kier and van Dalen, 2014).

Similar criticism about economic and business coverage has been observed in the aftermaths of previous economic crises; once the economy improves, however, it often transpires that little has changed. Roush (2006, p. 232) observed that business reporters broadened their perspective and distanced themselves from the inside world of banking after a speculative bubble in the Internet sector burst in the early 2000s (the so-called dot-com bubble). But critics have argued that this critical outsider perspective disappeared again during the 2003–2007 economic boom (Starkman, 2014).

Nonetheless, the Great Recession has apparently served as a true critical juncture with a longer lasting impact on how economic journalists see their role and do their work—similar to the effects of the Watergate scandal on investigative reporting and the Vietnam War on foreign war reporting. For the reasons described, criticism of economic coverage was much more visible during the Great Recession than earlier financial crises. In fact, a massive wave of criticism aimed at press conduct was evident in public and scholarly debate (e.g., Kier and van Dalen, 2014; Tambini, 2010). This severe criticism coincided with conditions that were perfect for a change away from elite-oriented, passive economic journalism towards more proactive and audience-oriented reporting. Based on a historical analysis, Feldstein has identified two prerequisite conditions for a surge in critical reporting: an increase in demand from the public and an increase in media supply. Both these conditions were present for economic news during the Great Recession. The crisis, starting in 2007, was longer and more severe than other economic crises in recent history. Its strong impact on people's lives created a new audience for economic news and an increase in demand for business news aimed at non-business insiders. This growing demand occurred at a time when new technologies and a need to find new sources of income led to a sharp increase in the supply of economic news (Kjær and Langer, 2005). From the late 1990s, the mass media prioritized economic news more, creating special business sections in newspapers, business magazines on television, and news economic blogs and economic news portals online. At the same time, new specialized economic and business news outlets entered the market (Kjær and Langer, 2005). Increased demand and supply combined with severe criticism provided the perfect breeding ground for economic journalism to revamp itself and to become more meaningful and helpful to the general audience.

Indeed, Kier and van Dalen (2014) report that the style of Danish economic news was significantly different in 2010 than in 2007. Their results point to a further mainstreaming of economic news as a consequence of the recession. News on the dedicated business pages of broadsheet newspapers in 2007 was characterized by a passive dissemination of business plans and future strategies, with few investigative exposés[2] (see Figure 1.1). The degree of proactive, critical economic journalism trebled in 2010. In that year most of the articles on the business pages were initiated by journalists, who took on a more proactive approach. This change in economic reporting led not only to more critical coverage but also to journalism that is more accessible to the general audience and that is written in the interest of the general public rather than business insiders. The share of articles using conflict framing on the business pages of broadsheet newspapers doubled while the share of articles making abstract developments concrete by explaining how individuals are affected by them more than trebled (Figure 1.1).[3] As we will show in this book, such news characteristics help people to better understand important developments (see also Jebril, de Vreese, van Dalen, and Albæk, 2013).

Clearly, the Great Recession was not the only event that led to this transformation in economic journalism; the changes are in line with a trend that had already started decades earlier. We do argue, however, that the Great Recession was an important catalyst in this process.

Combined, the aforementioned developments have led to the following:

- Growing attention to the economy in the news;
- A broadened definition of economic news that goes beyond information about macro-economic developments and the financial section and that gives more attention to individuals' personal economic decisions;
- A changing target audience for economic news, such that the interests and demands of a general rather than a specialist audience have become more central;
- A changing style of economic news, aimed more at informing and engaging the broader audience.

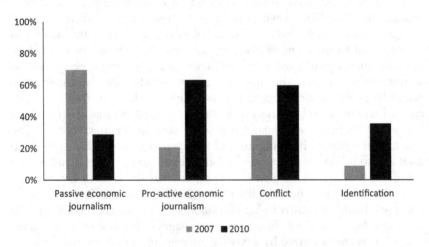

Figure 1.1 Change in economic coverage from 2007 to 2010

Note: Percent of economic news articles. Economic coverage on the business pages of broadsheet newspapers *Berlingske* and *Jyllands Posten*. 2007: *n* = 227, 2010: *n* = 206.

Source: Kier and van Dalen (2014).

In sum, over time economic news has become more like mainstream news, especially since the Great Recession of the late 2000s and early 2010s. While these changes are more pronounced in some countries than in others (see Davis, 2018 for a discussion of the United Kingdom), several studies of Western countries after the start of the Great Recession indeed confirm that economic news resembles mainstream news. Strömbäck, Todal Jenssen, and Aalberg (2012) showed that during 2008 and 2009 economic news was highly visible in Norway, Sweden, Belgium, Netherlands, the United Kingdom, and the United States. In four of these countries economic issues received even more attention than domestic politics. Doyle (2006, p. 443) argues that "for UK newspapers, selection of economic news items involves a constant effort to reflect and capture the concerns of as wide a lay audience as possible." In line with this, proximity, personalization, and negativity were important news values in Dutch economic coverage, in particular in the popular press (Boukes and Vliegenthart, 2017). Content analysis in ten European countries furthermore showed that news values like national relevance and personal consequences played an important role in the coverage of the Euro crisis (Arrese and Vara, 2015). According to this study, over half of the articles about the economy appeared outside the business and finance section.

Mainstreamed Economic News as an Information Source

The changes in economic news have given rise to concerns. Media critics argue that due to its change in style, economic news now focuses more on superficial human-interest and personalized stories and less on investigative accounts and thorough reporting—considered to be one of the reasons why journalists did not see the Great Recession coming (Starkman, 2014). Journalists themselves have blamed the media for keeping the economic downturn alive by focusing on negative economic developments and giving less attention to signs of economic improvement (Sennov, 2014). These critical voices of economic news join a broader chorus of media critics who warn against the negative effects of the mediatization of political information and the "dumbing down" of news (cf. Temple, 2006 and Chapter 3). In the same vein, the changing journalistic style in economic news is criticized for being of no benefit to the audience and for possibly resulting in misperceptions and ill-informed audiences.

In this book we challenge this pessimistic view on the state and effects of economic news. We argue that the mainstreaming of economic news—by adopting modern mediatized news values and reporting styles from the coverage of politics—in actual fact helps people understand the economy. We ask *who*, in particular, might benefit from this mainstreaming (e.g., through an increased interest in, and knowledge of, the economy), as well as *how* and *why*.

An analysis of whether media inform citizens about the economy and help them understand economic affairs requires a clear normative starting point of what type of information citizens require to fulfil their democratic duties. We take the competitive model of democracy as a starting point (Strömbäck, 2005). According to this model of democracy, the main requirement of citizens is to participate in democratic elections. To cast their vote on an informed basis, citizens should be knowledgeable about how society developed over the last years and what role the government played in these developments, and be informed about the most important issues of the day. It is well documented that economic perceptions play an important role in vote decisions (Powell and Whitten, 1993), and that assessments of whether the government is to be held accountable for economic developments affect government support (Nannestad and Paldam, 1995). This shows that economic knowledge, according to the competitive model of democracy, is a clear prerequisite of democratic citizenship.

Establishing that knowledge about the economy is important for democracy is one thing. Another is to determine what *type* of knowledge is required and *how much*. In order to assess whether the media do a good job informing citizens about the economy, it needs to be specified what citizens should learn from their media consumption. Knowledge about the economy can range from knowing the exact level of inflation in a specific month to a deep understanding of how changes in international trade agreements affect the worldwide trade balance. Sanders (2000) argues that in order to make voting decisions the average citizen neither needs to know the exact level of unemployment nor the precise interest rate, but mainly needs to be aware of major developments in the economy and to know in which direction it is heading. Similarly, Schudson (1998) argues that people can function as monitorial rather than fully informed citizens. Instead of continuously following all developments closely, monitorial citizens keep an eye on their environment and look for cues about important developments that require their attention. This monitorial citizen model acknowledges that full, detailed knowledge about all societal developments is not achievable for citizens in today's complex societies.

Building on these observations, we show in this book that mainstreamed economic news helps citizens to fulfil their democratic duties in line with the normative requirements of the competitive model of democracy. We show that economic news helps people to correctly assess economic developments. This *awareness of national economic developments* is a prerequisite of informed voting decisions about whether the current national government should be re-elected. When the economy improves, this is vital information which could lead citizens to re-elect the government. If the economy declined over time, this information could lead citizens to give opposition parties a chance.

To use this information in their voting decisions, citizens need to assess whether responsibility for developments in the national economy should be attributed to the national government. In today's global economy and multilevel government structures, citizens face the question whether they should attribute responsibility for national developments to national governments or to factors outside of the reach of the national government, such as global developments or decisions at the EU level (Hobolt and Tilley, 2014). As we will show, mainstreamed economic news provides cues that affect how citizens *attribute responsibility* for economic developments.

Mainstreamed economic news furthermore triggers interest in the economy and helps audiences gain factual knowledge, thus becoming more sophisticated economically. *Interest in the economy* helps citizens pay attention to economic news when their attention is required. Although factual knowledge about the economy is not a prerequisite to make informed assessments about economic developments, such knowledge can still play an important role in electoral participation. Knowledge about a nation's current economic situation can help voters assess how realistic are the promises made by parties participating in elections. It is well documented that *sophistication* is positively related to political participation broadly (de Vreese and Boomgaarden, 2006), and voting behaviour in particular (MacDonald, Rabinowitz, and Listhaug, 1995).

The complexity of the economy can be overwhelming for voters. Previous research has shown that when they feel that they lack understanding of important political events and information, people may abstain from voting (Kaid, McKinney, and Tedesco, 2007). Thus, in order for citizens to take part in elections and take into account economic developments, it is important that they believe in their own competences not only when it comes to understanding political developments, but also economic developments—so-called *internal economic efficacy*. As we will show, exposure to mainstreamed economic news helps develop internal economic efficacy.

Surprisingly, particularly people who are not intrinsically interested in the economy and are not motivated to follow economic news (the inattentive audience) benefit from mainstreamed economic coverage that is characterized by negativity, consequence framing, domestication, and a human-interest focus.

Mainstreamed economic news informs the inattentive audience through three mechanisms. First, it functions as an *alarm bell* (Zaller, 2003); big headlines and extensive coverage of the economy when economic developments are dramatic or highly relevant raise the awareness of even the inattentive audience. Second, mainstreamed economic news raises the interest and attention of inattentive audiences by using *elaboration-inducing* news-telling techniques (e.g., human-interest framing, focus on negativity), which invite mental elaboration and reflection. Elaboration-inducing elements make the audience process information more extensively, which in turn makes them better informed. Third, the level of domestication of economic coverage provides the audience with *mental shortcuts and heuristics*, which affects whether citizens hold the national government accountable for economic developments.

These conclusions are the results of a unique research project combining content analyses, panel survey data, an experiment, and time-series analysis. These studies were conducted to provide the data needed to assess how mainstreamed economic news informs the inattentive audience. First, we analyse European-wide data from 2014 to show that people across Europe have, in fact, adequate perceptions of their national economic climates and that media exposure helps them form these perceptions. Our in-depth analysis is based on data collected in one country, Denmark. We assess how the Danish media report on the economy, relying on automated content analysis of economic news in three broadsheet newspapers over two decades and on a comprehensive content analysis of economic news of 16 diverse news outlets over a one-year period. Based on the comprehensive content analysis, we assess the presence of human-interest framing, negativity, consequence framing, and domestication in economic news. Additionally, we study the *effects* of mainstreamed economic news on citizens' economic perceptions, evaluations, and political behaviour using a four-wave panel survey design, experiments, and time-series analysis. All information about the methods, measures, and data collection can be found in the Methodological Appendix to this book.

Collectively, these methods allow us to make strong causal claims, which cross-section data do not allow. In the analyses special attention is given to how effects are moderated by characteristics of the receiver (in particular, economic interest), allowing us to trace differences at the individual level and not just media effects across the board. This combination of methods provides a unique resource to link economic developments, media content, and effects at both the macro and the micro levels. The design allows us to link the effects of media exposure with specific content characteristics and to find out which mechanisms drive the effects.

Structure of the Book

The book proceeds as follows. Chapter 2 gets the ball rolling by presenting how accurately people perceive developments in the general economic climate. Despite the economy's extreme complexity, we show that citizens generally have a good perception of the direction in which the economy is heading. This applies not only to the general population but also to people who lack interest in economic news (the so-called inattentive audience). We furthermore show that media exposure is an important predictor of these correct perceptions. We test our findings in 28 countries and show that these results hold cross-nationally. This chapter provides the basis for our argument and it challenges common criticisms about the media's distorting role in forming people's economic perceptions. We show that people's perceptions of general economic developments are surprisingly accurate overall and that people learn about the economy from the media.

In Chapter 3 we lay out our argument that mainstreamed economic news helps inattentive audiences, in particular, to make sense of economic developments. Combining insights from debates about information processing, inattentive audiences, and monitorial citizens, we elaborate on the three mechanisms by which mainstreamed economic news informs people who are not intrinsically interested in economic news. Central are five key aspects of mainstreamed media coverage: visibility, negativity, human interest, consequence framing, and domestication. A content analysis of economic news over two decades and a comprehensive study of economic news in 16 news outlets show the presence of these content features in economic news. This chapter sets the scene for the subsequent chapters, where we show how these content characteristics influence citizens' perceptions and understanding of the economy.

The subsequent chapters present evidence that mainstreamed economic news helps inform the inattentive audience. In the different empirical chapters, we address each of the three central mechanisms. Chapter 4 uses time-series analysis on the first mechanism, the alarm bell function of economic news, showing that extensive negative economic coverage alerts the inattentive audience when it really matters—during economic downturns and especially in times of prolonged recession. Further, this heightened media attention helps the audience correctly perceive economic developments.

Chapters 5, 6, and 7 turn the focus to the individual level. They show that elaboration-inducing elements of economic news make the inattentive audience more interested, more economically efficacious, and more sophisticated by providing content that engages them in news elaboration. Chapter 5 shows that human-interest framing makes people relate the news more to their own lives, which makes them more interested in economic developments. Chapter 6 shows that negative news makes people pay more attention to economic news, which in turn improves their internal economic efficacy (i.e., the belief that one is capable of understanding economic information and making economic evaluations and decisions). Chapter 7, in turn, shows how exposure to economic news featuring consequence framing leads to higher levels of sophistication. In each of these chapters, we explore who benefits the most from these elaboration-inducing elements in economic news, and we show it to be people with low motivational interest, in particular.

In Chapter 8 we turn the focus to mainstreamed economic news as a provider of cues and mental shortcuts as we explore the role of economic news in economic voting. The domestication of economic news is central. Media make global developments relevant to domestic audiences by connecting the coverage to national actors and discussing the impact on home audiences. We argue that such domesticated coverage makes people associate the economy with national (political) actors. Results of the panel study and an experiment show that exposure to domesticated news leads to the attribution of responsibility to national actors. Media exposure affects attribution of responsibility, particularly in people with low levels of economic interest.

Table 1.1 gives an overview of how the empirical Chapters 4 to 8 support our overall argument. It shows which mechanisms are central in each of the chapters and which characteristics of mainstreamed economic news help the audience understand the economy in the broadest sense. The arguments will be further developed in each chapter.

While Chapters 4 to 8 show that mainstreamed economic news helps inform the inattentive audience, in Chapters 9 and 10 we explore the effects of economic news beyond understanding, showing that economic news affects government approval and consumer expectations. These two chapters underline the relevance of economic news by emphasizing that it has real-world consequences. In Chapter 9 we show that economic news affects how citizens evaluate the way the government handles the economy, which in turn influences overall approval of the government. In Chapter 10 we study the impact of uncertainty in economic news and argue that the mainstreaming of economic news is accompanied by more uncertainty in economic coverage. We show that news stating uncertainty about where the economy is heading lowers consumer confidence. These findings add a cautious note to our story, showing that mainstreamed economic news may also have negative side effects.

Chapter 11 is the final chapter and presents the book's main conclusions. First of all, it summarizes the evidence of the empirical analysis and gives an overview of how the influence of news on economic perceptions is moderated by interest in the economy. We conclude that particularly people with low interest in the economy benefit the most from mainstreamed economic

Table 1.1 Mainstreamed economic news informing the inattentive audience

Mechanism	Characteristic of mainstreamed economic news	Informed about the economy	Chapter
1. Alarm bell	Hyped coverage during crisis (negativity and visibility)	Accurate perceptions of the economic climate	4
2a. Induced elaboration	Human interest framing	Interest in the economy	5
2b. Induced elaboration	Negativity	Economic efficacy	6
2c. Induced elaboration	Consequence framing	Economic sophistication	7
3. Heuristics	Domestication	Attribution of responsibility for the economy	8

news. We discuss the boundary conditions of these findings and possible objections, and address the question: how much media exposure is necessary for mainstreamed economic news to have a positive effect? Based on our findings, we draw lessons that are relevant to economic journalists and argue for the need for more than one normative news standard. We conclude that when it comes to learning from the news, it is not necessarily the rich who get richer; when the right content features are present, the poorer get richer. Mainstreamed economic news helps narrow the knowledge gap.

Notes

1 Economic news is defined as "information reported by the news media about the state of the micro- meso- and macro-economy at home or abroad." Economic news is defined by the topic it covers rather than by the section of the newspaper in which it is printed or by the journalists writing it (approach similar to Hetsroni et al., 2014 and Soroka, 2006). The macro-level economy includes topics such as the welfare state, imports and exports, interest rates, and taxation and growth. The meso-level economy refers to news about the business section or corporations. The micro-level economy includes topics such as private consumption, personal economic stories, and mortgage rates.

2 The analysis is based on 432 economic news articles from the business sections of broadsheet newspapers *Berlingske* and *Jyllands-Posten* published before 2007 and after 2010, the start of the Great Recession. Passive economic journalism refers to articles that relay information about the plans and actions of a company or organization, such as a campaign, merger, or advancement into new markets. Proactive economic journalism refers to articles in which the journalists reveal information that is not already publicly available from press releases or reports. Often these articles build on interviews.

3 The study reported in Kier and van Dalen (2014) coded for news stories with conflict (articles that report about conflict and disagreement between persons or interests) and news stories that provide identification (articles that are made relevant to the audience by illustrating developments with reference to their impact on individuals).

2 A Baseline Understanding of the Economy

What do people know about the economy? As we shall see in this chapter, the economy is a complex issue that can be hard for people to grasp; indeed, several studies have shown that people often have limited knowledge about economic fundamentals. On the one hand, when asked about levels of unemployment or interest rates, people often get them wrong. On the other hand, they have a good sense of economic *trends*, which, as we will argue, provides a good baseline understanding of the economy. In this chapter we show that the population at large has a good perception of macro-economic developments. This case holds even for those with limited interest in the economy. We show that media exposure helps people form these correct perceptions.

These results are observed across Europe, in an aggregate-level analysis over a 16-year period in Denmark, and in an in-depth analysis of economic perceptions during a period of economic change in Denmark. We use the year 2013 as the focal point of the in-depth analysis because that year saw a change in the economic situation; after years of economic downturn during the Great Recession, the economy started to improve in the middle of 2013.

Being extremely complex, the national economy is generally seen as a difficult issue for citizens to understand. Research has highlighted the increasing complexity of economic measures, which the media must refer to in order to explain economic developments such as financial crises (Manning, 2013; Tambini, 2010). Political science literature distinguishes between easy and hard issues (Johnston and Wronski, 2015; Wojcieszak, 2014). Regarding easy issues, people can form opinions and preferences intuitively without having to rely on specific, highly technical knowledge. Examples of such issues are abortion or same-sex marriage—issues for which people can rely on predispositions or moral compasses without integrating hard facts per se. In contrast, hard issues are topics that are technical and more complex in nature. The economy is one such issue. Due to its complexity, citizens prefer to leave decision making about the economy to politicians rather than to the public at large (Wojcieszak, 2014). This inclination suggests that people are well aware of this issue's complexity.

One feature of hard issues is that, in general, they are unobtrusive, meaning that they are hard to observe in everyday life. Foreign politics is a commonly used example of an unobtrusive issue. In contrast to most hard issues, however, the economy *does* have a direct impact on people's lives, and changes in economic conditions can be inferred directly from gas prices or increased difficulties in getting a job. Haller and Norpoth (1997) therefore refer to the economy as a "doorstep issue."

Still, the economy's obtrusive nature does not necessarily make it easier for people to assess the state of the macro-economy. Personal experience has a strong influence on assessments of one's own personal economic situation (egotropic economic perceptions) but not necessarily of the country's situation at large (sociotropic perceptions) (Mutz, 1992). Although they are related, egotropic perceptions are not always in sync with sociotropic perceptions (Kinder and Kiewiet, 1979). Psychological biases might lead to a gap between assessments of one's personal situation and the situation of the population at large. Attribution bias, for example, may cause people to think that others are more affected by negative economic developments than they themselves are (Weiner, 1986).

Both the economy's complexity and the misleading influence of personal experiences on assessments of the national economy raise the question: how much do people actually know about the economy? It is well known that people's factual knowledge about similar topics, such as politics and public affairs, is limited (Delli Carpini and Keeter, 1997). Likewise, when it comes to knowledge about economic statistics, findings have been pessimistic. Blendon et al. (1997) observe a gap between the public's and the economists' views of the economy. Walstad and Rebeck (2002) found large deficits in factual economic knowledge among the population, confirming an earlier study by Walstad (1997). Wobker, Lehmann-Waffenschmidt, Kenning, and Gigerenzer (2012) found a considerable lack of basic knowledge about economic concepts, facts, and causal relations among German citizens. Lusardi (2008) and Lusardi and Mitchell (2011) examined factual knowledge about financial institutions and banking processes, and concluded that financial literacy is low. Curtin (2009) also demonstrated a lack of knowledge about economic statistics, even in 2009, in the middle of the Great Recession. He summarized several possible explanations:

> The lack of knowledge has been attributed to the limitations in the cognitive capacity of the public, the challenging technical and mathematical jargon used in official announcements, the high costs and low benefits from updating knowledge of official economic statistics, the absence of a perceived importance of official statistics to people's everyday lives, and even the lack of credibility of the nation's statistical agencies.
>
> (Curtin, 2009, p. 1)

However, as we argued in Chapter 1, these findings are not necessarily problematic. In order to make informed voting decisions, citizens need, according to Sanders (2000), to be aware only of major *developments*. Curtin (2009) claims that being continuously up to date about unemployment figures or price indexes would require too much mental effort compared to the benefits such knowledge provides in everyday life. Outside the economic domain, Barabas and Jerit (2005) likewise argue that surveillance knowledge about recent developments is more important than factual information. Thus, one may argue that correct assessments of economic developments and trends should serve as a baseline understanding of the economy. Before turning to the media's role in shaping these perceptions, we first assess how aware citizens are of economic trends.

Assessing the Economy

Following the argument by Sanders (2000) and Curtin (2009), that correct assessments of economic developments and trends should serve as a baseline understanding of the economy, we analyse how closely perceptions of economic developments are related to actual economic trends.

One common question in standard consumer sentiment analysis makes this assessment possible. Surveys of consumer sentiment regularly include a so-called retrospective sociotropic question that asks respondents whether they believe that the general economic situation in their country has improved or worsened over the last 12 months. This question is appropriate for assessing whether people have baseline knowledge of the economy because it asks about trends over a concrete period and about developments in the national economy rather than people's own economic situations. To get a sense of how accurate the perceptions of economic trends are, the answers can be compared to the actual developments of a nation's economic situation over the preceding 12 months. Gross domestic product (GDP) numbers are widely available and are a commonly accepted indicator of a nation's economic situation. By comparing the answers (to the retrospective sociotropic consumer sentiment question) to changes in GDP over the last year, we assess how closely perceptions of economic trends are related to actual developments.

A comparison of economic perceptions and actual developments in 28 European countries in 2014 offers an interesting test for whether people have a baseline understanding of the economy. The year 2014 marked a period of economic improvement across Europe after the start of the Great Recession. The economies across Europe improved at different paces, however, according to Eurostat (see Figure 2.1).[1] Change in GDP was over 3 percent in the Baltic states and in several central European countries. In the United Kingdom and Ireland, the economy likewise significantly improved. Although it also improved in northern European countries—such as Germany, the Netherlands, and Sweden—the change in GDP was below 2 percent. In four countries, change in GDP was negative: Cyprus, Finland, Croatia, and Italy. Thus, cross-national variation in economic developments across Europe in 2014 was substantial. If people are aware of economic developments, their understanding should be reflected in cross-national differences in retrospective sociotropic economic perceptions.

To test this possibility, we analyse the general sense of economic developments in different European countries using the 2014 European Election Study (EES; Schmitt, Hobolt, Popa, and Teperoglou, 2015). The 2014 EES was conducted in 28 European countries about the time of the European parliamentary elections. A representative sample of each population answered the same questions, including a question about the perceived change in the general economic situation in the country in question over the past 12 months. In Figure 2.1 we show the mean score for each country on a scale from 1 (got a lot worse) to 5 (got a lot better). These scores are compared to the real change in GDP as measured by Eurostat.

Across countries, country ranking based on economic perception scores closely resembles the ranking based on change in GDP. The countries where people are most negative about economic developments (Croatia and Italy)

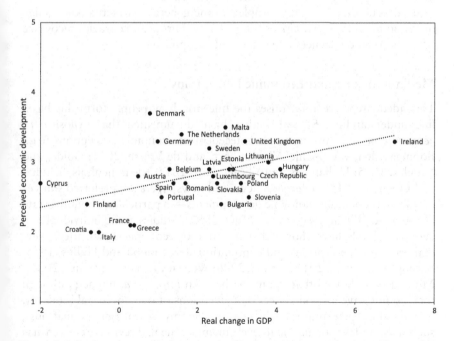

Figure 2.1 Real and perceived economic developments over the last 12 months across Europe

Note: Perceived economic development on scale from 1 (a lot worse) to 5 (a lot better).

Source: 2014 European Election Study (Schmitt et al., 2015).

are two of the four countries where the economy declined. In the four countries where the economy declined, perceptions are significantly lower than in the other countries. The countries with the most economic growth (Hungary, Ireland, Lithuania, and the United Kingdom) are among those where people are most positive about economic developments.

It must be noted that some countries do not match the pattern. Poles are somewhat more negative than can be justified by real economic developments; the average Polish perception is close to the middle position on the scale, even though GDP grew around 3 percent over the previous year. People in the northern European countries of Belgium, Denmark, Germany, the Netherlands, and Sweden are significantly more positive about the economy than the Poles. This result might be the consequence of the Great Recession, which hit harder in northern Europe than in Poland. In fact, Poland was the only European country to avoid economic decline during the Great Recession, so Poles might have been less aware of positive economic developments than northern Europeans.

Despite these few countries that do not fit the overall pattern, at the country level the relation between the economic situation and perceived economic change is strong. The correlation of real change in GDP and perceived economic developments across countries is strong and robust ($r = .46, p < .01$).[2] Thus, despite the economy's complexity and general low factual knowledge of economic indicators, citizens in different European countries recognize cross-national differences in economic developments.

Media Exposure and Economic Perceptions

This adequate correlation raises the question how people form this baseline understanding. Several studies have documented that *exposure to economic news* is an important antecedent of economic perceptions (e.g., Boomgaarden, van Spanje, Vliegenthart, and de Vreese, 2011; Goidel and Langley, 1995; Hollanders and Vliegenthart, 2011; Kleinnijenhuis, Schultz, and Oegema, 2015). Television news and newspapers are preferred sources of information about economic developments—in particular, about the state of the national macro-economy (Mutz, 1992). Studies at the individual and aggregate levels have shown that the tone of economic news affects several economic perceptions and expectations (e.g., Blood and Philips, 1995; Boomgaarden et al., 2011; Soroka, 2006; Wu, McCracken, and Saito, 2004). Mutz (1998) showed that the media have an *impersonal* impact; although they do not have a strong effect on perceptions of one's personal economy, they do affect perceptions of the macro-economy (sociotropic evaluations), such as state-level or national-level unemployment. Previous research has shown no or limited media effects on confidence about one's own economic situation (egotropic evaluations; Boomgaarden et al., 2011).

Most of these studies have explored whether exposure to economic news affects optimism and pessimism about the economy without assessing whether these perceptions are justified given the economic climate. However, critiques of how the media cover the economy lead to pessimistic expectations about the contribution of economic news exposure to correct perceptions of economic developments. The media's attention to the economy fluctuates heavily and primarily focuses on economic developments when they are negative while giving less attention to positive developments. This bias has led to negative views of how economic news influences economic perceptions. The argument goes that by distorting people's perceptions of the economic climate and making them overly pessimistic, the media contribute to keeping the economy down (e.g., Sennov, 2014). If this criticism is justified, media exposure should be related to overtly pessimistic economic assessments, and in the economic climate of 2014, media exposure would make correct perception of positive economic developments less likely across Europe.

We further analyse the 2014 EES data to test whether media exposure actually leads to a distorted picture of economic trends. We operationalize correct perception of economic trends based on the retrospective sociotropic consumer sentiment question introduced earlier. In Croatia, Cyprus, Finland, and Italy—which all suffered economic downslides—people who answered that the economy declined are coded as correctly perceiving economic trends. In countries where GDP grew over the preceding year, people who answered that the economy improved are also coded as correctly perceiving economic trends. We then tested for a positive relation between traditional media consumption (television and newspapers)[3] and correct perception of economic developments after controlling for age, gender, position on the economic staircase, and support for the government.

The results show that, contrary to the pessimistic view of the media's role in forming economic perceptions, following the news helps people to correctly perceive economic developments.[4] This association is, first of all, true for countries where the economy decreased (Table 2.1); here the more one is exposed to television and newspapers, the more likely one is to correctly perceive economic decline. Still, this result is not yet proof that media exposure helps people to correctly perceive the economy. It may simply show that media exposure makes people more pessimistic, as media critics claim. Looking at the countries where the economy improves, however, we see that media exposure does not necessarily make people pessimistic. In a positive economic climate, media exposure helps people to correctly perceive economic growth.[5] This result becomes even more remarkable when the effect of media exposure is compared to the effect of the other variables in the model. For the variables gender, position on the economic staircase, and whether one is a government supporter, the direction of the effects on correct perceptions is different in countries where the economy improved from countries where the economy declined. While demographic background and political leaning are consistently related to more pessimistic or optimistic perceptions of the economy, the media effect depends on the economic

Table 2.1 Explaining correct perception of economic development over last 12 months across Europe

	Model 1			Model 2			Model 3		
	Countries where economy declined			Countries where economy improved			All countries combined		
	B	SE B	Exp(B)	B	SE B	Exp(B)	B	SE B	Exp(B)
Constant	0.11	0.19	1.11	-1.34	0.08***	0.26	-1.42	0.07***	0.24
Age	0.003	0.002	1.003	-0.01	0.001	1.00	-0.004	0.001***	0.99
Male	0.20	0.07**	1.22	-0.27	0.03***	0.76	-0.20	0.03***	0.81
Low on economic staircase	0.24	0.10*	1.27	-0.56	0.04***	0.57	-0.42	0.04***	0.66
High on economic staircase	-0.17	0.09*	0.84	0.47	0.03***	1.60	0.38	0.03***	1.46
Government supporter	-1.05	0.08***	0.35	1.28	0.03***	3.61	0.98	0.03***	2.65
News exposure[1]	0.09	0.03**	1.09	0.13	0.01***	1.14	0.15	0.01***	1.16
Countries where economy declined							2.52	0.13***	12.37
Countries where economy declined × media use							-0.21	0.03***	0.81
Nagelkerke R^2	.08			.17			.18		
N	3,602			24,913			28,515		
Percentage correctly classified	66.3			72.6			70.5		

Note: ***$p < .001$, **$p < .01$, *$p < .05$, #$p < .1$ (two-sided t-tests). [1]News exposure = television and newspaper exposure combined.

Source: 2014 European Election Study (Schmitt et al., 2015).

climate. When the economy improves, media exposure is correctly related to a more optimistic outlook; when the economy declines, people who are more exposed to the media are, correctly, more negative.

The media's constructive role in shaping economic perceptions is evident in one final result, which we attain when countries with economic growth and countries with economic decline are included in one statistical model. Here we find a negative interaction between a decreasing economy and media exposure, meaning that media exposure has a weaker effect when the economy declines. This finding speaks against the criticism that overtly negative media coverage makes people overtly pessimistic; instead, media effect on correct perception is strongest when the economy improves.

Figure 2.2 shows the relation between media exposure and correct economic perceptions for each country individually. Although the relation is not significant in all of the countries, in most of them the results point in the expected direction. In countries like Germany, Greece, Hungary, and the United Kingdom, media exposure helps people to correctly perceive economic developments. We observe this trend not only in countries where the economy improved but also in Croatia and Finland—two

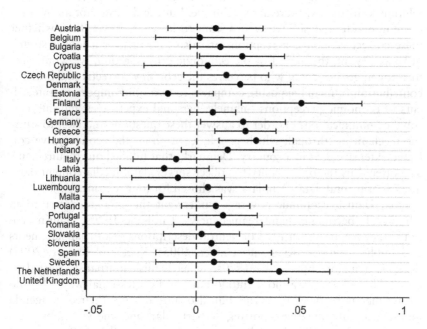

Figure 2.2 Effect of news exposure[1] on correct perception of economic development over last 12 months across Europe

Note: Standardized coefficients with 95% confidence intervals. [1]News exposure = television and newspaper exposure combined.

Source: 2014 European Election Study (Schmitt et al., 2015).

of the four countries where the economy declined. This effect is mostly driven by newspaper exposure, but in several countries also by television exposure. In only one country was exposure to the mass media negatively related to correct perceptions of the state of the economy; in Italy more newspaper exposure leads to more optimistic judgements about the economy than real economic developments justify. The partisan nature of the Italian media system (Gnisci, van Dalen, and Di Conza, 2014) or specific economic developments around the time of the survey might have played a role.

In sum, Italy aside, the comparative analysis supplies evidence that across Europe exposure to the media, if anything, *helps* the audience develop correct perceptions about the economy. This result is true both in countries where the economy is declining and in countries where it is improving. Media exposure is an even better predictor of whether people correctly perceive economic trends than "traditional" predictors of factual knowledge like gender, age, or position on the economic staircase.

Case Selection

The EES 2014 allowed for a broad look at economic perceptions and their relation to media exposure across Europe, but the data do not allow for a more in-depth analysis. We would want to know, however, first, whether these correct economic perceptions are also present over a longer stretch of time, beyond the period of the economic crisis. Second, we would like to study in greater detail who perceives the economy correctly and how the contribution of media exposure compares to two other important antecedents of economic perceptions—namely, personal experiences and interpersonal communication. In order to answer these questions and later to study the mechanisms through which people learn about the economy, we collected extensive data in a country (Denmark) that fulfilled our requirements and offered us the opportunity to collect survey data, media content data, and experimental data. Denmark was chosen for four reasons.

First, Danish economic coverage underwent the changes described in Chapter 1, becoming mainstreamed news. Until the 1970s, Danish economic news mainly consisted of neutral descriptions of official statements and public meetings (Kjær and Langer, 2005). Kjær and Langer (2005) describe a major shift in the 1970s, when Danish journalists started to cover the economy in a more autonomous and professional way. They no longer merely reported on events but also started to set their own agenda and increase investigative reporting. In particular, since the 1990s, business news—including news about the macro-economy—has become an integral part of the Danish newspaper agenda and has featured increasingly on the front pages. Kjær and Langer (2005) argue that in business coverage, just as in economic coverage in general, journalists have increasingly taken a more autonomous stance.

Second, Denmark has a diverse media landscape, with a concomitant diversity in the television, newspaper, and online media markets. Television news is provided by both a public broadcaster (DR) and a commercial station (TV2). Newspaper readers can choose between newspapers that have various political leanings and that hold different positions on the broadsheet–tabloid dimension. In addition, Denmark has a specialized business newspaper, *Børsen*. The television channels and newspapers also have online versions. As we shall see in the coming chapters, these different types of outlets have their own reporting styles and special content characteristics. Variety of news content is necessary for our comprehensive analysis, which aims not merely to study the effect of news exposure but also to identify the content characteristics that help people learn about the economy.

Third, the news media are used by much of the Danish population. Danish newspaper readership is lower than in other countries, but although it is declining, it is still high (Albæk, van Dalen, Jebril, and de Vreese, 2014). A Danish public service tradition is to air a lot of news during prime time, which may help expose even uninterested people to news about the economy (Bos, Kruikemeier, and de Vreese, 2016; Curran, Iyengar, Lund, and Salovaara-Moring, 2009). Thus, in Denmark, even people little interested in the economy are generally exposed to a certain degree of economic news. This circumstance makes it possible to study how these groups learn from mainstreamed economic news. Although a small minority, news avoiders are not entirely absent from Danish society. Figure 2.3 shows how news access in Denmark compares to news access in another 26 countries, as reported in the 2016 Reuters Digital News Report. The figures show that news access in Denmark closely resembles news use internationally. Furthermore, interest

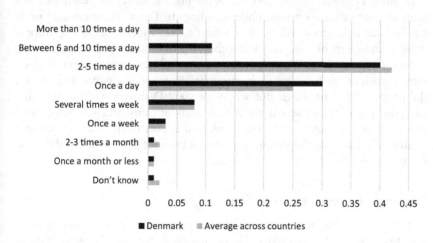

Figure 2.3 News access in Denmark compared to news access in 26 countries

Note: Share of the population.

Source: Reuters Digital News Report 2016 (Newman et al. 2016).

in economic news in Denmark is comparable to countries like Germany, the Netherlands, Spain, Sweden, and the United Kingdom (Newman, Fletcher, Levy, and Kleis Nielsen, 2016). Denmark is therefore a suitable case because news avoidance is uncommon, while news use and economic interest are comparable to various other Western countries. We will return to the generalizability of our findings beyond Denmark in the final chapter of this book.

Fourth, just like other European countries, Denmark experienced economic malaise from 2008. In fact, Denmark was the first European country to enter into recession (Goul Andersen, 2010). Although the economic malaise was not as strong as in other European countries (e.g., Greece and Spain), it took a long time before economic growth reached pre-crisis levels. In our analysis we provide a study of general developments in economic news and of economic perceptions over a 14-year period as well as an in-depth study of one year, 2013, in which the economy changed from decline to growth. A time of economic change provides an interesting context for the study of economic developments, media coverage, and perceptions: first, because the economy is highly visible in this period; and second, because these changes provide interesting variation, which allows for a test of our hypotheses. The year 2013 started with economic decline; GDP in the first quarter was 1 percent lower than in the first quarter of 2012.[6] Thereafter, GDP improved from quarter to quarter. In the second quarter, the economy was still worse than a year earlier (−0.6 percent), but in the third quarter, GDP was only slightly below the level of the year before (−0.2 percent). In the last quarter, the economy started to recover as GDP grew by 0.3 percent compared to a year earlier. This increase reflects broader European developments.

In sum, Denmark is suitable for studying the effect of mainstreamed economic news on economic understanding. In Denmark, economic news has become mainstreamed, media content varies widely, media exposure is diverse and resembles exposure in other Western countries, and economic contexts are changing. These factors provide an interesting context to study individual-level differences in learning from economic news and to test the proposed mechanisms. But while we view Denmark as an interesting case, our presentation here is not a case study of Denmark. We test general theory-driven expectations in this book and expect them to apply to other contexts. In the final chapter, we return to a broader perspective and discuss the boundary conditions of our findings.

Economic Perceptions Over Time

Earlier we saw that across Europe, media exposure helps citizens form correct assessments of developments in the national economy. We now want to investigate this finding in greater detail, examining a longer period of time and comparing different subgroups of the population. We do so by focusing on one country, Denmark. We take a longitudinal perspective and explore how retrospective economic perceptions reflect developments in the real economy between 1996 and 2012. The grey line in Figure 2.4 depicts developments in the national economy based on quarterly GDP data.[7] For each quarter, the graph shows how the economy performed compared to a year earlier. Developments in the Danish economy clearly reflect developments in the world economy, as can be seen from two periods of economic boom and bust. Between January 1999 and June 2000, the economy boomed. This period has come to be known as the dot-com hype. In late 2000, the bubble burst and the economy declined. In 2003, the economy entered several years of economic expansion. This period of sustained growth was followed by a period of economic contraction and stagnation from January 2008 onwards. Although the worst economic decline was over in 2009, economic indicators did not regain pre-2008 levels until the end of 2012.

To investigate how aware the general population was of these economic developments, we observe time-series data collected by the national Statistics Denmark.[8] As in other Western countries, data are collected monthly on how the general population perceives the economic climate. Questions are answered by a random sample of around 1,000 respondents at the start of each month. To assess how aware consumers are of economic developments, we can look at the retrospective sociotropic data. Survey participants

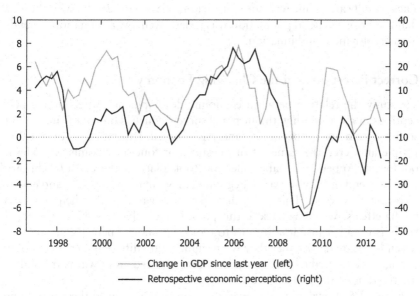

Figure 2.4 Comparing *real* developments in the national economy (grey line) and *perceived* economic developments over the previous 12 months (black line), 1996–2012

Note: The scale for change in GDP can be found on the left. The scale for retrospective sociotropic economic perceptions can be found on the right. Quarterly data.

are posed the following question, which was also used in the 2014 European Election Study: "How do you think the general economic situation in this country has changed over the past 12 months? It has got a lot better; got a little better; stayed the same; got a little worse; got a lot worse; don't know." Answer categories are weighted to calculate the aggregate perception of the population: got a lot better, 100; got a little better, 50; stayed the same, 0; got a little worse, –50; got a lot worse, –100. As can be seen from the black line in Figure 2.4, sociotropic retrospective economic perception data are generally above zero, meaning that people perceive the economy to have grown compared to one year ago. There is also considerable variation; between 1996 and 2012, the data range from –40 to +30.

How well do these economic perceptions reflect economic developments? Because GDP is only measured every quarter, we compare trends in GDP to economic perceptions in the first month of each quarter (Figure 2.4). At the aggregate level, developments in economic perceptions closely mimic changes in the national economy. In some periods the perceived economic development did not reflect the real economic development, but in general, economic perceptions reflect economic developments well. Two statistical analyses support this conclusion. The first is a strong correlation between the two series ($r = .68$, $p < .01$). And the second—despite the small number of cases in the analysis—is a significant effect of real change in GDP on economic perceptions after controlling for previous economic perceptions. These results are in line with the conclusions of Sanders (2000), who showed that the British general population was indeed well aware of national *trends* in unemployment and inflation.

Correct Perceptions of the Changing Economy

We study the relation between economic development and economic perceptions in more depth with our panel survey, which is one of the main data sources upon which this book's analysis is based. During 2013, over 1,000 people answered the same set of questions at four time points (see Methodological Appendix). Data collection took place at the end of February (wave 1), end of May (wave 2), beginning of September (wave 3), and end of November (wave 4). This design has specific advantages that help to assess media effects. We come back to this point in later chapters. Now, the panel study is used because it allows us to look at economic perceptions in more detail by studying whether they were significantly different as the economy changed. As described earlier, the economy showed an upwards trend during the time of the panel survey.

Figure 2.5 shows how our survey respondents perceived these economic developments. We asked respondents how they thought the general economic situation in Denmark had changed over the past 12 months. We show the mean score per survey wave on a scale from 1 (got a lot worse) to 5 (got a lot better). The results show that also during times of changing economic

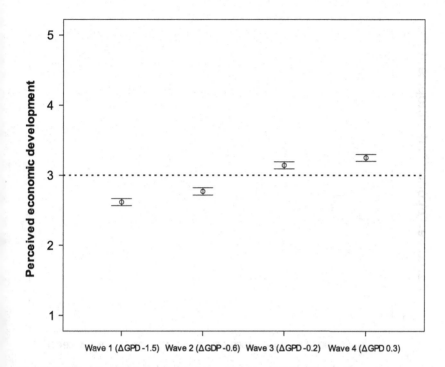

Figure 2.5 Perceived economic development over the last 12 months

Note: Mean score with 95% confidence intervals. Perceived economic development on scale from 1 (a lot worse) to 5 (a lot better).

developments, average perceptions of economic development closely resemble real changes in the economy. As the economy improved, the perceptions likewise became more positive. For each wave the mean score was significantly higher than for the previous wave ($p < .05$). In sum, the panel study confirms the results of the time-series presented earlier. People generally have good baseline knowledge of the economy because they are aware of changes in major macro-economic trends.

Does this result also apply to the inattentive audience—that is, to people who are not intrinsically motivated to follow economic developments? Like the population at large, people with low interest have a good perception of national economic developments (Figure 2.6). We asked respondents to indicate how interested they are in the economy. Those who indicated that they are uninterested or indifferent (neither interested nor uninterested) were defined as people with low interest. This group makes up 23 percent of our respondents.

In the first and second waves of the panel survey, the inattentive audience perceived the economy to have declined compared to a year ago. This perception is in line with real developments in GDP. In wave 3 the economic

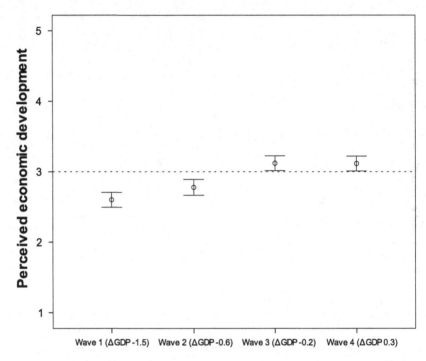

Figure 2.6 Perceived economic development over the last 12 months (inattentive audience)

Note: Mean score with 95% confidence intervals. Perceived economic development on scale from 1 (a lot worse) to 5 (a lot better).

development was deemed significantly better than in waves 1 and 2. The only development that was not picked up by the inattentive portion of the population was the improvement between waves 3 and 4; the scores for the two waves did not differ significantly.

Exposure, Discussion, and Personal Experiences

In the beginning of this chapter we showed that across Europe, media exposure is related to correct assessments of the national economy. However, economic news is not the only relevant source shaping people's economic perceptions. Next to media exposure, interpersonal communication and personal experiences can also be expected to matter for economic perceptions (Mutz, 1992). It is widely accepted that interpersonal communication is related to higher levels of sophistication and participation (e.g., Bennett, Flickinger, and Rhine, 2000; Eveland, 2004; Holbert, Benoit, Hansen, and Wen, 2002). Personal experiences are one of the main predictors of people's personal economic evaluations (Boomgaarden et al., 2011). Likewise, these personal experiences may matter for macro-level perceptions. A study of economic sophistication in the United States showed important gains in the public's awareness of economic statistics between 2007 and 2009—which included time immediately prior to and after the financial crisis of 2007–2008 (Curtin, 2009). In this period many US citizens had direct or indirect negative experiences with the economy.

So how is media exposure related to economic perceptions after controlling for the effects of personal experiences and interpersonal communication? For each of the four waves, logistic regression was used to explain whether respondents correctly perceived economic improvement/deterioration compared to 12 months earlier[9] (Table 2.2). For waves 1, 2, and 3, the correct perception was deterioration in the economy, and for wave 4, improvement. Similar to Albæk et al. (2014), we examine the effect of exposure to five of the most used news sources: broadsheets *Jyllands-Posten* and *Politiken*, tabloid newspaper *Ekstra Bladet*, and the television news of DR and TV2.[10] The effect of exposure is compared to the effect of interpersonal communication about the economy, measured by asking respondents to indicate on a 5-point scale how often they discuss the economy with others.[11] Experiences with the economy were measured by posing four questions that asked whether the respondents themselves, or somebody they knew, had recently had negative experiences with the economy, such as losing a job or struggling to pay bills.[12]

Looking first of all at wave 1, we find that media exposure is related to correct perceptions. The more a person is exposed to the news, the higher the chances that his or her perceptions of economic developments are accurate. The same goes for direct experiences with the economy; the more a person is affected by the economic crisis, the more likely he or she is to correctly perceive the economy's decline.[13] Conversing about the economy with family or friends does not help create a better perception of the economy.

The finding that media exposure and personal experiences with the economy help form correct perceptions of the economy is confirmed in waves 2 and 3. The results also confirm that there need not be a trade-off between learning from the news and learning from personal experience. Mutz (1992) argues that media may help *enhance* the effects of personal experiences on preferences and perceptions about unemployment by exposing people to the similar experiences of others, which helps people realize that being fired or invited to a job interview are all part of a broader societal pattern. In waves 2 and 3, interpersonal communication was not significantly related to correct economic perceptions.

Wave 4 of the survey was the only one in which the real economy had improved compared to a year ago. The more one is exposed to media coverage, the more likely that this improvement will be correctly perceived. The effect, however, is not significant. In this last wave, people who felt the negative consequences of the economic crisis are less likely to correctly

Table 2.2 Explaining whether respondents correctly[1] perceived that the economy was improving/declining compared to 12 months earlier

| | Model 1 | | | Model 2 | | | Model 3 | | | Model 4 | | |
| | Wave 1 | | | Wave 2 | | | Wave 3 | | | Wave 4 | | |
	B	SE B	Exp(B)	B	SE B	Exp(B)	B	SE B	Exp(B)	B	SE B	Exp(B)
Constant	-0.71	.151***	0.49	-1.00	.19***	0.37	-1.92	.24***	0.15	-0.52	.22*	0.59
Interpersonal communication	-0.05	.040	0.95	-0.07	.05	0.93	-0.05	.07	0.96	0.22	.06***	1.25
News exposure	0.19	.038***	1.20	0.16	.05**	1.17	0.13	.06#	1.14	0.06	.06	1.06
Personal economic experiences	0.25	.036***	1.28	0.29	.05***	1.34	0.40	.06***	1.49	-0.47	.06***	0.63
Nagelkerke R^2	.04			.04			.05			.09		
N	2506			1666			1288			1043		
Percentage correctly classified	58.0			62.7			77.8			61.3		

Note: ***$p < .001$, **$p < .01$, *$p < .05$, #$p < .1$ (two-sided t-tests). [1]Correct perception for waves 1, 2, and 3: economy declined; correct perception for wave 4: economy improved.

perceive the change in the economic climate. Interpersonal communication is significantly related to more correct economic perceptions. The results suggest that over the whole period of the panel study, interpersonal communication points towards more optimistic view of the economy. This optimism means that personal discussions are not related to more correct economic perceptions in the first three waves, but are significantly related to more correct perceptions during the last quarter of 2013. We see the opposite effect for people with negative economic experiences. They are more pessimistic across the board, which means that they have correct perceptions of economic developments in the first three waves and false perceptions in wave 4. Of the three sources of economic information, media exposure was the only one whose effect changed depending on the economic climate. In the first three waves, people with more exposure correctly perceived economic decline. In the last wave, people with more exposure were more optimistic (although the effect was not significant, perhaps because this phase was one of positive economic growth following a long period of economic decline).

In sum, this analysis shows that media exposure is generally positively related to correct perceptions of the economic climate, even when taking interpersonal communication and personal experiences into account. In the rest of the book, we focus on the effect of media exposure on economic perceptions and understanding. We return to the other two sources of information in the final chapter of this book.

Moving Beyond Simple Exposure and Descriptive Evidence

This chapter has shown that although the economy is extremely complex, people generally make accurate assessments of economic developments. This case applies even to people who are not intrinsically interested in the economy—the inattentive audience. Across Europe, media exposure is an important antecedent of these correct perceptions, both in countries where the economy improved and in countries where the economy declined. This first correlational evidence challenges commonly heard criticisms of economic news and is the starting point for the rest of our book. In the following chapters, we argue that specific content features of mainstreamed economic news actually help the audience understand (in the broadest sense) economic developments. We argue that these content characteristics are beneficial for the inattentive audience in particular. Our argument will be tested with time-series analysis, panel data, and survey data, which provide stronger causal evidence than the descriptive and correlational results presented in this chapter. As we argue in the next chapter, to observe these effects we have to go beyond correlational evidence and simple exposure, and study exposure to particular content characteristics, such as human-interest framing, negativity, consequence framing, and domestication (Schuck, Vliegenthart, and de Vreese, 2016).

Notes

1 Eurostat. Gross domestic product, volumes. Percentage change q/q-4. Code: teina011. Downloaded 12 July 2016. At http://ec.europa.eu/eurostat/web/products-datasets/-/teina011.

2 When the outlier Ireland is excluded from the analysis, the correlation between real change in GDP and perceived economic trends remains significant ($r = .43$, $p < .05$).

3 Question wording: "How often do you follow the news . . . on television; . . . in newspapers." Scale recoded to range from 1 (never) to 6 (every day, almost every day).

4 Analyzing the data in a multilevel model leads to the same conclusion.

5 The same results are found when we do the analysis for television and newspaper exposure separately.

6 Eurostat. Gross domestic product, volumes. Percentage change q/q-4. Code: teina011. Downloaded on 12 July 2016. At http://ec.europa.eu/eurostat/web/products-datasets/-/teina011.

7 Yearly change in GDP is calculated based on B.1*g Bruttonationalprodukt, BNP, seasonally adjusted. Source: Danmarks Statistik. Nationalregnskab og offentlige finanser. Last modified 22 August 2017. At www.statistikbanken.dk/10175. Change in GDP is strongly related to quarterly levels of the Composite Leading Indicators ($r = .072$, $p < .05$), which is an aggregate measure of several indicators of the national economy, including employment figures and total volume of retail sales. Based on this strong correlation, we argue that GDP is a useful benchmark to assess how accurate economic perceptions are.

8 Source: Danmarks Statistik. Forbrugerforventninger: FORV1: Forbrugerforventninger (nettotal) efter indikator. Danmarks økonomiske situation i dag, sammenlignet med for et år siden. Last updated 22 August 2017. At www.statistik banken.dk/statbank5a/default.asp?w=1188. The value for the first month of each quarter is used in the analysis.

9 Question wording: "How do you perceive the general economic situation in Denmark to be now, compared to 12 months ago?" Answer categories: a lot better, somewhat better, the same, somewhat worse, a lot worse.

10 The respondents indicated how many days, if any, they use the following outlets during a typical week: news on DR1, news on TV2, *Politiken, Jyllands-Posten, Ekstra Bladet*. Responses were given on an 8-point scale ranging from 0 to 7 days a week. News exposure was measured by summing the exposure to the five outlets and dividing by 5.

11 The question wording was as follows: "How often if at all, do you discuss about the economy?" Answer categories: never, once a month or less, a few times a month, a few times a week, every day, or almost every day.

12 The question wording was as follows: "Have you, or someone you know, lost his job recently? Have you, or someone you know, not been able to pay his bills recently? Did you restrict your summer vacation spending?" (In waves 1, 2, and 3): "Will you limit the expenses related to Christmas?" (In wave 4): "Do you feel comfortable with your retirement savings?" Answer categories: yes, no, do not know/do not wish to answer. The answer "yes" to the first three questions and the answer "no" to the last question were coded as a negative experience. These scores were summed into a scale which runs from 0 (no negative experiences) to 4 (several negative experiences).

13 The results are significant after controlling for political leaning, economic interest, and levels of education.

3 How Economic News Informs the Inattentive Audience

As we have seen in Chapter 2, people's baseline understanding of economic developments may not be as deplorable as is often claimed, and media exposure is associated with correct economic perceptions. These findings stand in contrast to commonly heard criticisms of economic news. During the economic crisis, criticism was especially tough. The media were criticized for overdramatizing the economy and keeping the crisis alive with overly negative and highly visible coverage. Such criticism resonates with the argument that political news is softening or "dumbing down"—rational, factual, and extensive coverage aimed at an audience of rational citizens is being replaced by entertainment-driven, emotional, and sensationalist coverage aimed at an audience of consumers (Otto, Glogger, and Boukes, 2016; Temple, 2006). Further (so the argument continues), this transformation, during which relevant information takes a backseat to sensational trivialities, has a deteriorating effect on citizens' knowledge of, and interest in, public affairs. Not only does this type of dumbed-down news lack information that serves to educate people, but it might actually impede their engagement in public affairs by addressing them as spectators rather than active members of society.

In this chapter we challenge this view, arguing that such criticism overlooks the different ways of processing information by different audiences. Rational, factual, and extensive economic coverage may indeed be the most rewarding for people with strong internal motivation and extensive previous knowledge, but many others process news differently and therefore benefit from different types of economic news (see also Graber, 2001). People who are not intrinsically motivated benefit from news that is focused and engaging. This theoretical discussion forms the backbone of our empirical chapters, in which we present in-depth analyses of how the characteristics of mainstreamed economic news help the audience to develop an interest in the economy, to grow in economic efficacy, to learn about the economy, and to attribute responsibility for economic developments.

The argument unfolds as follows. First, we review literature about the knowledge gap and discuss how audiences with a high motivational interest in economic news process (economic) information. We then argue that their way of processing news does not apply to the large parts of the population who are not intrinsically motivated to follow economic news and who might most adequately be described as the inattentive audience. We then present three mechanisms through which mainstreamed economic news informs the inattentive audience: (1) sounding the alarm bell, (2) increased elaboration, and (3) heuristic processing. At this point we introduce the characteristics of mainstreamed economic news that help the inattentive audience: visibility, human-interest framing, negativity, consequence framing, and domestication. As we will demonstrate in subsequent chapters, visibility is an indicator of the severity of economic developments (mechanism 1); human-interest framing, negativity, and consequence framing increase elaboration (mechanism 2); and domestication serves as a mental shortcut (mechanism 3).

The Inattentive Audience and Motivational Interest

The question whether people learn from the news and public information has received extensive academic attention. Most studies about learning from the news have focused on the conditionalities of learning from the news: under which circumstances do people learn? Who learns most? And what content characteristics are most beneficial to the audience? The focus on conditionalities goes back to literature on the knowledge gap (Tichenor, Donohue, and Olien, 1970, pp. 159–160):

> As the infusion of mass media information into a social system increases, segments of the population with higher socioeconomic status tend to acquire this information at a faster rate than the lower status segments, so that the gap in knowledge between these segments tends to increase rather than decrease.

In other words, people with higher socioeconomic status learn relatively more from the same information than people with low levels of education and social status.

Next to socioeconomic status, *motivational interest* is another key factor driving knowledge gaps (Elenbaas, de Vreese, Schuck, and Boomgaarden, 2014; Ettema and Kline, 1977, p. 485; Genova and Greenberg, 1979; Shehata, Hopmann, Nord, and Höijer, 2015). Following the self-selection argument, motivated citizens are, first, more likely than nonmotivated citizens to be exposed to public affairs content (Bennett and Iyengar, 2008; Prior, 2005). In a high-choice media environment, people who are interested in public affairs and thus motivated to follow the news can find public affairs information (and learn from it), whereas people with low interest can choose to opt out of public affairs information and instead follow entertainment programmes (from which they learn less).

Second, and more relevant for our argument, once exposed to public information, people with high motivational interest in a topic pay more attention to this information, process it centrally, and therefore absorb it better and are better able to retain it. Support for this observation comes from different strands of communication literature. According to the Elaboration Likelihood Model (Petty and Cacioppo, 1986), people process information in one of two ways. When following the peripheral route, people engage in minimal mental processing without evaluating the information in detail and instead rely on shortcuts to process it. But when following the central route, people pay close attention to information, weighing up the strength of different arguments instead of relying on shortcuts. The central way of processing results in new information being retained longer because the processing requires more mental effort. Motivation to be informed about a topic is one of the key variables explaining whether the central or peripheral route of information processing is chosen. Under high motivation conditions, information is processed through the central route, which is related to more mental effort and more information retention. Under low motivation conditions, people process information through the peripheral route, which is characterized by less mental effort and less information retention.

Motivation likewise plays a central role in the *cognitive mediation model* (Eveland, Shah, and Kwak, 2003, p. 362). According to this model, "motivations for media use . . . drive media information processing behaviors . . . during and after exposure to news content." When people are motivated to follow the news by their desire to be informed about public affairs, they will pay more attention to news and engage in more elaborative processing, which leads to greater knowledge gains "because of the connections made between news content, past experiences, and existing knowledge." In their study Eveland and colleagues indeed show that surveillance motivation affects knowledge through attention and elaborative processing. This finding resonates with the albeit slightly different argument by Blumler (1979) about the role of gratification (which the audience seeks through the news) on media effects. Blumler (1979, p. 18) argues that "the person who is more strongly and more exclusively moved to consume media materials for their informational content is more likely to acquire knowledge from them."

If people who are highly motivated to attend to information learn more from it, then the inattentive audience—that is, citizens who are neither intrinsically interested in the economy nor motivated to follow economic news—will be left behind and learn less from economic news. In general, interest is an important motivational resource (Katz, Assor, Kanat-Maymon, and Bereby-Meyer, 2006), and interest in politics is an important motivation to watch television news (Wonneberger, Schoenbach, and Van Meurs, 2011). Likewise, Baum (2003, p. 96) argues that inattentive audiences are unlikely to pay attention to hard news because the expected costs in terms of time and effort are too high compared to what they gain from it.

Nevertheless, in this book we argue that *mainstreamed* economic news might reach out to the inattentive audience because this type of economic news includes content features that are tailored to the way the inattentive audience processes information, helping them to develop an understanding of economic developments. To illuminate how people with different levels of motivational interest benefit from different types of economic news, we first look at how people with high motivational interest use economic news.

Economic News for the Highly Informed Audience

Different audiences have different motivations to follow economic news and subsequently benefit from different types of economic content. A close look at how highly motivated, elite audiences consume news about the economy illustrates this point. Davis (2006) interviewed such a hyper-attentive audience: fund managers at the London Stock Exchange, "an elite, rational audience par excellence" who "make conscious, well-thought-out decisions, based on the information gained from media and communication sources that are widely circulated and consumed"(Davis, 2006, p. 603). Thus, these people get their information from a wide variety of sources, but at the same time, they remain heavy users of financial news. Davis (2006) reports that in 2000, around half of professional investors saw newspapers as the most important information source. Their news consumption is goal oriented. They use newspapers to get a broad overview, assess the public mood, find out what other investors are doing, and see whether a consensus is forming. The information-gathering objective becomes clear from one interviewee's description of his use of the *Financial Times*, a specialist financial newspaper read by all interviewees in Davis's study and described as the most authoritative one.

> Often it is relaying information rather than necessarily being a commentator. And that relay of information is obviously important because you can miss things. So reading the FT every morning you make sure you have a relatively broad set of updates.
>
> (Hugh Sergeant, in Davis, 2005, pp. 311–312)

The interviewee's words reveal that the specialist financial press provides a constant, broad overview of information. Investors know that if information is relevant, it will appear in the *Financial Times*. The investors then actively pick out the information relevant to them and combine it with other information. Being *homines oeconomici*, they then use this information to make conscious decisions about investments that they think will maximize profits for their clients and themselves.

This process of knowledge acquisition fits in with what we know about knowledge gaps based on *motivational interest* (described earlier). The financial traders are highly motivated and are goal-oriented consumers of specialized news. They can be considered the extreme category of the attentive audience of economic news—people who will benefit from more information about the economy and whose knowledge will grow quickly from new information. The ideal of a rational audience benefitting from media content is often depicted as the standard to be expected of *all* audiences and news media. Be that as it may, the presence of a rational, active audience needing media that provide broad overviews of events to help them monitor the market is the exception rather than the rule. As Davis (2005, p. 307) argues, a

> quite different production-consumption dynamic is taking place than that associated with the pleasure-seeking consumer or vaguely interested citizen-voter. The way the media and information is produced and encoded and the way the audience receives and consumes it are also quite different.

Economic News for the Inattentive Audience

The inattentive audience might not be best served by the same content as attentive and economic elite audiences. The original account of the knowledge gap hypothesis applied to newspapers. Tichenor et al. (1970, p. 162) refer to the content of newspapers as one of the explanations for the knowledge gap, arguing that newspapers were mainly aimed at the "interests and tastes of [the] higher-status segment." Eveland and Scheufele (2000) argue that the particular *style* of newspapers is part of the explanation. By way of example, they refer to the work by Graber (Graber, 1994). According to Graber, an inverted pyramid structure is prevalent in news coverage, such that new information is presented before being given a context, which might be more advantageous for highly interested people who already have prior knowledge about the topic.

The preceding description of how the *Financial Times* covers the economy resonates with what Zaller (2003) calls the *police patrol model* of public affairs coverage. The media is likened to a police patrol; they systematically cover the whole political environment and report on political developments in "sober, detailed, and comprehensive coverage," even when not much is going on (Zaller, 2003, p. 114). It is exactly this coverage that makes the rich richer and fosters a gap in knowledge gain between people with high motivational interests and those with low motivational interests. The majority of the public has neither the same incentives nor the intrinsic motivation to continuously monitor the economic and political environment. For much of the audience, the benefits of paying such close attention to the economy would be minimal. As argued in Chapter 2, the average citizen does not need to know the exact unemployment level or a precise interest rate but needs to be aware only of major developments and of the direction in which the economy is heading. Being continuously up to date on unemployment figures or the price index would require too much mental effort compared to the benefits such knowledge yields in everyday life. In politics, Downs (1957) speaks of rational ignorance, arguing that individuals' potential impact on election outcomes is so small that people lack real incentives to follow politics closely and to carefully study different candidates' policies. Similarly, Schudson (1998) argues that people can function as monitorial rather than fully informed citizens. Instead of continuously following all developments closely, monitorial citizens keep an eye on their environment, which means that they can be triggered to pay close attention when close attention is required.

Central to this line of thinking is the idea that even without actively seeking and engaging with public affairs information, a large part of the population has sufficient knowledge of economic trends and feels sufficiently informed to make economic decisions. We argue that mainstreamed economic news plays an important role in informing the inattentive audience about the economy in three ways: (1) raising awareness by extensive negative coverage when economic developments require broad awareness; (2) raising interest and attention to the news, which leads to more knowledge elaboration and retention; and (3) providing mental shortcuts and heuristics, which allow people with low intrinsic motivation to behave as informed citizens.

With any of these three mechanisms, the mental costs of absorbing new information are low, and the information can be acquired as an accidental by-product without being actively sought. In addition, we believe that each mechanism will be more beneficial to the inattentive audience than to the already informed citizen, thus allowing for a narrowing of the knowledge gap. Each of these mechanisms will now be described in depth.

Informing the Inattentive Audience I: Sounding the Alarm Bell

The first way in which the news media inform the inattentive audience about the economy is by providing eye-catching coverage of important developments that the general public should be aware of. As early as 1948, Lasswell (1948) argued that the media should fulfil a surveillance function. The journalist's task is not to continuously cover each aspect of society but rather to focus on significant developments. In the domain of politics, Zaller (2003) argues that the media serves the monitorial citizen best when they function as a burglar alarm rather than a police patrol, as described in the preceding section. As a burglar alarm, the media should focus on specific political developments when these require the awareness of the audience. When important developments should be known by the audience at large, the coverage of these topics should dominate the media agenda at the expense of other topics. When they no longer require the same level of public salience, they can disappear from the agenda and make room for other subject matter.

Extensive coverage helps the inattentive audience to learn about these important developments. In line with the agenda-setting thesis (McCombs and Shaw, 1972), an issue's position on the media agenda influences its position on the public agenda. Thus, when the media focus on the economy, it will also be higher on the public agenda. Indeed, Doms and Morin (2004) and Carroll (2003) showed that people update their expectations about the economic climate more often when the topic is high on the media agenda. More frequent updates can, in turn, be expected to lead to better perceptions of the economic climate. Outside the economic domain, evidence suggests that the availability of information in the information environment leads to higher levels of knowledge among the population. Comparing Switzerland with the United States, Iyengar, Hahn, Bonfadelli, and Marr (2009) found that international news is more present in Swiss news. Accordingly, the Swiss are more exposed to it and are better informed than Americans. In keeping with this finding, Jerit, Barabas, and Bolsen (2006) showed that policy-specific knowledge is higher for issues that are widely covered in the media. Because information is easily available in Switzerland, Swiss citizens face less opportunity costs when they are exposed to the news. de Vreese and Boomgaarden (2006) and Shehata et al. (2015) showed that people also learn from watching public service broadcasting channels on which public affairs information is more widely available.

It can be expected that the inattentive audience, in particular, benefits from this broad availability of information. In their original paper, Tichenor et al. (1970, p. 159) already argued that the knowledge gap closes when "the stimulus intensity of mass media publicity is maintained at a high level." People with high levels of education and prior knowledge will pick up the information the quickest, but if the media keep their focus on a relevant issue long enough, even the information poor will eventually be exposed to the information.

Arguably, this levelling effect was stronger in the 1970s, when the media environment was less fragmented, than nowadays when the inattentive audience has more possibilities to opt out when it comes to following the news (Bennett and Iyengar, 2008). For the alarm bell function to work, even the inattentive audience must consume at least some news. A counterargument against the positive effect of changes in media content comes from the increased importance of selective exposure. At the same time as economic news has become mainstreamed, technological, economic, and societal developments have led to a large increase in available media channels that news consumer can choose from. This has given individual media users more control over which media content they can consume or avoid. Thus, despite the changes in the style of economic news described in Chapter 1, audiences who are not intrinsically motivated to stay up to date about the economy simply have the possibility to tune out and stop following complicated and demanding genres like economic news altogether. Previous research has indeed shown that the gap in exposure to political news between interested and uninterested citizens has grown over time (Strömbäck, Djerf-Pierre, and Shehata, 2013). This is accompanied by a growing knowledge gap between so-called news seekers and news avoiders (Hopmann, Wonneberger, Shehata, and Höijer, 2015). Although the increased choice has increased the gap in media exposure, there is little evidence that people turn away from news completely (Newman, Levy, and Nielsen, 2015). Despite growing possibilities to tune out, in 2014 Elenbaas and colleagues still found that greater availability of information can help the inattentive audience to catch up. They showed that people with high motivation are quick to pick up new information, but as long as information remains high on the media agenda for long enough, people with less motivation will eventually catch up. This finding shows that the general availability of information in the information environment constrains and sometimes overrides the moderating influence of individual motivations, even in today's high-choice media environment.

Such knowledge gains among the inattentive audience are not the result of motivated learning but rather of inadvertent learning (Shehata et al., 2015). "When availability abounds, even the weakly motivated cannot help but encounter some of the available information and absorb it" (Elenbaas et al., 2014, p. 481). Indeed, the studies on the role of the availability of information in explaining knowledge gains by Iyengar et al. (2009) and Shehata et al. (2015) show that the less attentive and the less interested audience learn the most in relative terms. Applying this result to the economy, in order to inform the inattentive audience, economic developments should dominate the media agenda when they are highly important to the audience. Besides making the economy more visible when economic developments require it, the burglar alarm function of mainstreamed economic news can also be fulfilled by covering the economy in a more negative tone. As we will see later in this book, the tone of mainstreamed economic news is generally negative, and the audience is attentive to this negative news. If economic developments require more awareness of economic developments than is normally the case, the media should sound the alarm bell and report about the economy with a "negativity bonus"—that is, with a negativity that is above and beyond regular levels.

Several authors have related the visibility of economic coverage to its negative tone (MacKuen and Coombs, 1981; Mutz, 1998), and others have argued and shown empirically that negativity strengthens agenda-setting effects (Wu and Coleman, 2009). In the words of Mutz (1998, p. 71), it "is not simply the amount of news coverage that leads to greater salience, but rather the effect of negative economic news on perceptions of collective economic reality, which in turn heighten the salience of the issue."

In sum, the media can sound the alarm bell by covering important economic developments like economic crises more extensively and with a more negative tone. As we will show in Chapter 4, this is exactly how the mainstreamed media cover the economy.

Informing the Inattentive Audience II: Elaboration-Inducing Content

The second way in which the inattentive audience learn from mainstreamed economic news is when the media provide content that raises the likelihood that they will engage in elaboration when exposed to economic news. Whereas the previous discussion focused mainly on whether audiences are *reached*, here the focus is on what they *do* with the information when they are exposed to it. The emphasis is therefore on the *processing* of information—in other words, on what happens during and after exposure to economic news. Cognitive activity is a key condition for absorption and retention of new information. By contemplating new information and by relating it to existing information and to personal experiences, the chance that the information is remembered increases substantially (Eveland et al., 2003). This cognitive activity consists of two closely related aspects: first, paying attention to the news, referring to "the amount of mental focus given to the news or even to particular types of stories" (Eveland et al., 2003, p. 363), and second, elaborating the news, referring to "the use of news information to make cognitive connections to past experiences and prior knowledge and to derive new implications form news content" (Ibid.). Together, these two elements are much like the central route of information processing in the Elaboration Likelihood Model.

Whether people pay attention to news and engage in elaboration depends not only on the consumers of news but highly on the news content itself. In other words, information can be presented in such a way that people will be either more likely or less likely to pay attention to what they see or read, and in turn, to engage in elaboration. This finding is well established in public communication campaign literature (Rice and Atkin, 2012, p. 9), which advises that information should be made personally relevant and engaging through the provision of "interesting or arousing substantive content." In her discussion of the audience's potential to learn from television, Graber (2001, p. 146) argues that television content has particular characteristics that make the audience likely to pay attention. She argues that "most American audiences are attracted by vivid information, which means that it is (a) emotionally interesting, (b) concrete and image-provoking, and (c) proximate in a sensory, temporal, or spatial way" (Nisbett and Ross, 1980, p. 45 in Graber, 2001, p. 146).

The positive effects of attention-inducing elements on learning, such as personalization, are not uncontested. Prior (2005) provides a critical analysis of the idea that soft news—mixing news and entertainment and presenting news in a more sensational and personalized way—leads to knowledge gains among the audience. He argues that viewers might pay attention to such soft news, but that the positive effects are limited if people only pay attention to the entertaining aspects of the news. His empirical analysis showed that, across the board, exposure to soft news had limited impact on political knowledge. In a similar vein, others have argued that commercial pressures lead journalists to produce news "with emphasis on attractive visuals and emotions over social significance" (Mujica and Bachmann, 2018, p. 2). In an experiment, Grabe, Zhou, Lang, and Bolls (2000) found that such tabloid-style packaging of news did increase attention to the news, but they did not find any effect on learning. Millburn and McGrail (1992) even showed that television stories with an overemphasis on drama, including violence and emotions, distracted the audience and decreased recall and learning of information.

These studies underline that news stories have to find the right balance between information and attention-grabbing elements, where the attention-grabbing elements should support and supplement the substantive information. They also show that not all news elements that grab the audience's attention will also lead them to learn about the subject matter. While overtly vivid visuals may distract the audience, stories with a personal angle have positive effects on learning (Mujica and Bachmann, 2018, p. 7). In addition, while attention-grabbing story elements may have limited or no effects on recall and comprehension of information across the board, specific audiences, such as people with low economic status, may actually benefit the most from this type of content (e.g., Mujica and Bachmann, 2018). Similarly, we argue that attention-inducing content will catch the attention specifically of audiences who are not intrinsically motivated. The attention of people who are intrinsically motivated to expose themselves to hard news about the economy does not need to be triggered by engaging news. Audiences who lack motivation may be drawn into the news story and triggered to elaborate on what they see and read when it is presented in an attractive and relevant way. In defence of so-called dumbed-down political information, Temple (2006) makes a similar argument, saying that "what is needed are quality 'dumbed down' pieces, aimed at the tabloid market, talking about politics from an informed, analytical perspective, but in a matter that might (just) draw in the uninterested tabloid reader."

In this book we look at three ways in which economic news raises attention to itself and stimulates elaboration of its content: human-interest framing, a negative tone, and consequence framing. Human-interest framing "brings a human face or an individual's story to the presentation of an event, issue or problem" (Semetko and Valkenburg, 2000, p. 95). For example, a journalist may make a recession visible by focusing on the difficulties of job-seekers to find employment or of shop owners to sell their goods. Human-interest framing is a way for journalists to make the news personally relevant and thereby raise economic interest (Bennett 1995, in Semetko and Valkenburg, 2000, p. 96). Neuman (1992, p. 71) showed that people who were exposed to the human-interest frame felt compassion and empathy for the people involved and "used their imaginations to put themselves in someone else's shoes." Genova and Greenberg (1979) have also argued that people constantly scan their environment to look for information that may affect them personally and influence their daily lives. As we argue in Chapter 5, when information has personal relevance, people are most likely to pay the amount of attention required to learn.

A second content characteristic inducing elaboration is negative tone of the news. Research from various fields such as neuroscience, psychology, and political science tends to agree that information processing is subject to a *negativity bias* (Kahneman and Tversky, 1979; Soroka, 2014). This type of bias means that individuals pay more attention to negative information than to positive information. Negativity may affect a person's motivation to understand and make use of information in order to help that person better deal with the threats, challenges, or obstacles at hand. According to affective intelligence theory, negativity activates the surveillance system that identifies novel and threatening information. When the surveillance system is activated, it "invokes greater attentiveness, greater thoughtfulness, and greater motivation for learning in just those situations that demand greater attention" (Marcus, Neuman, and Mackuen, 2000, p. 57). As we argue in Chapter 6, greater awareness and motivation to learn should increase elaboration and, in turn, be beneficial to people's understanding of the economy.

The third elaboration-inducing content characteristic of mainstreamed economic news is consequence framing. By not only presenting information and broad societal trends but also by explaining what these trends mean for people personally, their family, or the country they live in, the media improve the ability to recall information. As we elaborate in Chapter 7, contemplating consequences and the impact they might have on one's own life or direct environment is a key aspect of the elaboration process, which helps to later retain new information (Eveland, 2001).

Informing the Inattentive Audience III: Heuristics and Information Cues

A third way in which the media help the inattentive audience become informed about the economy is by providing them with mental heuristics and cues. According to Lupia (2016, p. 44), cues are "pieces of information that can take the place of other information as the basis of competence at a particular task." These pieces of information provide a shortcut for arriving at informed decisions. In politics, people rely on cues like partisanship or standings in the polls to decide who to vote for. Several researchers have documented the importance of heuristics and information cues in economic decision making (Schellinck, 1983; Slovic, Finucane, Peters, and MacGregor, 2002). People rely on heuristics, particularly when they are faced with difficult decisions and complex assessments (Lau and Redlawsk, 2001). Mass media coverage can be an importance source of information cues. Given the complexity of the economy, information cues in economic news are expected to allow inattentive citizens to keep the mental transaction costs low and still make a reasonable assessment of the economic situation.

People rely on heuristics and information cues when faced with complex information because humans are generally economical with their mental resources (Kahneman and Tversky, 1979). Fiske and Taylor (1991) speak of people as "cognitive misers." They argue that people's reliance on such shortcuts makes sense, given the enormous amounts of information that people are exposed to and the complexity of many decisions and assessments. Relying on heuristics and information cues resembles the peripheral route of the Elaboration Likelihood Model of information processing (Van Raaij, 1989).

Several scholars have argued that the information provided by shortcuts puts average citizens in a good position, such that their decisions are similar to those they would make were they fully informed. Lupia (1994) showed that Californian voters with relatively low levels of factual knowledge resembled well-informed voters in insurance reform elections. These inattentive voters compensated for their lack of encyclopaedic knowledge by using their knowledge of insurance preferences as a proxy.

Nevertheless, reliance on information cues and heuristics does not always lead to the best possible decisions and, at times, can lead the inattentive audience astray (Lau and Redlawsk, 2001). Thus, we should not overestimate the advantages of information shortcuts, but neither should we completely reject their usefulness. In the words of Lupia (2016, p. 55),

> the right question to ask is not whether cues always (or never) yield competent decisions, because we know the answer to both questions is "no." The constructive question to ask is, "Under what conditions are particular cues necessary or sufficient for competent decision-making."

Therefore it is most useful to study which type of cues help the inattentive audience. Here, the mass media have an important responsibility to provide cues that help the inattentive audience. Kuklinski, Quirk, Jerit, Schwieder, and Rich (2000) have shown that misinformation can be a powerful source of information and can lead people to poorer political judgements than if they had made uninformed decisions. Such examples underline the media's important role of providing heuristics of sufficient quality to allow the inattentive audience to form correct economic perceptions.

In Chapter 8 we focus on one particular heuristic offered by mainstreamed economic news; the degree of domestication in economic news provides cues that help the inattentive audience determine whether economic developments are the responsibility of national governments or foreign actors (Hobolt and Tilley, 2014). According to attribution theory (Weiner, 1985), people constantly ask the *why* question, searching for explanations for what they see happening around them. This need for causal explanations is particularly strong when people are faced with unexpected and negative situations, such as an economic recession or crisis. An important dimension of causal thinking is establishing whether a situation is internal or external: is the situation due to an actor's actions and abilities, or is it rather the consequence of external causes beyond the actor's control? Similarly, people will assess whether an economic situation results from the national government's actions or from developments outside the country. When causes are seen as internal, people will hold the government accountable; when causes are seen as external, they will not.

Coverage of global and transnational developments is often characterized by a high level of domestication (e.g., Cohen, 2013). Domestication of the news can be defined as "a process of presenting distant events as relevant to a domestic audience and constructing them as compatible with the culture and dominant ideology of the country of broadcast" (Gurevitch, Levy, and Roeh, 1991, p. 207). The level of domestication in economic news coverage is expected to be an important cue for inattentive audiences, which affects to whom they attribute responsibility for economic developments. If a crisis is primarily covered with a focus on foreign places, actors, and developments, people will be cued to see it as a foreign development beyond the national government's control and responsibility. But if the media systematically cover the crisis from a national angle—focusing on how the national population is affected and how national politicians, firms, interest organizations, and the like behave—then the news should trigger the audience to see the crisis as an internal, national affair.

What Drives the Three Underlying Mechanisms? Unpacking the Content Characteristics of Mainstreamed Economic News

Figure 3.1 shows that economic news in the mainstreamed media is characterized by the content characteristics that were identified earlier as informative for the inattentive audience: visibility, human-interest framing, negativity, consequence framing, and domestication. The description of the content characteristics is based on a comprehensive content analysis of national economic news (see Methodological Appendix). The content analysis covers economic news over the whole year, in 16 news outlets. These outlets include the offline and online versions of tabloid and broadsheet newspapers, commercial and public service television news, and one specialized business newspaper. In the description of the content features, we compare economic coverage on television, in newspapers, and in the specialized business newspaper. The same patterns were present in the online versions of these outlets.

First, economic news is indeed broadly visible in the news.[1] In television news and in newspapers, more than one out of five news stories dealt with the economy. This visibility is an important condition for the described mechanisms to kick in.

The second relevant feature of economic news is human-interest framing, which is a news frame that "brings a human face or an individual's story to

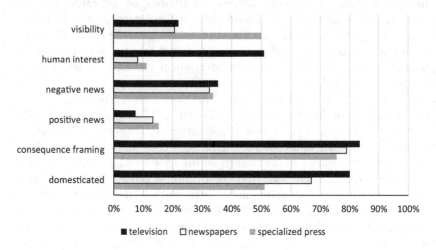

Figure 3.1 Content characteristics of mainstreamed economic news

Note: Offline and online versions combined. See Methodological Appendix for details.

the presentation of an event, issue or problem" (Semetko and Valkenburg, 2000, p. 95). The human-interest frame is used extensively in journalism and is present in the coverage of a wide range of topics and themes (de Vreese, 2005; Semetko and Valkenburg, 2000). The closely related concepts of personalization and identification are generally considered important news (Boukes and Vliegenthart, 2017; Galtung and Ruge, 1965; Harcup and O'Neill, 2001). The human-interest frame is a way for journalists to personalize the news and thereby produce news stories that capture audience interest. Thus, human-interest framing can be seen as part of the trend that is making economic news more mainstreamed and interesting for the general audience. This type of economic coverage is present in 5–10 percent of newspaper articles.[2] On television, however, human-interest framing is a common way to present economic news and is used in around half of the economic news stories.

The third relevant content characteristic of mainstreamed economic news is negativity. The content analysis reveals that the tone in the news media is predominantly negative.[3] The negativity is especially striking when compared to the low share of articles with a positive tone. When examining these figures, we need to take into account that the economy was on the way up and grew during the latter part of 2013. Still, around one-third of all the articles reported negatively about the news and fewer than 15 percent reported positively. The predominantly negative tone was present across the board, with limited variation depending on type of news outlet. This result confirms that negativity is an important news value (Harcup and O'Neill, 2001). Revenue models and competition (Lischka, 2014) are other explanations for the dominance of articles with a negative tone over articles with a positive tone. According to Alsem, Brakman, Hoogduin, and Kuper (2008), the competition between news organizations leads them to focus more on negative than on positive news. Negative news is simply expected to sell better (Soroka, 2014). Even in the specialized economic press, most of the articles were negative, although positive articles made the overall tone more balanced than it was in other outlet types.

Across the studied outlets, there is broad consensus on the use of the economic consequence frame when reporting about the economy.[4] This frame is the fourth relevant content characteristic of mainstreamed economic news. When using it, journalists present "an event, problem, or issue in terms of the economic consequences it will have on an individual, group, institution, region, or country" (Valkenburg, Semetko, and de Vreese, 1999, p. 552). Economic news often focuses on consequences—for example, when journalists discuss what economic developments mean for employment figures, housing prices, or taxes. According to Graber (2009), the focus on consequences is an important news value. It explains why the economic consequence frame is a common feature of economic news that is aimed at mainstream audiences.

The fifth relevant characteristic of mainstreamed economic news is domestication, which can be defined "as a process of presenting distant events as relevant to a domestic audience and constructing them as compatible with the culture and dominant ideology of the country of broadcast" (Gurevitch et al., 1991). Domestication manifests itself in news coverage that links international developments to actors from the home country and that describes the impact on the home country (Cohen, 1996, p. 85). The news value of proximity, the desire to make news relevant to domestic audiences, and commercial motivations have been identified as explanations for why domestication is a common practice in the coverage of broad international developments like climate change or terrorism (Olausson, 2014; Van Leuven, Heinrich, and Deprez, 2015). The share of articles that has Denmark as their location can serve as an indication of the degree of domestication (Cohen, 1996).[5] Across all outlets, over half of the coverage has Denmark as the main location, indicating a considerable domestic focus. Television news has a clear domestic focus on the economy. These results are in line with Nienstedt, Kepplinger, and Quiring (2015), who showed a high level of domestication in the coverage of the Euro crisis in 11 European countries. Again, the specialized economic press stands out; this outlet type has the least domesticated coverage.

Mainstreamed Economic News and the Inattentive Audience

In sum, this chapter puts forward the argument on which the rest of this book builds. We discussed the important moderating role of motivational interest in the likelihood that people learn from media exposure. We illustrated this point with a discussion of how an audience with high economic interest and motivation to follow economic news (financial analysts) quickly picks up new knowledge from specialist financial newspapers, which provide a broad overview of economic developments. As we have seen, the average individual is not motivated to consume economic news in this manner. Many people lack intrinsic motivation and do not systematically follow economic developments. The inattentive audience requires news that (1) makes the economy highly visible when the economy requires heightened awareness, (2) includes elements that raise audience attention and the likelihood of news elaboration, and (3) provides heuristics and mental shortcuts that lead to correct assessments of the economic situation. The content analysis of economic news showed that the content characteristics that help the inattentive audience learn about the economy are features of mainstreamed economic news. Economic news is highly visible, uses consequence and human-interest framing, focuses on negative rather than positive developments, and has a high level of domestication. When analysing the content, we see that the potential for positive effects is present, and the evidence does not warrant us jumping to quick conclusions about the inadequacy of economic news. In subsequent chapters we test each of the three proposed mechanisms, starting with the alarm bell function in the next chapter.

Notes

1 To measure the visibility of economy in the newspapers, we calculated the total number of printed news stories and the total number of economic stories on the days that are included in our content analysis. More details on the operationalization of economic news and the sampling strategy used can be found in the Methodological Appendix. The share of these stories gave us the numbers for visibility of economy in each outlet for each wave. For the television outlets, the coders who watched the broadcasts were asked to note the total number of stories and the total number of economic stories in the newscast. We only calculated visibility for the offline version of the outlets.

2 To measure the presence of human-interest framing in economic news, the coders coded whether the news story provides a human example or human face to the story in order to illustrate developments in the economy. Inter-coder reliability (Krippendorff's alpha) was .95.

3 The question used by coders in our content analysis to identify tone was "What is the evaluation of the general economic climate?" where general climate referred to macro-economic stories concerning the national or international economies. To decide the tone of an article, coders relied primarily on the heading and subheading. The tone of an article was coded as negative when only negative evaluations of the economy were present in either the heading or subheading. If the tone of an article was absent from the heading or subheading, or if the tone of the remaining article contradicted the heading and subheading, coders counted and compared the number of times a positive or a negative tone appeared in the article. If a negative tone outweighed a positive tone, the article was coded as negative or vice versa. Coders only included tone that was *explicitly* expressed in the articles. An acceptable inter-coder reliability result was obtained for the tone measure (Krippendorff's alpha = .75).

4 The figure shows the percentage of articles about economic news that "reported an event, problem or issue in terms of the economic consequences it had/has/can have on an individual, a group, a company, an institution, a region or a country" (de Vreese et al., 2001). The Krippendorff's alpha inter-coder reliability score on the coding of this variable was .72.

5 To measure the location, coders identified whether the story took place in Denmark or outside of Denmark. Inter-coder reliability tests showed satisfactory levels of coder agreement (Krippendorff's alpha = .83). In Chapter 8 we will expand the operationalization of domestication with three additional indicators.

4 Sounding the Alarm When It Matters

In this chapter we look at the first mechanism through which mainstreamed economic news is expected to inform the inattentive audience, which is by raising their awareness when it matters, thereby helping them form correct assessments of economic developments. We consider correct economic assessment to be a core requirement for democratic citizens (see Chapter 1). How can the economy be covered in such a way that the awareness of the inattentive audience is raised when the economy requires their heightened awareness? Two aspects of economic coverage are particularly relevant in this regard. The tone and visibility of economic news provide signals alerting the inattentive public about important economic developments. The *tone* of economic coverage refers to a favourable or unfavourable evaluation of the state and future of the national economy. People are generally attentive to negative news (cf. Chapter 6). When the news about the economy becomes *more* negative, the public pays more attention and are more likely to update their economic perceptions (Soroka, 2006). Similarly, the *visibility* of the economy in the news is an important indicator of the importance of economic developments. When more articles are written about the economy and when news moves from the dedicated business pages to the front page, these changes are signals to monitorial citizens that the economy requires their consideration. The tone and visibility of the economy are strongly related: when news about the economy becomes more negative, it also becomes more prominent (see also Mutz, 1998, p. 71).

In line with Zaller (2003), we argue that in order to serve the monitorial citizen well, the visibility and tone of economic news should vary considerably depending on the state of the economy. If the economy were always prominent in the news with overly negative headlines, the journalist would be continually sounding the alarm (Bennett, 2003). Were this the case, highly visible economic news would become business as usual, and it would not raise the awareness of the audience when really needed (Zaller, 2003, p. 121). Economic news should grab audiences' attention with negative and visible coverage when these audiences need to be aware of important developments.

Thus, the media should function more like a burglar alarm than a police patrol on a month-to-month basis. The police patrol function would entail systematic coverage of the whole environment and "sober, detailed, and comprehensive coverage" of developments (Zaller, 2003, p. 114). As a burglar alarm, the media should focus on specific developments whenever these require the audience's consideration. According to Ju (2008) and Goidel and Langley (1995), economic news has a similar alarm function: "In the absence of a fire alarm, media coverage of the economy is fairly routine. When something is, or appears to be wrong, however, the economy demands front page, and generally, negative media attention" (Goidel and Langley, 1995, p. 325). Thus, the visibility and tone of economic news should be increased or decreased depending on the course of the economic cycle. Functioning as a magnifying glass, the media should amplify periods of prolonged economic contraction by making the economy *more visible and reporting with an overly negative tone*. In periods when the economy is stable, there is no need to raise the awareness of the inattentive audience, and the media can thus reduce the visibility of economic news.

Burglar Alarm Rather Than Police Patrol

Previous research has shown that the media cover economic developments more like a burglar alarm than a police patrol. The visibility and tone of economic news vary depending on the economic situation. First, economic news reflects *change* in economic developments rather than the absolute state of the economy. That the economy is doing well is not newsworthy per se (De Boef and Kellstedt, 2004, p. 640), but how the economy is developing and where it is heading is newsworthy (Martenson, 1998). Second, economic news reacts *asymmetrically* to economic developments; it becomes more negative when the economy declines but not more positive when the economy improves (Blood and Philips, 1995; Goidel and Langley, 1995; Soroka, 2006). Harrington (1989) showed that American networks give more attention to negative than positive developments. Soroka (2006) showed that newspaper coverage of the economy in the United Kingdom reflected negative but not positive developments. Such a negativity bias was confirmed for newspaper coverage in South Korea (Ju, 2008) and in the United States (Fogarty, 2005; Hester and Gibson, 2003). One notable exception is reported by Casey and Owen (2013, p. 21), who found no asymmetric responsiveness in a model where several economic indicators were included simultaneously.

While the change effect and asymmetry effect have been confirmed in several studies focusing on the tone of economic news, fewer studies look at whether the *visibility* of economic news is responsive to (negative) change in economic indicators. Harrington (1989), Fogarty (2005) and Soroka, Stecula, and Wlezien (2015) found that the visibility of economic news reflects changes in economic indicators, but with notable variation. Harrington (1989) showed that US television news paid more attention to the economy when unemployment increased and gross national product (GNP) deteriorated, but only during non-election years. The study of economic coverage on the front page of the *New York Times* by Fogarty (2005) showed that more stories about the economy appeared when unemployment changed.

Previous studies have explained these patterns in macro-economic coverage by pointing to professional norms, personal predispositions of journalists, audience interests, and organizational influences. It is the media's task to hold governments accountable for negative economic developments (Casey and Owen, 2013, p. 4), which automatically leads to more attention to negative economic developments than to positive developments. Economic journalists might be personally more aware of negative economic change because they are naturally inclined to surveil their environment (Ju, 2008, p. 238). Psychological research has shown that individuals pay more attention to negative than to positive developments (cf. Chapter 6). Soroka (2006, p. 374) argues that this inclination leads journalists to place more emphasis on negative developments, "not just based on their own (asymmetric) interests, but also on the (asymmetric) interests of their news-consuming audience." These explanations are all in line with the idea that economic news has become mainstreamed, caters to a broad audience, and follows news values.

Key Questions

In this chapter we study whether mainstreamed economic news helps the audience learn about important economic developments by sounding the alarm bell when it matters. Our first expectation is that economic news highlights negative developments by increasing its visibility and negative tone. Furthermore, we study whether economic news functions as a magnifying glass by raising audience awareness with highly visible economic coverage and negative headlines in times of economic recession when the audience really needs to be aware. To strengthen our argument that the magnifying-glass function is a feature of mainstreamed economic news, we show that economic experts and the specialized economic press react differently to economic developments. Finally, we study the relation between real economic developments and economic perceptions when the economy is highly visible in the news and when media attention is low. If our expectations are correct, perceptions should reflect real economic developments more closely when the economy dominates the media agenda.

The Tone and Visibility of Economic News

In our analysis, we study how the tone and visibility of economic news react to real-world economic developments, operationalized as the Composite

Leading Indicators series (CLI).[1] Our automated content analysis of the visibility and tone of news about the macro-economy between 1996 and 2012 confirms that economic news functions as a burglar alarm and focuses on change and negativity. We study economic coverage in broadsheet newspapers. Because the political leaning of newspapers may influence economic coverage (Larcinese, Puglisi, and Snyder, 2011), three broadsheet newspapers with different political leanings were included in the analysis: *Berlingske*, *Politiken*, and *Jyllands-Posten*. These outlets are expected to give a good indication of the overall economic coverage in the mainstream media because they can be considered newspapers of record. Ideally, we would base the time-series analysis on a broader set of news outlets, including television news broadcasts. However, due to data availability this was not possible. Previous research has shown that monthly aggregated content characteristics of economic news show strong similarities across different mainstream media outlets (Hollanders and Vliegenthart, 2011). Therefore, we assume that the monthly tone and visibility of economic news in the three analysed newspapers reflect overall media coverage. The visibility and tone of economic news in these newspapers were measured with dictionary-based, automated content analysis. Because we are interested in the effect of economic coverage on perceptions of national economic developments, we analyse national macro-economic news items (see Methodological Appendix).

The CLI is an aggregated measure of the following indicators of the national economy: (1) total volume of retail sales, (2) new passenger car registration, (3) employment figures, (4) production figures, (5) official discount rates, (6) deflated money supply, (7) petrol exports, and (8) consumer confidence. The same measure has been used as an independent variable in previous studies of economic news (Blood and Philips, 1995; Soroka, 2014). The CLI gives an indication of the economy's future development. This indicator is used here because Soroka et al. (2015) have shown that media coverage is more responsive to indicators of the economic future than indicators of the past or current state of the economy.

Figure 4.1 shows how the Danish economy (represented by the grey line) and the tone of economic news (black line) developed between August 1996 and December 2012. Between January 1999 and June 2000, the economy boomed. This period has come to be known as the dot-com hype. In late 2000, the bubble burst and the economy declined. In June 2003, the economy entered several years of economic expansion. This period of sustained growth was followed by a period of economic contraction and stagnation from January 2008 onwards.

The black line shows the average tone in economic news. The tone of economic news and the CLI are positively and significantly correlated ($r = .13$, $p < .05$), which suggests that economic news and economic developments are related. Throughout the whole period of analysis, the news is predominantly negative. The only exception is between 2003 and 2007, when,

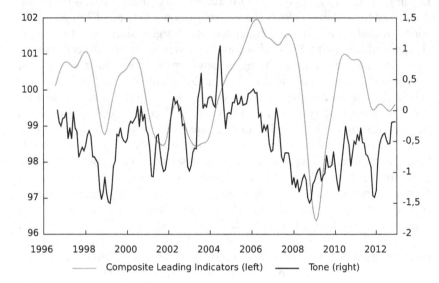

Figure 4.1 Economic developments (grey line) and the tone of economic news
(black line) in three broadsheet newspapers between August 1996 and
December 2012

Note: The scale for the Composite Leading Indicators can be found on the left. The scale for
the tone of economic news can be found on the right. Monthly data. The three-month moving
average of tone is displayed.

during several months, the news had on average a slightly positive tone.
The start of the period of economic growth coincided with a positive peak
in the tone of the news in June 2003, when the Danish press wrote about
"surprisingly positive sales numbers"[2] and "surplus [on the balance of pay-
ment] against all odds."[3] At the end of 2007, the tone of economic news
decreased sharply. Although it later improved slightly, it remained negative
until the end of 2012.

Figure 4.2 shows the results of a time-series analysis studying the relation between the tone of economic news and CLI in more detail. Time-
series analysis allows to study how longitudinal developments in the tone
of economic news are affected by economic developments, operationalized
by the CLI (see Methodological Appendix). Previous research has shown
that there is a large degree of stability in the news (Vliegenthart, 2014): if
the news was negative in the previous months, it is also highly likely to be
negative in the current month. This is confirmed in our analysis. The tone of
economic news is first and foremost determined by the tone in the previous
three months. In Figure 4.2 we show the summed coefficient of the tone t-1
to tone t-3. This represents the combined influence of the tone in the previous three months on the current tone.[4]

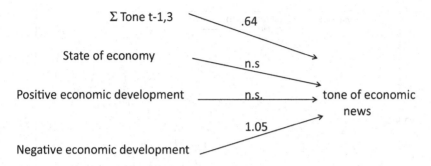

Figure 4.2 Explaining the tone of economic news (August 1996–December 2012)

Note: Unstandardized beta-coefficient. Significant at $p < .05$ (two-sided t-tests). See Appendix table 4.1.

The tone of economic news does not reflect levels of CLI. Positive economic developments have no significant influence on the tone of economic news either, but negative developments have a significant effect. In other words, how well the economy is doing or whether it improves does not affect the tone of economic news. What matters is whether the economy is declining. When the economy declines, the downturn is reflected in a more negative tone in the news. Economic growth does not lead to more positive news.

Figure 4.3 compares the development in the leading economic indicators (represented by the grey line) to the visibility of news about the national economy in broadsheet newspapers (black line). Until 2008, between 20 and 40 articles per month explicitly dealt with the state or development of the macro-economy. After that, when the economy entered the Great Recession, economic news became twice as visible as during the previous years. After 2009, the visibility of economic news remained high.[5] The tone and volume of economic news are closely and inversely related ($r = -.38$, $p < .001$). This relationship agrees with the argument by Mutz (1998) that salient economic developments are negative developments. It also supports our argument that both visibility and tone matter for the alarm bell function of mainstreamed economic news and that both should be studied in combination.

Figure 4.4 studies the relation between economic developments and the visibility of economic news in more depth. The visibility of economic news shows a large degree of stability. How much news deals with the economy is primarily determined by the visibility of economic news in the four previous months. On top of that, economic decline matters. Like the tone of economic news, visibility reacts to decreases in the CLI but not to increases or the absolute level of the CLI. On average, each of the three newspapers responds to a 1-point decrease in economic conditions, with six more articles about economic news per month. Thus, mainstreamed economic

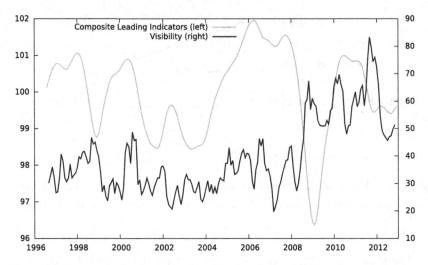

Figure 4.3 Economic developments (grey line) and the visibility of economic news in three broadsheet newspapers (black line) between August 1996 and December 2012

Note: The scale for the Composite Leading Indicators can be found on the left. The scale for the visibility of economic news can be found on the right. Monthly data. The three-month moving average of visibility is displayed.

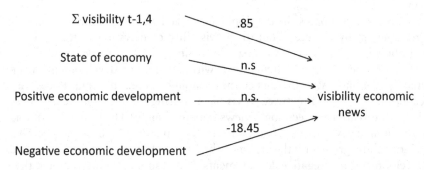

Figure 4.4 Explaining the visibility of economic news (August 1996–December 2012)

Note: Unstandardized beta-coefficient. Significant at $p < .05$ (two-sided t-tests). See Appendix table 4.1.

news not only becomes more negative in tone but also more visible when the economy decreases (for similar findings see Damstra and Boukes, 2018).

Both the analysis of tone and visibility of economic news confirm that the mass press covers economic news like a burglar alarm, raising the awareness of the audience with visible and negative coverage when the economy declines. To see whether these results are specific to the mainstreamed press

Table 4.1 Explaining the tone and visibility of economic news in specialized business newspaper *Børsen*

	Model 1		Model 2	
	Tone		Visibility	
	B	SE B	B	SE B
Constant	−5.86	7.94	75.13	73.87
Tone t-1	0.06	0.12		
Σ Visibility t-1,2			0.33	0.15*
Composite Leading Indicators (CLI)	0.05	0.08	−0.61	0.73
Positive Δ CLI	0.15	0.92	10.09	8.86
Negative Δ CLI	1.11	0.75	−1.44	6.70
Adj. R^2	.03		.12	
AIC	204.35		651.67	
HQC	209.18		567.43	
SBC	216.39		576.04	
N	82		81	
Breusch-Godfrey	0.02	(p = 0.88)	2.43	(p = 0.12)
Ljung Box Q	0.01	(p = 0.99)	0.17	(p = 0.68)

Note: From April 2006 until December 2012. Unstandardized beta-coefficients with standard error. *$p < .05$ (two-sided t-test).

or whether they are also present in the specialist press, we repeated the analysis for the financial daily *Børsen*, for which data were available between 2007 and 2012 (Table 4.1). Looking at the tone of economic news in *Børsen*, we found that the absolute state of the economy and a positive change or negative change in the economy had no significant effect on whether the newspaper reported positively or negatively about the economy. The same results were found for the visibility of economic news, which did not react to the CLI either. In other words, the elite economic press functions as a police patrol, consistently covering the economy. From this we can conclude that *Børsen* probably serves the elite, attentive audience well—an audience that looks for broad, comprehensive coverage of the economy on a daily basis and for whom information on economic upturn or stability might be just as useful as information on economic decline. However, the paper is not widely read by the inattentive audience.

Economic News Through the Magnifying Glass

So far, our analysis of economic news coverage has shown that economic news becomes more visible and more negative in tone when the economy is declining. These features are desirable for the alarm bell function of economic news. At times, economic developments are so severe that they require extra awareness from the audience—for example, at times of economic crisis or sustained economic growth. Previous research has indeed shown that occasionally the tone of economic news deviates from normal patterns of coverage (Doms and Morin, 2004; Wu, Stevenson, Chen, and Güner, 2002). Studying economic news between the early 1970s and 2003, Doms and Morin (2004) conclude that the news sometimes reports in overly negative or positive tones about the economy. This overemphasis cannot be explained by the journalistic focus on change and negativity alone. We turn to the literature on media hypes and news waves to better understand these processes. Journalism research in areas other than the economy has given insight into why media coverage intensifies in certain periods. Studies on the coverage of, for example, the threat of street violence have shown that journalists periodically open the gates and focus on specific societal problems (Fishman, 1978). Likewise, research on climate change coverage has identified sharp peaks in media attention (Schäfer, Ivanova, and Schmidt, 2013). Similar mechanisms may increase attention to the economy and lead to an overly negative or positive tone of economic news, depending on the economic cycle.

One of the mechanisms driving these periods of intensive coverage is the emergence of a dominant news theme or frame, which provides a common interpretation or labelling under which diverse events can be summarized. When journalists cover a complicated topic, they orient themselves towards their "competitor colleagues" to reduce ambiguity. This convergence can lead to the development of one dominant journalistic interpretation, which is shared across different outlets. Known as "pack journalism," this phenomenon is strengthened by increasing competition among media outlets as well as journalists' fear of missing the important stories of the day (Frank, 2003). Once such a dominant news theme emerges, it "leads to a high degree of uniformity in the news selection and a pressure on every news desk to join the pack" (Vasterman, 2005, p. 514). Consequently, the threshold for reporting about events that fit the dominant news theme is lowered, and the media gates are opened to the coverage of similar stories. When stories that do not fit the dominant perspective are simultaneously shut out, the result is continuous reinforcement of the dominant frame. Framing studies have shown that such dominant news themes (or "organizing devices used to construct news stories"; Shah, Watts, Domke, and Fan, 2002, p. 341) are hard to change once they become mainstream among journalists and societal actors (Huxford, 2012; McCarthy and Dolfsma, 2009).

"Recession" or "crisis" are examples of common news themes that can trigger self-reinforcing spirals of coverage about the economy. Due to the economic system's complexity and the availability of a wide variety of sometimes contradictory economic indicators, the economy's state is often ambiguous. The themes of recession or crisis give both journalists and their audience a common interpretation, which helps to simplify economic reality. Huxford (2012, p. 350) argues that during the economic downturn in

2000, journalists simplified the economy by "corralling the multitude of economic states and indicators within the label 'recession,' and then treating that as a single entity." Later, McCarthy and Dolfsma (2009) showed that crisis-related terms in the *Economist* increased sharply in 2007 and 2008. Kleinnijenhuis et al. (2015) showed that frame complexity decreased during the beginning of the crisis in 2007 and 2008, which may indicate that a dominant frame emerged. Once a dominant frame is established, it can lead to more stories about the economy's negative state, which spread from the financial section of the newspaper to other sections. The crisis frame lowers the threshold for negative stories but raises it for stories with a more optimistic outlook. This threshold adjustment may result in more economic coverage with an overly negative tone.

During periods of economic boom, the same mechanisms can magnify the positive state of the economy in media coverage. "Economic boom" or "economic growth" may become common themes to which positive economic news is connected. Stories that temper economic optimism might be difficult to place within the common interpretation and have less chance of being covered. During the Internet bubble at the end of the 1990s, the media reported overly optimistically about the state of the economy (Roush, 2006). Mercille (2014) argues that during the Irish housing bubble, critics of the economic situation had limited access to the media because their message did not fit the "Celtic Tiger discourse" that dominated Irish economic coverage.

Such amplification processes are the result of not only internal media routines. Sources play an important role as well. Vasterman (2005) argues that the way sources define events can trigger intense coverage, while Wien and Elmelund-Præstekær (2009) argue that sources can prolong periods of intensive coverage. Business journalists and generalists who report about the economy rely heavily on economic experts and analysts who act as primary definers and shape the journalists' interpretations of the economic situations (Doyle, 2006; Guerrera, 2009; Thompson, 2013). These analysts and experts might misperceive the state of the economy during an economic boom (Helleiner, 2011), or they may have an interest in spinning economic news in a certain way, such as playing down threats when the economy is doing well (Guerrera, 2009). This self-reinforcing process in economic coverage does not stem only from source influence on journalists. The reverse is possible, too. At times the relation between economic information and markets can become self-referential. In this case the news not only reflects but also reinforces consensus in the market (Thompson, 2013).[6]

We tested whether the magnifying processes that have previously affected the visibility of societal problems (e.g., street violence, crime) also affect macro-economic news during times of economic boom and bust. During the period under analysis, the economy went through two periods of economic boom and bust. Based on quarter-to-quarter change in gross domestic product (GDP) data[7] and change in leading indicators (see Figure 4.1), the first boom period was identified between January 1999 and June 2000. This was followed by a period of bust between January 2001 and March 2002. The economy grew between July 2003 and June 2006, followed by a period of decline between January 2008 and June 2009.

As a first step in our analysis of whether economic coverage deviates from normal coverage during these periods of economic boom or bust, we conducted structural break tests, which can identify turning points in the development of the tone of economic news. A turning point was found in July 2003 (Chow test $F(5, 116) = 3.34, p < .001$), coinciding with the start of the extended period of economic growth. Another turning point was found in May 2007 (Chow test $F(5, 184) = 2.32, p < .05$). Statistical tests confirm that the negative tone of economic news was magnified for the bust periods between 2007 and 2012.[8] May 2007 marks the change between a period of overly positive tone and a period of overly negative tone. The timing is early in comparison to the contraction of the real economy. The boom period between 2003 and 2007 was also magnified with overly positive coverage.

No structural breaks were found in the data marking the start and end of the growth and downturn periods around the turn of the millennium. The absence of structural breaks indicates that economic news was business as usual during this period. Based on structural break tests, it seems that the tone of economic news only deviated from normal coverage during the second boom and bust period. The periods of economic upturn and downturn around 2000 were not magnified in the news. Arguably, these periods were less intense than the later period of growth and recession, but still, the media could have raised extra awareness of these developments. This finding raises the normative question of how severe an economic recession should be in order to require the awareness of the inattentive audience.

If the magnifying effect also applies to the visibility of economic news, the economy should be significantly more visible during periods of economic decline. Increased visibility, however, did not occur during the first period of decline (January 2001–March 2002) or between January 2008 and June 2009. Nonetheless, Figure 4.3 shows an increase in the visibility of economic news in the last four years of the study period. This increase is confirmed in a structural break test, which shows a change in the dynamics of the data in October 2008 (Chow test $F(5, 181) = 4.51, p < .001$). Additional analysis shows that economic news did indeed become more visible between 2008 and 2012 than economic indicators would predict. Economic news did not magnify the positive state of the economy around the turn of the millennium or in 2003–2006.

The sudden increase in visibility of news about the economy seems to result from the emergence of "crisis" as the dominant news frame. As can be seen from Figure 4.5, the use of the term "crisis" increases sharply in the second half of 2008. In line with the theory on pack journalism and media hypes, this common way of understanding and labelling economic

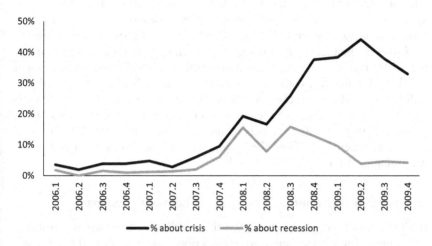

Figure 4.5 References to crisis and recession in national economic news (2006–2009)

Note: Percent of economic news articles which mention crisis and recession (results based on economic coverage in broadsheet newspapers Berlingske, Jyllands-Posten and Politiken). Quarterly data.

developments seems to have opened the news gates and lowered the threshold for stories related to the economy to make it into the news.

In conclusion, our analysis showed that economic news sounds the alarm bell when it matters. Month by month, journalists react only to negative changes and not to positive changes in the economy. An asymmetry exists in the magnification of economic booms and busts. Although economic news became more positive in tone during the boom period, it did not become more visible. When the economic news magnified the negative state of the economy, however, it also became more visible. This pattern of increasing visibility should be seen as positive in light of the media's alarm bell function because the need to raise awareness of inattentive audiences during economic decline is greater than during economic growth. The tipping points identifying the start and end of the magnification periods were close to the tipping points in the macro-economy. This result shows that the media did not ring the alarm all the time but raised awareness of the economy when needed.

The media were even early to adjust the tone of the economic coverage in the wake of the economic crisis. The time-series analysis shows a structural break in the data for May 2007, after which media coverage becomes significantly more negative. Kleinnijenhuis, Schultz, Oegema, and van Atteveldt (2013) also showed that the media expressed early warnings before the start of the economic crisis. Fogarty (2005, p. 169) argues that the media are "quick to point out when the economy is doing poorly." To boot, our analysis shows that the media are quick to point out negative predictions about economic developments—presumably based on early warnings by economic experts—even before economic indicators show a clear decrease.

However, the media did not ring the burglar alarm loudly until November 2008. For over a year, the negative tone remained confined to a small number of articles, mostly on the business pages. Without increased visibility and headlines on the front page, it is questionable whether the inattentive audience will notice the change in the tone of economic news. All in all, despite some points of criticism, news coverage of economic booms and recessions generally fulfilled the burglar alarm function as described in the beginning of this chapter.

Mainstreamed Economic News Versus Economic Experts

In the previous section it was shown that neither the tone nor the visibility of economic news is a one-on-one reflection of economic reality. Instead, the news makes significant economic developments more salient by making them more visible. Can the focus on change and negativity as well as the magnifying effect really be attributed to journalistic routines? One alternative explanation is that economic coverage reflects the views of economic experts. Experts play an important role in the coverage of complex issues (Albæk, 2011; Albæk, Christiansen, and Togeby, 2003). Financial analysts and academic experts often provide interpretations of economic trends. If journalists rely heavily on these experts, they might be the reason for the observed patterns of coverage rather than the routines of journalists who cover economic news for mainstream audiences. We can therefore pose the question whether economic experts have similar biases.

Luckily, data are available that allow us to test expert bias. Between 2003 and 2007, the *Economist* regularly asked professional forecasters for their predictions about economic developments in a number of countries, including Denmark. Interestingly, large differences are apparent in how professional forecasts and how the tone of economic news relate to economic developments. In the 46 months for which professional forecast data are available, the tone of economic news is significantly related to change in economic indicators ($r = .41$, $p < .01$) but not to the levels of these indicators. This result is in line with the analysis for the longer period presented earlier. In contrast, professional forecasts are related to the levels of the economic indicators ($r = .36$) but not to change in these indicators.

These differences between professional forecasters and journalists become more pronounced in a regression analysis. We first look at the tone of economic news to see if we find the same pattern that was in the analysis over the longer period (see Table 4.2). Here, too, the tone reflects negative economic developments but not positive developments. How professional forecasters see the economic future has no impact on the tone of economic news.

Table 4.2 The influence of economic developments on the tone of economic news and on professional forecasts

	Model 1		Model 2	
	Tone		Professional forecast	
	B	SE B	B	SE B
Constant	−2.39	6.30	−2.39	1.56
Tone t-1	0.11	0.16		
Professional forecast	−0.38	0.51		
Σ Professional forecast t-1,2			0.37	0.13***
Composite Leading Indicators (CLI)	0.03	0.07	0.04	0.02**
Negative Δ CLI	5.82	2.51**	0.40	0.58
Adj. R^2	.09		.51	
AIC	71.92		−63.81	
HQC	75.35		−60.51	
SBC	81.07		−54.89	
N	46		44	
Breusch-Godfrey	0.82	($p = 0.37$)	0.07	($p = 0.80$)
Ljung Box Q	0.07	($p = 0.80$)	0.01	($p = 0.90$)

Note: From March 2003 until December 2006. Unstandardized beta-coefficients with standard error. ***$p < .001$, **$p < .01$ (two-sided t-tests).

Table 4.2 furthermore shows that professional forecasters are not affected by negative economic developments, thus confirming that their predictions are affected purely by the state of the economy. These results show that the focus on negative economic developments is due to journalistic routines and does not reflect how journalists' sources see economic developments. In a way, professional forecasters illustrate what the news would be like according to the full news standard; economic coverage would merely report about how the economy was doing, without highlighting significant developments (like an economic decline) or booms and busts. This way of covering the economy might be beneficial for attentive audiences, who are interested in economic developments and do not need to be triggered to be aware of them. But the inattentive audience would likely tune out; it would not be warned of significant developments and could not use the tone and volume of economic coverage as a heuristic for economic developments.

Magnified Economic News and Correct Economic Perceptions

After having shown that the tone and visibility of economic news work as an alarm bell and that the alarm bell does not ring all the time, the question remains whether the alarm bell function helps the audience correctly perceive the economy. If our argument holds, when the media alert the monitorial citizen by visible coverage, he or she should be more aware of economic developments and thus be better able to assess the state of the economy.

The idea that media attention to an issue influences the awareness of that issue among the audience is in keeping with the agenda-setting thesis (McCombs and Shaw, 1972), which has been confirmed in several studies. Two studies by economists support the idea that heightened attention to the economy on the media agenda drives an issue higher on the public agenda, which in turn affects the public's assessments of the economy. An analysis of the antecedents to inflation expectations (Carroll, 2003) suggests that people are not aware of economic developments all the time. Carroll's analysis shows that inflation expectations are updated almost four times as fast when inflation is high on the media agenda than when it is absent. Doms and Morin (2004) later showed that the same holds for general economic expectations, which "are much less 'sticky' during periods of high news coverage than in periods of low news coverage" (Doms and Morin, 2004, p. 2).

Does this more frequent updating also mean that assessments are more accurate? Carroll (2003) hints that it may be so. He compares the inflation expectations of the general public and of professional forecasters. When the economy was high on the media agenda, the public's assessments overlapped strongly with the inflation assessments of professional forecasters. However, as inflation disappeared off the news agenda, the gap widened. Nonetheless, the question remains whether these assessments of the economic situation were accurate. Because Carrol's study dealt with conjectures about the future, a link between audience perceptions and those of professionals does not give conclusive evidence that the perceptions are correct or that they reflect the current state of the economy.

To test this expectation, we return to the comparison between real change in the economy and perceived change in the economy, which was presented in Chapter 2. While the correlation between real change and perceived change was strong ($r = .68$), Figure 2.4 also demonstrates that the overlap between real and perceived changes was stronger at some times than at others. If highly visible economic news helps the monitorial citizen perceive the economy correctly, then the relation between real and perceived economic developments should be stronger in times of heightened economic coverage. Table 4.3 shows that this is indeed the case. The figure shows the influence of real change in GDP on the perceived change of the economy in both a low and a high visibility period. The cut-off point is October 2008, as indicated by the structural break test reported earlier. Two differences between the two regression analyses suggest that highly visible news is beneficial to economic perceptions. First, perceptions of the economy's state in the previous month have a stronger influence in the low than in the high visibility period ($\chi^2 = 2.95$, $df = 1$, $p < .05$). Confirming Carroll (2003) and Doms

Table 4.3 Explaining perceived economic developments during periods when the visibility of economic news was low and high

| | Model 1 | | Model 2 | |
| | Low visibility of economic news[1] | | High visibility of economic news[2] | |
	B	SE B	B	SE B
Constant	−4.52	2.31*	−16.27	4.56***
Perceived economic developments t-1	0.85	0.07***	0.33	0.18*
Δ GDP	1.13	0.51**	2.16	0.71***
Adj. R^2	.80		.67	
AIC	0.806		135.48	
HQC	285.56		135.96	
SBC	288.98		138.32	
N	45		19	
Breusch-Godfrey	0.64	(p = 0.43)	0.56	(p = 0.47)
Ljung Box Q	0.58	(p = 0.45)	0.54	(p = 0.46)

Note: [1]January 1997 until September 2008. [2]October 2008 until December 2012. Unstandardized beta-coefficients with standard error. ***$p < .001$, **$p < .01$, *$p < .05$ (two-sided t-test).

and Morin (2004), this fluctuating influence shows that consumer perceptions are updated more in the period when visibility is high, and they are more "sticky" when visibility is low. Second, the effect of the real economy is larger in the period with high visibility (2.13) than in the period with low visibility (1.13) ($\chi^2 = 12.92$, $df = 1$, $p < .001$). This shows that the perceptions of the general population are more strongly linked to real economic developments when the economy is highly visible on the media agenda than when it is less visible.

Before we can conclude that the visibility of economic news influences how much people update their perceptions, we need to assess at least one alternative explanation. As the analysis at the start of this chapter showed, visibility of economic news is not exogenous but reflects changes in the state of the real economy. Thus, we must consider the possibility that the state of the economy rather than the visibility of economic news raised the public's awareness. In our quarterly data, real change in the economy and the visibility of economic news are significantly correlated (Pearson's correlation −.37, $p < .01$).

Thus, an alternative explanation might be that visibility does not necessarily trigger people's awareness but, instead, that the severity of economic developments influences people to seek new information and to update their perceptions. This reasoning would be in line with Boczkowski and Mitchelsteins's analysis of people's interest for public affairs news online in times of high political activity (Boczkowski and Mitchelstein, 2013). They showed that during these times (such as elections), the audience demanded more political information. The availability of political news also increased, but not as much as the demand. They therefore conclude that "the agenda-setting function of the news media should be seen as highly context-dependent. . . . [T]his dependence on context . . . is primarily premised on fluctuations of the public's interest" (Boczkowski and Mitchelstein, 2013, p. 56). Although their study dealt exclusively with online news, whereas this chapter's focus is on broadsheet newspapers, it is plausible that the increased awareness of the economy from 2008 onwards was triggered not by heightened media awareness but by real-world economic developments, namely the Great Recession. Lischka (2015) showed that economic news has more influence on economic perceptions during times of economic recession. She argues that this is the case because the severity of the economic situation increases people's need for orientation (Weaver, 1980), which raises people's interest in economic developments.

Ideally, by means of time-series analysis, we would distinguish between the effect of the real economy and the effect of economic coverage on correct perceptions of the economic climate. However, this is difficult to do due to the low number of observations—the overlap in periods of high visibility and low economic development. We therefore separately analyse the moderating role of visibility on the one hand and economic developments on the other hand. First, we look at the role of visibility and divide the quarters in the analysis into four groups of equal size depending on the visibility of economic news. Then we look at the correlation between the real and the perceived economy in each period (top half of Table 4.4). In line with our theoretical expectation and the analysis shown above, we find that the link between real and perceived economic developments is stronger for periods when economic news is more visible. For the 16 quarters when economic

Table 4.4 Correlation between real and perceived economic developments

During quarters with different levels of visibility of economic news	
Low visibility ($n = 15$)	.16
Medium low visibility ($n = 16$)	.34
Medium high visibility ($n = 16$)	.52*
High visibility ($n = 17$)	.83***

During quarters with different levels of economic growth	
Negative/low economic growth ($n = 15$)	.77**
Medium low economic growth ($n = 15$)	−.13
Medium high economic growth ($n = 16$)	−.13
High economic growth ($n = 17$)	.08

Note: Pearson's correlation. ***$p < .001$, **$p < .01$, *$p < .05$ (two-sided t-tests).

news was least visible, there is no significant correlation, whereas for quarters with the highest visibility, there is a strong correlation. In the periods with medium high visibility of economic news, there was a significant relation between real and perceived economic developments.

How do these results look when we split the quarters according to the state of the real economy? The lower half of Table 4.4 shows that in the quarters when the economy was at its worst, there is again a strong significant correlation between the real and the perceived economy. However, in the other periods, the pattern is less clear than it was for news visibility. There is no significant relation between real and perceived economic change in the period with medium low economic growth. The comparison between the moderating effects of the visibility of economic news and of the economic climate suggests that both factors can influence economic awareness and the correctness of economic perceptions. The comparison also suggests a difference between the moderating influence of economic news and of the real economy. In regard to the latter, only the most extreme situations trigger updating and yield a significant correlation between real and perceived economic developments. Visibility has a more systematic influence on correct perceptions of the economy because a significant relation between real and perceived economic developments exists in the quarters when economic news has medium high visibility.

Taking Stock

This chapter focused on the first of three mechanisms by which mainstreamed economic news informs the inattentive audience. An analysis of economic coverage between 1997 and 2012 shows that economic news does indeed function as an alarm bell. It alerts the inattentive audience with visible negative coverage when the economy changes, deteriorates, or enters into recession—in short, when it matters. We contrast mass press coverage to experts' economic assessments to argue that media logic rather than reliance on expert sources is responsible for this type of coverage. In addition, we show that the specialist business press, which caters to the attentive audience, does *not* react to economic developments in the same way. Finally, we show that, on the aggregate level, the media's alarm bell function helps the audience develop correct perceptions of the economy. When the economy is highly visible, there is a strong correlation between economic perceptions and the real state of the economy. When media attention is low, this relation is significantly weaker. These findings show that mainstreamed economic news informs the audience through the first of three mechanisms described in Chapter 3—the alarm bell mechanism. With this aggregate-level analysis in place, it is now time to turn our attention to the individual level. In the next chapters, we will draw on our integrated panel study and content analysis to study the second mechanism: the effect of elaboration-inducing content elements.

Notes

1 The data were downloaded from the website of the Organisation for Economic Co-operation and Development (OECD). Leading indicators and tendency surveys. 2017. At www.oecd.org/std/leading-indicators. In the analysis the amplitude-adjusted Composite Leading Indicator (CLI) is used, which the OECD describes as "the most straightforward way to present the CLI."

2 Optimisme i butikkerne [Optimism in the shops]. *Politiken*, 11 July 2003, p. 12.

3 BMA, Ledende artikel: Eksportsucces [Editorial, Export success]. *Berlingske*, 17 July 2003, p. 4.

4 Including the tone of the three previous months, or in other words three lags of the dependent variable in order to account for autocorrelation in the time-series. Including three lags gives the most parsimonious model without autocorrelation based on the Akaike Information Criterium (AIC).

5 There is no significant correlation between the state of the economy and the visibility of economic news ($r = -.09$, n.s.).

6 This relation does not necessarily imply that economic news can independently influence economic markets and create market bubbles. Empirical evidence for such an effect of economic news is mixed (Lee, 2014, p. 717).

7 B.1*g Bruttonationalprodukt, BNP, seasonally adjusted. Source: Danmarks Statistik. Nationalregnskab og offentlige finanser. Last modified 22 August 2017. At www.statistikbanken.dk/10175.

8 As a robustness check, the analysis was repeated with different economic indicators. Our expectations were supported when level of unemployment, consumer confidence, business confidence, or the price index were included as indicators of the economy instead of the CLI. Finally, we repeated the analysis for the three newspapers separately, which led to the same results for *Politiken* and *Jyllands-Posten*. For *Berlingske*, the economic boom between 2003 and 2007 was not magnified in tone.

5 Making the Economy Relevant and Interesting With Human-Interest Framing

In this and the following two chapters, we turn to the *second* mechanism by which mainstreamed economic news informs the inattentive audience: the elaboration-inducing content characteristics of mainstreamed economic news. In the current chapter, we study to what extent exposure to economic news that is presented with a human-interest frame influences interest in the economy. Our main assumption is that exposure to this type of framing stimulates interest because it increases perceived personal relevance of news. Even people who are not intrinsically interested in the economy will automatically allocate mental resources to processing information when they perceive it to be personally relevant and important to their lives (Graber, 1988; Lang, 2000; 2009, p. 195). Consequently, news consumers become more motivated to invest cognitive effort in the news that they are exposed to. In other words, personal relevance induces elaborative processing (Berent and Krosnick, 1995).

Perceived personal relevance of news is affected by both what and who is covered (So and Nabi, 2013). We argue that human-interest framing (illustrating broader societal developments with an individual story; see Chapter 3) is a way for journalists to produce a news story that makes economic news more personally relevant (Graber, 1988). A news story with a human face may be perceived as personally relevant because it makes the news consumer identify with the person depicted. Identification, in turn, triggers interest in the economy. Before unfolding our argument and presenting empirical evidence, we first elaborate on what we mean by interest in the economy.

Interest in the Economy

Interest in the economy is relevant to how much people learn from the economic information that they are exposed to in the news media. People with high interest in the economy are intrinsically motivated to find out more about the economy. Increased motivation is conducive to more information searching and facilitates the retrieval of new information. Moreover, because the economy is deeply intertwined with politics, interest in economic matters seems to be a prerequisite for political engagement. If citizens are uninterested in economics, they are likely to be ignorant of opportunities to defend their own economic well-being or that of their fellow citizens through political participation. Despite the importance of economic interest, the concept is underdeveloped, especially when compared to political interest, which has received much more scholarly attention. In politics, interest is considered one of the most important determinants of engagement. If citizens have no interest in politics, they fail to "be aware of the political process or of the opportunities to defend their well-being, to contribute to collective actions, or to select a representative" (Van Deth, 2000, p. 119). Political interest is often defined as "an evaluative statement or judgment about how appealing the realm of politics is" (Boulianne, 2011, p. 152; Strömbäck and Shehata, 2010). More elaborately, Van Deth (2000, p. 119) defines political interest as "the degree to which politics arouses a citizen's curiosity." Following this definition, we can see interest in the economy as "an evaluative statement or judgment about how appealing economic issues are."

Although some people may feel obliged to be interested in politics to fulfil their duty as good citizens, not everyone considers politics to be important or relevant to their lives (Van Deth, 2000, pp. 119–120). By contrast, people may have more personal incentives to be interested in the economy. Being informed about the economy is undoubtedly needed in today's society, particularly since the start of the Great Recession. The economy is not only a central topic in political debates; every day, people have to make economic decisions that affect them personally.

Interest and News Exposure

Little research has been conducted on interest in the economy as an outcome of media exposure. The same goes for the effect of news exposure on political interest. Compared to both political knowledge and political participation, political interest as an outcome of news exposure has largely been ignored. The reason may be that political interest is conventionally considered to be a steady personality trait that people either do or do not have (Prior, 2010). Despite a high degree of stability in political interest, a number of studies suggest that media exposure might affect political interest. The positive relation between political interest and media exposure is well established. Several studies have found that interest affects news exposure (Shah and Scheufele, 2006) because politically interested people seek out news or political information to a greater extent than those who are less politically interested. This view seems consistent with the notion of political interest as a steady personality trait or a political identity (Prior, 2010, p. 748).

Another group of studies demonstrates that the relationship between news exposure and interest is reciprocal, so that news exposure produces interest in information and this interest stimulates increased news exposure

(Atkin, Galloway, and Nayman, 1976; Boulianne, 2011; Strömbäck and Shehata, 2010). The theoretical reason for the positive effect of news exposure on political interest is that habitual exposure to news containing politically relevant content socializes people into being interested in politics (Delli Carpini, 2004, p. 404; Graber, 1988, p. 316; Strömbäck and Shehata, 2010, p. 509).

A few studies suggest that exposure to different kinds of news content (public service versus commercialized) has different effects on political interest (Boulianne, 2011; Shehata, 2014; Strömbäck and Shehata, 2010). Shehata (2014) investigates political interest as a direct outcome of exposure to news content. He found that exposure to game-framed news has a negative effect on political interest, whereas exposure to issue-framed news has a stimulating effect. Shehata (2014) argues that game framing alienates people from politics, thereby demobilizing their political interest. Issue framing may increase an individual's feeling of being involved in politics, which, in turn, increases political interest.

The Effect of Human-Interest Framing on Interest

Building upon the work of Shehata (2014), who showed that specific news content has the potential to stimulate interest, we investigate the association between exposure to human-interest framing and interest in the economy. We define the human-interest frame as a news frame that "brings a human face or an individual's story to the presentation of an event, issue or problem" (Semetko and Valkenburg, 2000, p. 95). News that is framed around an individual is likely to "describe courses, importance and consequences of a problem from the unique perspective of an individual" (Bosch, 2014, p. 218).[1] For example, a headline of a news story with a human-interest frame is "Benny Østerlund: The Thoughts Were Passing Through My Head," about a man who has lost his eligibility to receive unemployment benefits.[2] As we discussed in Chapter 5, such headlines and stories putting a human face on an abstract story should help the inattentive audience relate to broad economic developments. An essential tool of journalists is to present news stories with a human face to make news appealing and understandable to a broad audience (Temple, 2006). The person in a news story can be deemed representative of a larger group of people who are affected by the issue at stake (Zillmann, 2006).

Other research has found positive effects of exposure to human-interest framing on variables such as political knowledge (Jebril et al., 2013) and government evaluations (Boukes, Boomgaarden, Moorman, and de Vreese, 2015). Bartsch, Oliver, Nitsch, and Scherr (2016) found that television portrayals of Paralympic athletes elicit empathic feelings, which increases audience interest in para-sports and destigmatizes people with disabilities. Together, these studies show that illustrating a news story with a human face can have positive effects on news consumers.

There is reason to expect that human-interest framing can stimulate interest in the economy as well. The human-interest frame is used to illustrate abstract news stories with a human face and has the potential to "bring a news story home on a personal level" because it makes news seem less distant and more personally relevant (Brants, 1998; Graber, 1988, p. 213; Temple, 2006). We see perceived personal relevance of news as an evaluation that people make about the news content that they are exposed to. It concerns involvement with an issue, and people are more likely to perceive an issue to be personally relevant when they expect it to have consequences for their lives (So and Nabi, 2013, p. 320). According to So and Nabi (2013), personal relevance is a function of both what and who is depicted. They claim that people might view a story as personally relevant when it depicts a situation that could affect their own lives. People are more likely to think of how a news story relates to their own lives when they identify with the person presented in the story (So and Nabi, 2013)—even if the person featured in the story is not deemed socially close. Graber (1988) also pointed to this connection between human-interest framing and personal relevance. She found that news stories regarded as personally relevant involved human interest–framed information.

Personal Relevance Raises Interest

We expect that the ability of human-interest framing to increase the personal relevance of a news story also raises interest in the story's topic. Van Deth (2000) claims that even though political phenomena may arouse citizens' curiosity, it is not obvious that politics are considered to be relevant to their lives. Without this relevance, politics will be judged to be unappealing, and most people will quickly lose interest in it. In this sense, a lack of interest in politics is due to the "waning relevance of politics" (Van Deth, 2000, pp. 117, 119). But if the way that politics is presented in the news can incite perceived relevance, interest may increase and people will put in more mental effort to process the information presented. In regard to the economy, personal relevance may likewise be the key to raising people's interest. If the news triggers people to relate economic developments to their personal lives, abstract news (e.g., about the stock exchange or export figures) will be made more appealing.

Empirically, Graber (1988) showed that people are more interested in a news story when it has a personal angle. By contrast, people disregard stories when they are not personally affected by the topic covered. In a similar vein, Petty, Brinôl, and Priester (2009) acknowledge that not every message received from the media is sufficiently interesting to ponder. They argue that the perceived personal relevance of a message is the "most important variable in enhancing interest in a message" (Petty et al., 2009, p. 136). They further argue that information about a topic of high personal relevance will lead to thoughtful consideration and to greater motivation to process the presented information. These arguments correspond to the findings of She-hata (2014), showing that active news processing has a positive effect on political interest. This line of thought dovetails with our central argument—namely, that mainstreamed economic news using human-interest framing induces elaborative processing by raising personal relevance.

Key Questions

Against this theoretical backdrop, human-interest framing is the first charac-teristic of mainstreamed economic news that we expect to lead to elaboration of economic news, which in turn should raise interest in the economy. This expectation is consistent with the literature that shows that news exposure has a positive effect on political interest, and it builds on the scarce literature that shows that specific news content has the potential to influence interest. One underlying assumption in our argument is that human-interest framing makes economic news more personally relevant. The second assumption is that perceived personal relevance of the news mediates the effects of exposure to human-interest framing on interest in the economy. Figure 5.1 illustrates the expectations that we explore in this chapter.

News Exposure and Interest in the Economy

We will test our expectations using our panel survey. The respondents in this study were asked about their interest in the economy at two points in time.[3] This allows for a testing of the difference in interest at these time points, which in turn can be related to the exposure to economic news in between the two time points.

As a first indication of a possible relation between exposure to human-interest framing and economic interest, we first look at the level of inter-est in the economy in people with different degrees of news exposure. Our respondents indicated on a scale from 1 (not interested at all) to 5 (very interested) how interested they are in economic matters. By asking about interest in the economy in this way, we follow the convention in measuring

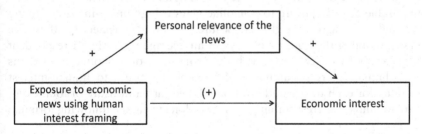

Figure 5.1 Anticipated relation between exposure to economic news using human-interest framing and interest in the economy

political interest (see Boulianne, 2011; Prior, 2010; Strömbäck and Shehata, 2010). The question was adjusted by replacing the reference to "politics" with "economic matters." After the adjustment, the item was "How interested or not are you in economic matters?"

To divide the respondents into three groups with different degrees of news exposure, we first calculated their total exposure. Each respondent answered the question, "How many days, if any, do you use OUTLET during a typical week?" for the eight Danish news outlets included in the year-long content analysis (see Chapter 3 and Methodological Appendix): DR1, TV2 (television), *Politiken, Jyllands-Posten, Berlingske, Børsen* (broadsheet newspapers), *BT* and *Ekstra Bladet* (tabloid newspapers). The respondents indicated whether they were exposed to the offline and online versions of the outlets. Responses were given on an 8-point scale ranging from 0 to 7 days a week. We then summed the days of exposure to each outlet to calculate a total exposure score for each individual respondent. Based on these results, we divided the respondents in three equal-sized groups: on average, the one-third with the lowest media exposure was exposed to fewer than two outlets per day. This was also the group with the lowest level of economic interest ($M = 3.69$, $SD = .88$ on a 5-point scale). The middle group, who was exposed to between two and three outlets per day, had significantly higher levels of economic interest ($M = 3.92$, $SD = .70$). One-third of the respondents was exposed to more than three outlets per day. This group with high levels of media exposure also had the highest economic interest ($M = 4.07$, $SD = .78$).[4] Thus, the results also clearly show that news exposure and interest in the economy are related.

Before exploring whether this relation between news exposure and interest in the economy is related to the prevalence of human-interest framing in economic news, we look at the aggregate-level changes in interest in the economy between the two waves. Interest in the economy declined modestly but significantly between the two points of time at which interest was measured, and it fluctuates considerably. For 32.6 percent of the respondents, the level of economic interest changed between the two-time points.

We conducted ordinary least squares (OLS) regression analysis to examine whether these individual differences in change in interest in the economy can be explained by exposure to economic news using human-interest framing (Table 5.1). Exposure to economic news using human-interest framing was measured with a weighted exposure measure (Schuck et al., 2016). We first multiplied the number of days in an average week that a respondent was exposed to each outlet with the proportion of economic news items with human-interest framing in the outlet. Exposure to human-interest framing for each media outlet was combined into a measure of total exposure to human-interest framing. This was done using the following formula:

Exposure to economic news using human-interest framing = ((Exposure to outlet 1 × share of human-interest framing in economic news outlet 1) + (exposure to outlet 2 × share of human-interest framing in economic news in outlet 1) + (. . .) + (exposure medium 16 × share of human-interest framing in economic news in outlet 16))/16 outlets.[5]

The regression models in Table 5.1 explain economic interest at time 2. Apart from exposure to human-interest framing between time 1 and time 2, we also included interest at time 1 in the regression model. In doing so, we can test whether exposure to human-interest framing has an effect above and beyond the levels of economic interest before exposure (see Markus, 1979). We do not include background variables like gender, age, or education in the model because these variables are expected to be stable between the waves. While these variables have likely affected economic interest at time 1, we do not assume that they had a direct impact on changes in interest between time 1 and time 2.

Exposure to economic news using human-interest framing has a significant effect on interest in the economy, after controlling for previous levels of interest in the economy (Model 1). The more one is exposed to economic news using human-interest framing, the higher the levels of economic interest. This confirms our expectation that exposure to economic news with a human-interest frame stimulates interest in the economy.

The question remains whether the increased interest is due to the increased personal relevance of the news. To test this question, we asked the respondents to indicate on a scale from 1 (disagree a lot) to 5 (agree a lot) whether they agree with the following statement: "I often think about how the news I watch on television or how the news I read about in the newspapers relates to my own life." The formulation of this question is similar to the one used by So and Nabi (2013).[6] When we add perceived personal relevance of news to the regression model, we find a significant positive effect of this variable on interest in the economy (Model 2 in Table 5.1). When perceived personal

Table 5.1 Explaining economic interest t2

	Model 1			Model 2		
	B	SE B	β	B	SE B	β
Constant	1.72	0.11***		1.36	0.13***	
Exposure to economic news with human-interest framing	0.91	0.16***	.15	.77	0.16***	.13
Economic interest t1	0.48	0.03***	.48	.46	0.03***	.46
Perceived personal relevance				.14	0.03***	.14
N	1,042			1,042		
Adj. R^2	.27			.29		

Note: ***$p < .001$, **$p < .01$, *$p < .05$, #$p < .1$ (two-sided t-tests).

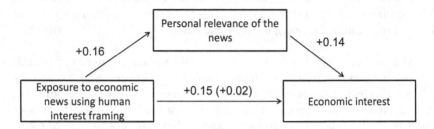

Figure 5.2 The indirect effect of exposure to economic news using human-interest framing on interest in the economy

Note: Standardized coefficients. Significant at $p < .05$ (two-sided t-tests).

relevance is included in the model, the effect of exposure to human-interest framing decreases. This might be an indication that perceived personal relevance mediates the effect of exposure to human-interest framing on economic interest.

We conducted a bootstrap analysis to test whether perceived personal relevance of news actually mediates the effects of human-interest framing on interest in the economy (Hayes, 2013).[7] Figure 5.2 shows that the independent variable, exposure to economic news using human-interest framing, has a significant positive effect on the mediating variable of perceived personal relevance of the news. As expected, exposure to economic news using human-interest framing has a significant indirect effect on interest in the economy. We thereby find support that human-interest framing has an effect on interest in the economy through perceived personal relevance of news. Additionally, exposure to human-interest framing has a direct effect on interest in the economy. Thus, perceived personal relevance is not the only explanation for the effect.

Human-Interest Framing and the Inattentive Audience

The inattentive audience benefits the most from economic news using human-interest framing. This can be seen from Table 5.2, which presents the results of a regression analysis explaining personal relevance of the news. Again, the results show that the more people are exposed to economic news using human-interest framing, the more likely they are to perceive the news as having personal relevance. People with high starting levels of interest in the economy perceive the news to have more personal relevance than people with low interest in the economy. An interesting result here is the negative interaction between starting levels of economic interest and exposure to economic news using human-interest framing. Thus, perceived relevance after news exposure increases the most in people with low levels of interest in the economy. Exposure to human-interest framing has only a limited effect on

Table 5.2 Explaining personal relevance of the news

	B	SE B	β
Constant	3.51	0.03***	
Exposure to economic news using human-interest framing	0.13	0.03***	.16
Economic interest	0.12	0.03***	.14
Exposure to economic news using human-interest framing × Economic interest	−0.05	0.03*	−.07
N	1,042		
Adj. R^2	.06		

Note: Variables were standardized to avoid multicollinearity. ***$p < .001$, *$p < .05$ (two-sided t-tests).

people who are already interested in the economy in the first place. Thus, the inattentive audience does indeed benefit the most from exposure to economic news using human-interest framing.

Two explanations for this finding come to mind. First, people who are already highly interested in the economy will automatically see the economy as personally relevant. For them, the connections between economic news about the stock exchange or international economies on the one hand, and their personal lives on the other hand, will be more obvious than to people with less interest in the economy. At the same time, people with a high interest in the economy might be active on the stock exchange themselves or actively looking, for example, to change their loan or improve their mortgage. If so, news about the economy will automatically be seen as personally relevant. When people automatically see economic news as personally relevant, they do not need the media to make the news relevant to them by using human-interest framing. Because perceived relevance is already high, the additional effect of exposure to human-interest framing will be small.

Second, people who are already highly interested in the economy are not stimulated to elaborate by the same type of content as the inattentive audience (Mujica and Bachmann, 2018). Compared to people with a low interest in the economy, people with a high interest in the economy are more likely to prefer hard news, as we discussed in Chapter 3. They may consider news that uses human-interest framing as infotainment, quite the opposite of the factual news that they prefer. More abstract news describing trends and general economic developments might be just as likely to trigger their elaboration as more concrete information.

Positive Effects of Human-Interest Framing

Our finding that exposure to economic news using human-interest framing (which is an oft-used journalistic tool in mainstreamed economic news, particularly on television) has a positive effect on interest in the economy is remarkable because, within the political realm, interest has mainly been considered a steady personality trait that does not change (Prior, 2010). In fact, our finding relates to previous research on the effects of news framing on changes in interest. Shehata (2014) found that political interest is influenced negatively by game-framed news exposure but positively by issue-framed news exposure. Human-interest framing certainly appears to affect interest, and empirical evidence supports the claim that the way in which information is presented in the news influences audience levels of interest in economic and political matters.

This chapter also revealed why human-interest framing stimulates interest. Perceived personal relevance of news was disentangled as a mechanism mediating the positive effect of human-interest framing on interest. At this point, we know of only one other study that theoretically addresses the potential mechanisms behind positive media effects on interest. Shehata (2014) suggests that *passive forms* of news use (e.g., framing exposure) and *active* or *motivated forms* of news use are different modes of media use that have different effects on interest. Considering these two forms of media use as independent variables, he demonstrates that motivated news use has a positive impact on political interest, whereas game-framing exposure has a negative effect on interest. In this chapter we have shown that framing exposure activates the mechanism of perceived personal relevance, which is a part of the motivation to processes information (Petty and Cacioppo, 1990). This finding indicates that framing exposure and more active forms of news use are not necessarily two different kinds of news use.

On the heels of this contribution, future research needs to further unravel the effects of exposure to human-interest news framing on changes in interest. In particular, the *what* and the *who* of a news story should be studied. According to theory, both the topic and the human face that appear in a news article are potentially important promotors of the article's increased personal relevance. In this regard, economic news coverage likely has a stronger effect on interest in the economy than political news coverage. Likewise, interest in a news story may be stimulated if the news audience identifies with the person in the story. Previous research supports that identification is key to determining personal relevance (Schweisberger, Billinson, and Chock, 2014; So and Nabi, 2013).

Overall, the findings challenge common criticisms of mainstreamed (economic) news. The news media has overwhelmingly been subject to media malaise accusations, which claim that news exposure fosters a spiral of negative consequences for various forms of civic interest and engagement. Our findings address the criticisms that have been directed at the tabloidization of news. As one of the characterizing content features of tabloidization, human-interest framing can be linked to a "downgrading" (Norris, 2000, p. 71) or "dumbing down" (Temple, 2006) of news. The present results question such worries and suggest that the tension between "'giving the public what it wants' and the desire to educate, reform and improve" (referred to by Norris, 2000, p. 72) need not end in a trade-off because human-interest framing can stimulate interest. In the next chapter, we look at another aspect of economic news that has been criticized in the past—namely, the focus on negative developments. Like human-interest framing, the focus on negativity also has surprisingly positive effects, especially for the inattentive audience.

Notes

1 Bosch (2014) refers to exemplification, which shares aspects of human-interest framing.
2 Lars Halskov and John Hansen. Benny Østerlund: Tankerne kørte rund I hovedet. *Politiken*, 31 March 2013, p. 4.
3 For this analysis, time 2 is the fourth wave of the panel survey, and time 1 is the first wave. The fourth wave was chosen because some of the variables in the analysis were not measured in the second and third waves.
4 Differences are significant at $p < .05$ (Anova with Tukey-b post hoc test).
5 Since some of the variables were not measured in waves 2 and 3 of the survey, we look in this chapter at developments between wave 1 and wave 4. We therefore combine three exposure measures to account for exposure to economic news using human-interest framing during this period: we weighted exposure to the different outlets measured at wave 2 by the share of items that uses human-interest framing in economic news measured between wave 1 and wave 2; exposure measured at wave 3 by the human-interest framing in economic news between wave 2 and wave 3; and exposure measured at wave 4 by human-interest framing in economic news between wave 3 and wave 4. We then calculated a combined exposure measure by adding the weighted exposure for the three waves and dividing by 3 ($M = .32$, $SD = .14$, minimum = 0, maximum = .78). Other ways of combining the exposure measure (like giving extra weight to the later waves) lead to the same results.

   Exposure to economic news using human-interest framing between waves 1 and 2 = (Exposure to EkstraBladet at wave 2*.28 + exposure to ekstrabladet. dk at wave 2*.13 + exposure to BT at wave 2*0 + exposure to BT.dk*.17 + exposure to TV2 nyheder at wave 2*.52 + exposure to TV2.dk at wave 2*0 + exposure to DR TV avisen at wave 2*.50 + exposure to DR.dk at wave 2*.08 + exposure to Politiken at wave 2*0 + exposure to Politiken.dk at wave 2*.12 + exposure to Berlingske at wave 2*.13 + exposure to Berlingske.dk at wave 2*.08 + exposure to JyllandsPosten at wave 2*0 + exposure to JyllandsPosten.dk at wave 2*.09 + exposure to Børsen at wave 2*0 + exposure to Borsen.dk*.17)/16.

   Exposure to economic news using human-interest framing at wave 3 = (Exposure to EkstraBladet at wave 3*.15 + exposure to ekstrabladet.dk at wave 3*.03 + exposure to BT at wave 3*.04 + exposure to BT.dk at wave 3*.08 + exposure to TV2 nyheder at wave 3*.42 + exposure to TV2.dk at wave 3*.01 + exposure to DR TV avisen at wave 3*.59 + exposure to DR.dk at wave 3*.03 + exposure to Politiken at wave 3*.19 + exposure to Politiken.dk at wave 3*.10 + exposure to Berlingske at wave 3*.07 + exposure to Berlingske.dk at wave 3*0 + exposure to JyllandsPosten at wave 3*.16 + exposure to JyllandsPosten.dk at wave 3*.03 + exposure to Børsen at wave 3*.12 + exposure to Borsen.dk at wave 3*0)/16.

   Exposure to economic news using human-interest framing at wave 4 = (Exposure to EkstraBladet at wave 4 *0 + exposure to ekstrabladet.dk at wave 4*. + exposure to BT at wave 4*.08 + exposure to BT.dk at wave 4*.08 + exposure to

TV2 nyheder at wave 4*.43 + exposure to TV2.dk at wave 4*.14 + exposure to DR TV avisen at wave 4*.52. + exposure to DR.dk at wave 4*.21 + exposure to Politiken at wave 4*.08 + exposure to Politiken.dk at wave 4*.13 + exposure to Berlingske at wave 4*.08 + exposure to Berlingske.dk at wave 4*.04 + exposure to JyllandsPosten at wave 4*0 + exposure to JyllandsPosten.dk at wave 4*.04 + exposure to Børsen at wave 4*0 + exposure to Borsen.dk at wave 4*0)/16.

Additionally, we tested our expectations with an alternative measure for exposure to economic news using human-interest framing where the share of economic news using human interest framing was multiplied by the visibility of economic news. This was done because it can be expected that the effect of exposure to human interest framing on economic interest is stronger when economic news is more visible (see Jebril et al., 2013 for a similar argument). Using this alternative exposure measure leads to the same conclusions.

6 To ensure that perceived personal relevance of news is different from economic interest, the correlation between these two variables is tested. A Pearson's r test reveals a relatively weak positive correlation between the variables ($r = .24$, $p < .01$). Moreover, a principal component factor analysis supports that perceived personal relevance and economic interest are different constructs because two components were extracted from the items measuring the variables.

7 We conducted a bootstrap analysis following the recommendations of Hayes (2013), model 4.

6 Good News in Bad News
How Negativity Enhances Economic Efficacy

In the previous chapter, we saw that economic news that uses human-interest framing makes the news more relevant, which in turn increases economic interest. We see this effect as evidence that mainstreamed economic news is beneficial to the inattentive audience because it includes elaboration-inducing elements. In this chapter we look at a second elaboration-inducing element: negativity. The focus on negativity is a central element of economic news coverage in the mainstream press. Others have observed that negativity is a "news ideology" (Lengauer, Esser, and Berganza, 2012, p. 181) and that the press is "negative-centric" (Trussler and Soroka, 2014, p. 361). We argue that the media's focus on bad news can, in fact, be good news because it enhances *internal economic efficacy*—the belief in one's own competence to understand economic information and to make economic evaluations and decisions.

This chapter looks at attention as the mechanism that links negative news and internal economic efficacy. Information processing is subject to a negativity bias (Soroka and McAdams, 2015, p. 15), which means that individuals automatically allocate attention to negative information. As we will argue, this increased attention is expected to lead to higher levels of internal economic efficacy. This process is particularly important for the inattentive audience. We will see that negativity arouses more attention to economic news among individuals with low interest in the economy.

News Exposure and Economic Efficacy

The belief in one's own competence to understand and act upon economic developments assists the public in making economic evaluations, judgements, and decisions. Internal economic efficacy is crucial for democratic citizens in a society where the economy and politics have become so closely intertwined. Nevertheless, internal economic efficacy has been overlooked by social scientists, and little is known about its relation to media exposure. The neglect of internal economic efficacy stands in contrast to the energy devoted to internal political efficacy, which has been studied extensively. The lack of research on internal economic efficacy is surprising because economic assessments and judgements affect not only evaluations of and support for the government but also contribute to important economic decisions (Hetherington, 1996).

Similar to Chapter 5, where we reviewed political communication literature to explain what media coverage can contribute to *economic* interest, it makes sense to turn to extant knowledge in the realm of politics when trying to understand *economic* efficacy. We know from politics that the related concept of *internal political efficacy* is an important determinant of political engagement, evaluations, and decisions (Kaid et al., 2007; Kidwell, Hardesty, and Childers, 2008; Rudolph, Gangl, and Stevens, 2000). An individual's self-perceived ability to understand what is going on in the political system is an important feature of internal political efficacy, defined as "beliefs about one's own competence to understand and to participate effectively in politics" (Neimi, Graig, and Mattei, 1991, p. 1407). Internal political efficacy is associated with less confusion in choice making (Raju, Lonial, and Mangold, 1995) and lower intimidation by challenges, conflicts, and disagreements (Valentino, Gregorowicz, and Groenendyk, 2009). Similarly, internal economic efficacy should give consumers more confidence to make economic decisions. We use the definition of political efficacy as a guide and refer to internal economic efficacy as "beliefs about one's own competence to understand and to participate in economic matters."

Internal economic efficacy bares resemblance to economic self-efficacy, which refers to "people's judgments of their capabilities to execute courses of action required to attain designated types of performances" (Bandura, 1986, p. 391). According to self-efficacy theory, efficacy judgements are not stable but develop as new information and experiences are acquired (Gist and Mitchell, 1992, p. 184). One type of information that affects efficacy judgements is information that conveys experiences of others. In order to choose the best course of action and to avoid making the same mistakes as others, an individual will observe another's actions and their consequences, and make inferences from them. Because the economy is a somewhat unobtrusive issue about which people learn from news reports (Boomgaarden et al., 2011), exposure to economic news may likewise play an important role in shaping internal economic efficacy.

Previous research on internal political efficacy suggests a positive effect of news exposure on internal efficacy. Kenski and Stroud (2006) found that online exposure to presidential campaign information increased internal political efficacy. Möller, de Vreese, Esser, and Kunz (2014) showed that internal efficacy changes positively when individuals are more exposed to newspapers and online news. These studies, however, relied solely on general measures of media exposure, without taking the actual news content into account. Other studies look at exposure to specific news to find out what type of news is particularly beneficial for political efficacy. Tewksbury, Hals, and Bibart (2008) showed that newspaper browsing, in the sense of looking for specific news content, is positively associated with internal political efficacy. Becker (2011) found that viewing late night political comedy on cable and on television had a positive effect on internal efficacy. Moreover, Baumgartner and Morris (2006) demonstrated that *negativity* in late night news led to higher levels of internal political efficacy.

Contrary to this study, however, Pedersen (2012) found that exposure to strategic game framing has a negative effect on internal political efficacy. Pedersen explains this negative effect with the limited substantial knowledge of politics that strategic game framing provides to news consumers. He also suggests that the game frame "may take up time and attention that would otherwise have been used to consume news containing factual knowledge about substantive politics and thereby lead to lower levels of political knowledge, which again lead to lower levels of internal efficacy" (Pedersen, 2012, p. 228). Pedersen's study clearly offers an alternative view to previous studies showing that news exposure increases political efficacy. These divergent findings underline the need to further explore the mechanisms linking exposure to specific content features and internal economic efficacy. We agree with the reasoning of Pedersen (2012) that *attention* may play a key role in this relationship.

Negativity, Attention, and Efficacy

News consumers have a limited capacity to process the huge amounts of information that they are exposed to in the news flow (Graber, 1988; Lang, 2000). In order to "tame the information tide" (Graber, 1988), news consumers select which information to process and which information not to process. Various research has shown that information processing is subject to a "negativity bias" (Soroka and McAdams, 2015, p. 15), which means that individuals automatically allocate *attention* to negative information because they scan the environment for unfavourable situations and are alerted by them (Chaffee and Kanihan, 1997; Lengauer et al., 2012; Marcus et al., 2000; Meffert, Chung, Joiner, Waks, and Garst, 2006; Smith, Cacioppo, Larsen, and Chartrand, 2003). This "asymmetrical attentiveness" (Soroka, 2014) towards negativity is assumed to be the main reason why negativity could have a positive effect on internal economic efficacy. Negative stories naturally draw the attention of the reader. Attention is defined as "the tendency to focus mentally on specific content during exposure to news" and is a necessary condition for processing information *elaborately* (Eveland, 2002, p. 29). Elaborative processing implies that information is carefully processed. This reasoning corresponds with previous research showing that negative information is better recalled and is processed more in depth than other information (Ito, Larsen, Smith, and Cacioppo, 1998; Neuman, Marcus, Grigler, and MacKuen, 2007).

Given such positive effects of attention on elaborative processing, attention may also have a positive impact on internal economic efficacy. News consumers who pay attention to economic news may feel informed about and better able to understand economic matters because they process economic information elaborately, learn more from it, and recall it better. This may not be the case when individuals do not pay attention to the news. A longitudinal panel study (Semetko and Valkenburg, 1998) found that individuals who paid more attention to news also felt more internally politically efficacious.

Apart from negativity's indirect effect on internal efficacy through increased attention, it may also have a direct effect. In addition to evoking attention, negativity offers clear guidelines on how to understand economic information and how to make economic evaluations and decisions. Negativity may assist individuals to better comprehend and may provide better guidance about which strategy to choose in order to deal with the economic matters at hand. Even though the news may be bad, at least one would feel that "there will be no unsettling surprises" (Graber, 1980, p. 6). This potential "usefulness" of negativity is also expressed by Trussler and Soroka (2014, p. 363), who claim that individuals strategically focus on negative information because it is more useful than positive information. Similarly, it is known from self-efficacy theory that individuals are better capable of learning from information when it has clear effects (Bandura, 1986, p. 300). For example, if economic news announces potential company collapses, it may be a bad idea to invest in these companies. Or at a household level, if the news media report that gas prices will increase, it may be a good idea to fill up the gas tank promptly. Such negative indicators of economic developments are likely to be useful information that can assist news consumers in making economic decisions or evaluations.

Key Questions

These considerations lead us to anticipate the relationship between exposure to negative news and internal economic efficacy shown in Figure 6.1. Based on the theoretical arguments that negativity guides individuals in how to act and increases motivation to make use of messages, we test the main expectation that exposure to negative economic news has a positive effect

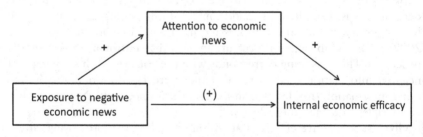

Figure 6.1 Anticipated relationship between exposure to negative economic news and internal economic efficacy

on internal economic efficacy. Moreover, we expect that exposure to negative economic news enhances attention to economic news. Our expectation is that this increased attention partially mediates the effect of negativity on internal economic efficacy.

Exposure to Negative Economic News and Internal Efficacy

Similar to Chapter 5, we use our panel study (see Methodological Appendix) to test how exposure to negative economic news affects internal economic efficacy, after controlling for previous levels of internal economic efficacy.[1] Before studying the effect of negative economic news exposure on internal efficacy, we first look at the relation between general news exposure and internal economic efficacy. We measured internal economic efficacy by asking respondents to indicate on a scale from 1 (disagree a lot) to 5 (agree a lot) how much they agree with the following statements:[2] (1) I see myself as well qualified for participating in discussions about the economy; (2) I think that I am better informed about the economy than others; and (3) I feel that I have a good understanding of the country's economic problems. These questions were derived from conventional items measuring internal political efficacy (items recommended by Neimi et al., 1991), which we adjusted to fit into the economic arena by replacing references to "politics" with "economy." Morrell (2005) applied a similar way of adjusting items. People who have higher levels of news exposure feel more internal economic efficacy ($M = 3.13$, $SD = .76$) than people with medium news exposure ($M = 2.93$, $SD = .79$) or low levels of media exposure ($M = 2.73$, $SD = .80$).[3] This result can be seen as preliminary support for our expectations because the economic news that these people are exposed to is predominantly negative (see Chapters 3 and 4).

How much did internal economic efficacy change between the two waves in the survey? On the aggregate level, there were only modest increases in the scores for internal economic efficacy between the two panel waves. At the individual level, however, fluctuations occurred frequently; for 35.2 percent of the respondents, economic efficacy changed between the two time points.

In the next step, we tested whether individual differences in changes are related to media exposure (Table 6.1). The independent variable *exposure to negative economic news* was measured by integrating the panel survey and the content analysis using a similar approach as in Chapter 5. To calculate exposure to negative economic news for each respondent, exposure to each of the 16 media outlets was multiplied by the respective outlet's negativity score. The degree of negativity in economic news was calculated for each media outlet by subtracting the number of news items with a positive tone from the number of items with a negative tone and dividing by the sum of positive and negative economic news items. Thus, the negativity score in each outlet can range from –1 (when the economic news is entirely positive)

Table 6.1 Explaining internal economic efficacy t2

	Model 1			Model 2		
	B	SE B	β	B	SE B	β
Constant	0.55	0.05***		0.27	0.06***	
Internal economic efficacy t1	0.79	0.02***	.78	0.75	0.02***	.74
Exposure to negative economic news	0.10	0.03***	.06	0.01	0.03*	.04
Attention to economic news				0.10	0.02***	.10
N	1,666			1,666		
Adj. R^2	.63			.64		

Note: ***$p < .001$, **$p < .01$, *$p < .05$ (two-sided t-tests).

to +1 (when the economic news is entirely negative). Based on these scores, exposure to negative economic news was measured by summing the exposure to negative economic news for each media outlet and dividing by the total number of media outlets. The following formula was used to calculate the exposure variable:

Exposure to negativity in economic news = ((Exposure to outlet 1 × negativity score in outlet 1) + (exposure to outlet 2 × negativity score in outlet 2) + (. . .) + (exposure medium 16 × negativity score in outlet 16))/16 outlets.

The weighted exposure measure that we use is a combination of exposure to negativity about sociotropic and egotropic developments.[4]

Model 1 shows that the more people were exposed to negative news between the panel waves, the higher their levels of internal economic efficacy after controlling for previous levels of efficacy. This finding is in line with the expectation that exposure to negative economic news increases internal economic efficacy.

Next, we study whether this relation is indeed moderated by attention to economic news. News attention is measured by the question, "In news in general, to what extent do you pay attention to economic news?" The response categories ranged from 1 (very inattentive) to 5 (very attentive; similar to Hollander, 1995; Strömbäck and Shehata, 2010). As expected, attention to economic news leads to higher levels of internal economic efficacy, even after controlling for previous levels of efficacy and exposure to negative economic news (Model 2). The effect of exposure to negative economic news becomes weaker when attention to economic news is introduced into the analysis. This may indicate that attention mediates the relationship between negativity and internal economic efficacy.

We now turn to our final expectation that attention mediates the effects of negativity exposure on internal economic efficacy. Figure 6.2 shows the

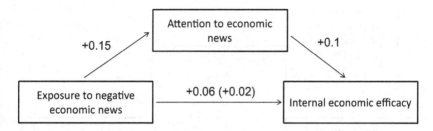

Figure 6.2 The indirect effect of exposure to negative economic news on internal economic efficacy

Note: Standardized beta-coefficients. Significant at *p* < .05 (two-sided t-tests).

results of the mediation analysis.[5] The analysis confirms our expectation that exposure to negative news increases attention to news. The indirect effect is significant, which means that the relationship between negative tone and efficacy is partly explained by the attention to news. The positive sign of the indirect effect shows that exposure to negative news increases attention to news, which in turn increases internal economic efficacy. Apart from the indirect effect through increased attention, exposure to negative news also has a direct effect on internal economic efficacy. However, this effect is smaller. The results suggest that mainly induced attention and subsequent elaboration drive the effect of negative news exposure.

Negativity and the Inattentive Audience

In line with this book's central argument, it is the inattentive audience that benefits the most from the attention-inducing effect of negativity (see Figure 6.3). The relationship between exposure to negative economic news and attention to economic news is weaker for individuals with a high interest in the economy than for individuals with a low interest (Figure 6.4). As we have already seen, exposure to negative economic news has a positive effect on attention. The significant positive effect of interest in the economy on attention to economic news shows that individuals with high interest in the economy also pay more attention to economic news than individuals with lower interest in the economy. The interaction between exposure to negative economic news and interest in the economy is negative and significant, in line with our expectations. Thus, people with low economic interest benefit the most from exposure to negative economic news. The more interested people are in the economy, the weaker the effect of exposure to negative news.

Figure 6.5 shows that the significant interaction between exposure to negative economic news and interest in the economy also affects internal economic efficacy. The declining slope illustrates that the indirect effect of

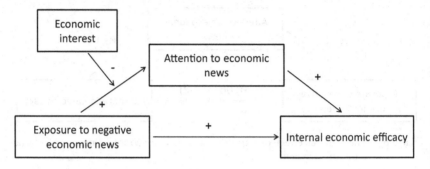

Figure 6.3 Conditional effect of economic interest

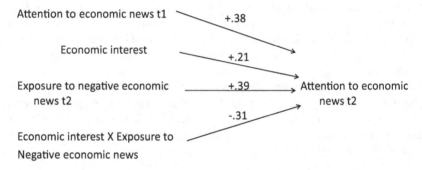

Figure 6.4 Explaining attention to economic news t2

Note: See Appendix table 6.1 standardized beta-coefficients. Significant at $p < .05$ (two-sided t-tests).

exposure to negative economic news on internal economic efficacy through attention to economic news lowers as individuals are more interested in the economy. For the inattentive audience, the effect is the strongest. For people who score 5 on the 5-point scale of economic interest, the effect of exposure to negative news is not significant.[6] Thus, exposure to negative economic news has no significant indirect effect on internal economic efficacy for people who are already highly interested in the economy.

The finding that economic interest moderates the indirect effect of attention on the relationship between negativity and internal economic efficacy is in line with previous research examining the relationship between *political interest* and *attention* (Holt, Shehata, Strömbäck, and Ljungberg, 2013; Strömbäck and Shehata, 2010). The relation between political interest and attention to news is well established. Holt et al. (2013) find that attention affects interest. Strömbäck and Shehata (2010) find the relationship to be reciprocal. Holt et al. (2013) agree with a reciprocal relationship,

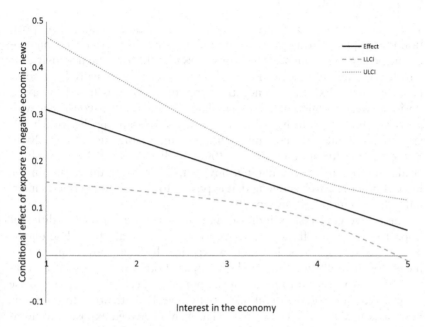

Figure 6.5 Conditional effect of exposure to negative economic news on internal economic efficacy at different values of interest in the economy

Note: $N = 1,666$.

such that political interest influences attention to political news and vice versa. In her seminal study, Graber (1988) found that interest in news makes individuals pay attention to specific stories, whereas individuals with low interest fail to pay attention. This finding explains why negativity's effect on attention arousal is conditioned by interest in the economy. Individuals with higher interest in the economy pay attention to economic news *regardless* of negativity. It would be more difficult for negativity to evoke attention in this group because their attention is already evoked by their interest in the economy. But regarding the inattentive audience, the attention induced by negativity compensates for their lack of intrinsic interest. In line with this reasoning, Young and Tisinger (2006) found that less interested individuals are more likely to increase attention to a particular issue when they are exposed to soft news or more accessible news. Likewise, Jebril et al. (2013) found that inattentive audiences were more affected by elaboration-enhancing news (e.g., using conflict frames and human-interest frames) than highly interested people. These results explain the negative moderating effect of economic interest on the relation between exposure to negativity and attention. In other words, the inattentive audience benefits the most.

Good News in Bad News

The present chapter offers an alternative view to the commonly held position that exposure to negative economic news has negative effects on economic perceptions. Our study demonstrates that the focus on negativity, for which economic journalism is heavily criticized, may actually have some positive effects. Exposure to negative economic news was found to have a positive effect on internal economic efficacy. This result is consistent with previous research, which also finds a positive relationship between news exposure and internal (economic) efficacy (Baumgartner and Morris, 2006; Becker, 2011; Kenski and Stroud, 2006; Möller et al., 2014; Tewksbury et al., 2008). The study's finding, however, is especially interesting in the light of other research showing that exposure to game framing *lowers* internal political efficacy (Pedersen, 2012).

These diverging results indicate that news exposure exerts a different impact on internal efficacy, be it economic or political, depending on the specific content features. In order to explain why some news content may have a positive effect on internal efficacy and other news content a negative effect, it is crucial to focus on the potential mechanisms driving these effects. Our study adds useful insights by revealing attention to economic news as a mediator of the positive relationship between exposure to negative economic news and internal economic efficacy. By focusing on news attention as a potential mechanism driving the effect of negativity on internal economic efficacy, we expand on prior research linking news exposure and internal political efficacy (Möller et al., 2014; Pedersen, 2012; Semetko and Valkenburg, 1998; Tewksbury et al., 2008). Our study suggests that news content that evokes attention (e.g., negativity) is likely to have a positive effect on internal efficacy. By contrast, news content that has a negative effect on attention may be assumed to have a negative effect on internal economic efficacy.

News consumers are not equally susceptible to the effects of negativity; negativity arouses more attention to economic news among individuals with low interest in the economy. This moderating effect of interest in the economy corresponds well with prior research showing that less interested individuals are more influenced by compelling news (Jebril et al., 2013). It also indicates that economic news content that attracts audience attention is the right strategy for capturing the attention of those who are not highly interested in economic issues. In this light, the mainstreaming of economic journalism—with its focus on viewers and readers as potential customers who want entertainment and generally demand negative news (Trussler and Soroka, 2014, p. 686)—may not have entirely "distracted public attention from the reality of global economies" (Chakravartty and Schiller, 2010, p. 670).

Despite its contributions, some limitations of our analysis need consideration. The coding of negativity did not differentiate between emotionally negative assessments of the economy and objectively negative ones (Soroka,

2014, p. 29). Whereas some characteristics of negativity appeal to reason, other characteristics may appeal to emotions. Both lots would be relevant to the processing of negative economic news and should therefore be studied. Conover and Feldman (1986) empirically demonstrated that one should consider not only cognitive responses to the economy but also affective responses. Taking emotional responses into account improves predictions of economic perceptions. This finding is in line with affective intelligence theory, suggesting that emotional responses to information are an important part of information processing. Thus, negative information may cause affective responses in relation to the economy. This type of information may therefore also increase internal economic efficacy because individuals seem to process information more intensely when they are emotionally affected (see Brader, 2006, p. 56). The coding of negativity did not distinguish between negativity reflecting political controversies and negativity reflecting solely developments in economic indicators. This lack of distinction means that the level of negativity found in news media outlets cannot be ascribed to political economic controversies or to developments in economic indicators. The coding of negativity could be strengthened in future research to determine whether different kinds of negativity affect attention and thereby internal economic efficacy differently.

Despite these limitations, the findings in this chapter are in line with our argument that mainstreamed economic news is beneficial to the inattentive audience. In the next chapter, we will show how the inattentive audience benefits from another elaboration-inducing content characteristic: consequence framing.

Notes

1 The time 2 measure is measured in the second wave of our four-wave panel survey. The time 1 measure is the first wave of the survey.
2 These items were combined into a reliable scale (Cronbach's alpha = .86, $M = 2.93, SD = 2.39$) and the unidimensionality of the items was supported by a factor analysis that extracted only one component. A similar scale was made for internal efficacy wave 1 (Cronbach's alpha = .86, $M = 2.86, SD = 2.45$).
3 Differences are significant at $p < .05$ (Anova with Tukey-b post hoc test).
4 We weighted exposure to the different outlets measured at wave 2 by the negativity score in economic news measured between wave 1 and wave 2. We first calculated one scale for exposure to negativity about the general economic climate and one scale for exposure to negativity about individual economic developments. The final exposure-to-negative-economic-news scale is calculated by adding the two scales and dividing by 2 ($M = .73, SD = .44$, minimum = −.04, maximum = 2.70).

Exposure to negative economic news (sociotropic) = (Exposure to EkstraBladet*.50 + exposure to ekstrabladet.dk*.78 + exposure to BT*.79 + exposure to BT.dk*.33 + exposure to TV2 nyheder*.75 + exposure to TV2. dk*.73 + exposure to DR TV avisen*1 + exposure to DR.dk*.73 + exposure to Politiken*.69 + exposure to Politiken.dk*1 + exposure to Berlingske*.23 + exposure to Berlingske.dk*.60 + exposure to JyllandsPosten*.50 + exposure to JyllandsPosten.dk*.83 + exposure to Børsen*.09 + exposure to Borsen.dk*.23)/16.

Exposure to negative economic news (egotropic) = (Exposure to EkstraBladet*.57 + exposure to ekstrabladet.dk*.33 + exposure to BT*.38 + exposure to BT.dk*.40 + exposure to TV2 nyheder*.45 + exposure to TV2.dk*.45 + exposure to DR TV avisen*.25 + exposure to DR.dk*.75 + exposure to Politiken*.60 + exposure to Politiken.dk*.60 + exposure to Berlingske*(−.43) +exposure to Berlingske. dk*.57 + exposure to JyllandsPosten*.78 + exposure to JyllandsPosten.dk*.60 + exposure to Børsen*0 + exposure to Borsen.dk*1)/16. Additionally, we tested our expectations with an alternative measure for exposure to negative economic news where the negativity score was multiplied by the visibility of economic news. This was done because it can be expected that the effect of exposure to negative news on economic efficacy is stronger when economic news is more visible (see Jebril et al., 2013 for a similar argument). Using this alternative exposure measure leads to the same conclusions.

5 We conducted a bootstrap analysis following the recommendations of Hayes (2013).

6 The precise region of significance for the indirect effects is $M \leq 4.52$ (identified by the Johnson-Neyman technique).

7 Learning From Economic Consequence Framing

In this book we argue that mainstreamed economic news informs the inattentive audience. We saw that although the economy is complex, people are well aware of economic trends, including the audiences who are not interested in economic affairs. Media exposure helps to form these correct perceptions. Furthermore, the media work as a burglar alarm; news organizations increase negative coverage of the economy when there are negative economic trends and thus help the audience form correct assessments of economic trends on aggregate. We then proceeded to study how two elaboration-inducing aspects of mainstreamed economic news coverage can affect the public at the individual level. In Chapter 5 we showed that human-interest framing affects interest in economic affairs on the individual level. In Chapter 6 we saw how negativity can be beneficial to the inattentive audience. In this chapter we will analyse a third elaboration-inducing element of mainstreamed economic news: consequence framing. Our main argument is that exposure to news frames focusing on the consequences of economic developments increases knowledge about economic affairs.

Economic Sophistication

In today's complex economic environment, it is important for the audience to be informed about economic matters. Political scientists have been exploring how informed the public is by studying the concept of political sophistication (Converse, 1964; Luskin, 1990). Following the political science literature, this chapter focuses on *economic* sophistication as an indicator of how informed the audience is about the economy. This approach parallels the one we took in the previous two chapters when we discussed economic interest in relation to political interest and internal economic knowledge in relation to political knowledge.

To understand political sophistication on the individual level, researchers have been interested in political cognition, particularly in its simplest form, which comprises knowledge of political facts and various bits of information about politics (Delli Carpini and Keeter, 1997). According to Carpini and Keeter (1993, p. 1180), "factual knowledge is the best single indicator of sophistication." Awareness of facts denotes exposure to various forms of communication and is correlated with the capacity to critically assess facts (Zaller, 1992). Political sophistication has many societal implications, and in most models of democracy the sophistication of citizens occupies a central place (Strömbäck, 2005). Other things equal, high levels of political knowledge among citizens are associated with a healthy democratic system. They have positive consequences for political participation (de Vreese and Boomgaarden, 2006; Neuman, 1986) and can affect attributions of responsibility (Rudolph, 2003). In addition, high levels of political sophistication influence evaluations of parties and candidates, and thus voting behaviour (MacDonald et al., 1995). Likewise, economic sophistication is an important phenomenon, which plays an important role in people's political behaviour, particularly in times when citizens need to hold politicians accountable for economic outcomes.

Extrapolating from the concept of political sophistication, we build a similar and parallel concept that measures how sophisticated individuals are in economic affairs. We conceptualize economic sophistication in terms of factual knowledge about economic current affairs (Zaller, 1992). We operationalize economic sophistication by measuring how knowledgeable individuals are about economic institutions, the country's economic situation compared to those of other countries, and the basic national economic structure.

To clarify how we understand economic sophistication, we need to distinguish it from other indicators of being informed about the economy. In Chapters 2 and 4, we looked at correct perception of economic trends, which is different to factual knowledge. We analyse factual knowledge in this chapter. We argued that people need not be fully informed about all economic facts and can function well as monitorial citizens if they are aware of broad economic developments. That is not to say, however, that economic sophistication does not matter at all. Citizens who are more knowledgeable about economic affairs make better informed economic decisions regarding their households—for instance, when it comes to retirement plans (Lusardi, 2008; Lusardi and Mitchell, 2011).

Economists wanting to measure the public's knowledge about financial concepts have studied a concept called "financial literacy." The questions used to measure this concept mainly focus on practical matters regarding financial institutions and banking processes—by asking, for example, how inflation or interest rates work (Lusardi and Mitchell, 2008, 2011). This is similar to the concept of civic education in political science. Civic education refers to citizens' knowledge about the workings of democratic processes and political institutions (Galston, 2001, 2004). Economic sophistication deals with the economy more broadly, beyond financial institutions. To measure it, we will focus on knowledge about the current affairs that are related to the economy and economic institutions rather than about general principles according to which the economy works.

Finally, the concept of economic sophistication should be distinguished from economic efficacy, which was central to Chapter 6. Economic efficacy refers to the self-perception that one is capable of understanding the economy. In other words, it is a subjective assessment of knowledge. Economic sophistication, however, is an objective measure of knowledge. Previous research has shown that subjective knowledge is correlated with objective knowledge but it affects consumer behaviour differently (Raju et al., 1995). It is therefore important to study actual knowledge and to look at how informed about the economy the audience actually is.

Consequence Framing and Economic Sophistication

Following research on political sophistication, we expect news exposure to be an important antecedent of economic sophistication. Research showing effects on learning about current affairs from the news can be traced back to the work of Lazarsfeld, Berelson, and Gaudet (1944). Since then, many studies have established a relationship between exposure to news and political sophistication (Albæk et al., 2014; Fraile, 2011; Gordon and Segura, 1997). In a review of the current literature, McLeod, Kosicki, and McLeod (2009, p. 231) suggested that "special forms of political communication, debates, and conventions, along with standard news coverage, convey discernible if modest amounts of information to their audiences." These gains in knowledge are the result of three factors: availability of information, the nature of the medium, and individual-level motivation.

When it comes to the availability of information, we have seen in many of the aforementioned studies that exposure to hard news influences political sophistication. We have also seen that people who prefer entertainment—in a fragmented media landscape where news can easily be avoided altogether—are less sophisticated about political affairs (Prior, 2005). Other studies have highlighted the effects of specific mediums in enhancing political sophistication; for example, the nature of television allows people to become informed even if they are not interested in politics (Schoenbach and Lauf, 2002). Last but not least, Iyengar et al. (2010) showed that the influence of personal motives on political knowledge is more important in countries with a fragmented media environment lacking a strong public broadcaster. Their influence is less important in Scandinavian countries, where a strong public broadcaster system exists. More recently, several studies have gone beyond a simple correlation between news exposure and political sophistication, and have examined how some news frames influence knowledge about political affairs (e.g., Albæk et al., 2014).

In this study, given the nature of economic sophistication, we are interested in the effect of the economic consequences frame. The economic consequences frame presents "an event, problem, or issue in terms of the economic consequences it will have on an individual, group, institution, region, or country" (Valkenburg et al., 1999, p. 552). According to experimental findings, exposure to economic consequences frames has an impact on readers' thoughts on economic and financial stories (Valkenburg et al., 1999). Furthermore, it helps citizens make connections between causes and effects of events (Price, Tewksbury, and Powers, 1997). Neuman (1992, p. 63) argues that it reflects the "preoccupation with the bottom line, profit and loss." Kostadinova and Dimitrova (2012) found a strong presence of the economic consequence frame in the economic coverage of specialized outlets. An example of a news story that uses a consequence frame concerns the latest economic figures for Denmark. They were published in *Jyllands-Posten* on 12 April 2013, when export showed a slight decline. The article discusses the implications of these numbers for the Danish economy. For example, an expert explains that "we will see a stagnation in the Danish economy which will continue into the second quarter and maybe throughout the year."[1] Another example is an article published in *Politiken*, which discusses inflation in Denmark and addresses the consequences of the continuous economic stimulus in countries like China. In the long run, inflation and price bubbles could result.[2] By relating development to the potential impact on people's wallets, this type of coverage should stimulate elaboration among the inattentive audience.

We argue that the crucial mechanism for learning and remembering about an event involves understanding an issue's causes and effects, something especially relevant to the complex issue of the economy.

Our expectation is that exposure to consequence framing in economic news increases *sophistication* about economic affairs. Elaboration is the process of connecting new information to information already stored in the memory. Research in psychology has highlighted that the way an individual processes information influences his or her recall capabilities. Mayer (1980) outlined three types of elaboration. Associative elaboration refers to meaningfully associating multiple stimuli; integrative elaboration refers to integrating new information based on prior knowledge about the stimuli; and comparative elaboration refers to explaining the relationship between two new concepts (Mayer, 1980; Van Blankenstein, Dolmans, Van Der Vleuten, and Schmidt, 2008). Experimental research has shown that these elaboration techniques improve the recall of information (Bobrow and Bower, 1969; Mayer, 1980).

These elaboration techniques have also been used in communication research on learning from the news. Eveland's study showed that elaboration processing (thinking and interpreting news stories in a way that it makes sense to the reader) is related to knowledge about political affairs (Eveland, 2001). For instance, as described by Eveland (2001), when a news user watches a news story about the decline of farming, she might elaborate on the story by thinking, for instance, about her own family background, by recalling a news article about farming or by considering the consequences of farming in the economy.

We expect that exposure to economic news that is reported with a focus on tangible consequences for an individual, group, company, institution, region, or country influences thoughts and recall abilities—in particular, in regard to concrete, factual knowledge. By elaborately processing news content, the news consumer will improve both memory and the ability to recall information. That being so, through elaborative processing, new economic information that is integrated with pre-existing knowledge structures will be easily accessible for individuals to form economic perceptions (Eveland, 2001). This process is called integrative elaboration: new information is integrated with previous information stored in memory, and thus the ability to recall is enhanced. For example, if an individual is aware of the significance of a downturn in gross domestic product (GDP), a news story about falling exports framed as a potential threat to GDP growth will enable this new information to be integrated with prior knowledge about the importance of GDP.

Key Question

Building upon a long tradition of studies on how political news exposure is linked to political sophistication (e.g., Baum, 2003; Prior, 2005; Zaller, 1992), this chapter examines the relationship between exposure to economic news and economic sophistication. More specifically, we are interested in knowing if the elaboration following exposure to economic consequence frames affects economic sophistication.

Consequence Framing and Economic Sophistication

We study the effect of exposure to consequence framing on economic sophistication with our panel study, comparing wave 1 and wave 2 (see Methodological Appendix). Before deciding how to measure economic sophistication, we looked at different ways political sophistication was tapped in relevant previous studies. Some measure factual knowledge (Delli Carpini and Keeter, 1997); others use individual perceptions of parties' ideological placements compared to the average placement (Gordon and Segura, 1997); and yet others use a combination of variables such as political interest, political knowledge, cognitive elaboration, and active processing of information (Guo and Moy, 1998) or only the level of education (Gastil and Dillard, 1999). Economic sophistication was measured differently in previous studies, ranging from open-ended questions on economic measures (Lewis and Scott, 2000) to student grades (Williams, Waldauer, and Duggal, 1992). In our study, we created a scale of four questions assessing factual information of the economy (see Box 7.1), a method that has also been argued to be a valid measure of political sophistication (Carpini and Keeter, 1993; Zaller, 1992). Apart from the validity of this measure, another argument for this choice of operationalization is that we are looking at the effects of *information* acquired through media.

Box 7.1　Questions asked to assess economic sophistication

(Bold indicates the correct answers)

1. How high is the unemployment rate in Denmark, according to Eurostat? (August 2012)*

    a. 2.3 percent
    b. 4.8 percent
    c. **8.1 percent**
    d. **11.2 percent**
    e. 13.5 percent
    f. Don't know

2. Who is the current managing director of the International Monetary Fund (IMF)?

    a. Dominique Strauss-Kahn
    b. Kofi Anan
    c. **Christine Lagarde**
    d. Bill Gates
    e. Don't know

3. Which of these countries is not among the top five export partners of Denmark?

    a. Sweden
    b. UK
    c. **Russia**
    d. Germany
    e. Don't know

4. What is Denmark's credit rating according to Standard and Poor's?

    a. **AAA**
    b. AA
    c. BBB
    d. C
    e. Don't know

*There are two correct answers to this question due to the different operationalizations that are used to report unemployment.

Finally, the panel study design restricts us from using stable measures as indicators, such as education.

The scale questions deal with a variety of topics: a measure of the latest unemployment figures, international economic institutions (in this case, the IMF), the national economy's structure (who are the country's main export partners?), and last, the national economy in comparison to other countries' situations (what is the national credit rating?). Each question had an option of four or five different answers as well as the answer "Don't know." Claims are made that the "Don't know" answer should be discouraged in knowledge studies so as to reveal a more knowledgeable audience (Mondak, 1999, 2001). However, an experimental study showed that discouraging "Don't know" answers does not affect the answers (Luskin and Bullock, 2011). We calculated our economic sophistication scale by summing the number of correctly answered questions.

Confirming previous studies, people with the highest levels of news exposure had higher levels of sophistication ($M = 2.43$, $SD = 1.29$ on a scale from 0 to 4) than people with medium levels of exposure ($M = 2.19$, $SD = 1.29$) or low levels of news exposure ($M = 1.68$, $SD = 1.26$).[3] To see whether exposure to economic consequence framing is related to economic sophistication, we take a similar approach as in Chapters 5 and 6, and study whether developments in sophistication over time are related to exposure to economic news that uses economic consequence framing. Following this design, the respondents answered the same questions twice to measure economic sophistication at time 1 and time 2. The inclusion of the same questions in both waves may seem problematic because the respondents may pay more attention to these issues because they were asked about them before. We choose this way of measuring, however, because creating questions with a similar level of difficulty is challenging. To test whether people answer the questions differently if they have seen them before, we recruited a fresh sample of 406 respondents and let them answer the questions, too, at time 2. Their level of economic sophistication was not statistically different from that of the people who answered the questions for the second time. Although insignificant, we did an extra analysis testing whether we could find a panel effect for the highly educated individuals. Our argument was that they might be more capable of learning or remembering the economic sophistication questions. The extra analysis showed that even for the highly educated, no panel effect occurred.

Between time 1 and time 2, the overall level of economic sophistication increased from a means score of 2.01 ($SD = 1.32$) to 2.10 ($SD = 1.31$). At the first measurement, 16.5 percent of the respondents answered all questions correctly, and at the second measurement, 18.5 percent.[4]

To test how exposure to economic consequence framing relates to these changes in economic efficacy, we ran an ordinary least squares (OLS) regression analysis, with economic sophistication measured at time 2 as the dependent variable. In this regression we controlled for the levels of economic

Table 7.1 Explaining economic sophistication t2

	B	SE B	β
Constant	0.55	0.05***	
Economic sophistication t1	0.71	0.02***	.71
Exposure to economic news with economic consequence framing	0.13	0.04***	.06
N	1,666		
Adj. R^2	.53		

Note: ***$p < .001$ (two-sided t-tests).

sophistication at time 1. Exposure to economic consequence framing was measured by combining the media exposure measures with the content analysis findings. The days of exposure to each outlet for each individual were weighted with the share of articles about the economy in each outlet that used economic consequence framing. We used the following formula:

Exposure to economic consequence framing = ((Exposure to outlet 1 × consequence framing in economic news in outlet 1) + (exposure to outlet 2 × consequence framing in economic news in outlet 2) + (. . .) + (exposure medium 16 × consequence framing in economic news in outlet 16))/16 outlets.[5]

In Table 7.1 we can see that after controlling for levels of economic sophistication at time 1, exposure to economic news using the economic consequence framing between the two points in time has a positive and significant effect on economic sophistication. This result supports our expectation.

Informing the Inattentive Audience

Exposure to news with an economic consequence frame is most beneficial to people with low interest in the economy. Table 7.2 shows the effect of exposure to economic news using consequence framing for citizens with low, medium, and high interest in the economy. After controlling for previous levels of economic sophistication, exposure has a significant and positive effect on the audience with low interest in the economy. For people with medium levels of interest in the economy, the effects were also positive but were only significant at $p < .1$. The effect was insignificant for those with high levels of interest in economic affairs. These results support the overall argument of this book and show that the inattentive audience benefits the most from exposure to economic news that uses consequence framing.

Our explanation for this finding is that citizens who are both interested in the economy and engaged in news already have a high level of economic sophistication, and their recent exposure to news information does not

Table 7.2 Explaining economic sophistication for people with different levels of economic interest

	Model 1			Model 2			Model 3		
	Low economic interest			Medium economic interest			High economic interest		
	B	SE B	β	B	SE B	β	B	SE B	β
Constant	0.38	0.09***		0.69	0.07***		0.55	0.13***	
Economic sophistication t1	0.65	0.04***	.66	0.68	0.02***	.68	0.76	0.04***	.75
Exposure to economic news with economic consequence framing	0.19	0.09*	.09	0.10	0.05#	.04	0.08	0.07	.04
N	348			977			341		
Adj. R^2	.47			.48			.58		

Note: ***$p < .001$, *$p < .05$, #$p < .1$ (two-sided t-tests).

contribute to knowledge gains. In addition, exposure to news framed in terms of economic consequences is particularly beneficial to citizens who are inattentive to current affairs and uninterested in the economy. Again, sophisticated and attentive citizens do not need the media to stimulate their elaboration because they are more effective in connecting the dots between previous stocks of knowledge, current developments, and potential future developments than inattentive citizens, who have larger gaps in their knowledge. Our argument follows the rationale of previous studies that have examined the moderating effect of political interest on political sophistication gain.

The Benefits of Consequence Framing

In this chapter we showed that exposure to economic news that is framed in terms of the consequences they have for an individual, group, institution, region, or country helped increase economic sophistication. We argue that this cognitive effect is a result of consequence framing helping citizens add new information into pre-existing structures of knowledge (Eveland, 2001) and thus facilitating better recall of issues (Valkenburg et al., 1999). While there are studies examining how framing influences political sophistication (Jebril et al., 2013; Price et al., 1997), to our knowledge, this study is one of the first to examine the effect of framing on economic sophistication.

In Chapters 1 and 2 we reasoned that people can function competently as monitorial citizens *without* having detailed factual knowledge about the state of the economy as long as they correctly assess economic trends.

However, our argument does not negate economic sophistication as an additional asset once the lower threshold of correctly assessing economic trends is met. As we discussed, economic sophistication helps people make informed economic decisions. We argue that although political sophistication is an important concept that is essential to democracy, economic sophistication can likewise be beneficial to the democratic citizen according to the competitive model of democracy. In the mandate version of the competitive model of democracy, citizens need to be informed about the positions of political actors to evaluate alternative political choices. Knowledge of positions on economic policy can play an important role here. In the sanctional version of the competitive model of democracy, the audience is expected to make informed decisions about whether to re-elect an incumbent government party or, instead, to give the opposition a chance. Factual knowledge, like party affiliation of the prime minister and minister of finance, can help make this assessment. Economic sophistication can also be beneficial to democratic citizens according to the participatory model of democracy, which expects citizens to engage in civic activities. In recent years, political participation has developed beyond traditional forms like voting or protesting. Economic activities, like boycotting or buying products for political reasons, have emerged as new forms of political participation (Ohme, 2017). Economic sophistication can help make informed decisions about these types of participation.

This chapter has shown that exposure to economic consequence framing increases economic sophistication. A question for further research is how this may play out in more polarized media environments. As we saw in Chapter 3, economic consequences were highly present in all the media outlets analysed. At the same time, the tone of economic news was homogenously negative in all outlets studied. We can speculate whether exposure to economic consequence framing would likewise have had a positive effect across the board if media outlets were more polarized in their depiction of economic developments. If such polarized coverage were received by strong partisans, they might connect this new information to already existing and biased preconceptions of the state of the economy. This reaction might lead to steadily more polarized assessments of the economy, especially when fake news plays an increasingly important role and "alternative facts" become available. We return to this discussion in Chapter 11.

The news exposure effect on economic sophistication was not evenly distributed in the population: citizens with low interest in economic affairs were the ones affected more positively by consequence framing, followed by those with a medium interest in economy. Thus, the findings of Chapter 7 support the overall argument of this book—namely, that mainstreamed news reporting of economic affairs benefits, in particular, people who most need to be informed about the economy and not those who are already interested. In a world in which the economy is becoming increasingly complex and where many economic actors are intertwined, different types of knowledge and understanding about the economy are required. Mainstreamed economic news helps citizens in different ways. In Chapters 2 and 4, we showed that economic news can help gain a better awareness of movements in economic trends. In Chapter 6 we showed that mainstreamed economic news fosters economic efficacy. And in Chapter 8, we examine how the degree of domestication of economic news affects the way people attribute responsibility about economic affairs.

Notes

1 Nielsen, Bo. Dansk økonomi balancerer på kanten af recession, *Jyllands-Posten*, 12 April 2013, Erhverv and Økonomi, p. 8.
2 Thomas Flensburg. En økonomi i slæbesporet tager toppen af prisstigningerne, *Politiken*, 22 January 2013, p. 15.
3 Differences are significant at $p < .05$ (Anova with Tukey-b post hoc test).
4 The low number of respondents in both the high response categories suggests negligible ceiling effects. In addition, only 69 percent of the respondents who correctly answered all questions in the second wave did so in the first wave.
5 We weighted exposure to the different outlets measured at wave 2 by the share of items that uses economic consequences framing in economic news measured between wave 1 and wave 2:
Exposure to economic consequence framing = (Exposure to EkstraBladet *.78 + exposure to ekstrabladet.dk *.88 + exposure to BT*.88 + exposure to BT.dk*.88 + exposure to TV2 nyheder*.84 + exposure to TV2.dk *.78 + exposure to DR TV avisen*1 + exposure to DR.dk *.83 + exposure to Politiken *.83 + exposure to Politiken.dk *.72 + exposure to Berlingske*.92 + exposure to Berlingske.dk *.80 + exposure to JyllandsPosten *.79 + exposure to JyllandsPosten.dk*.74 + exposure to Børsen*.75 + exposure to Borsen.dk*.78)/16 ($M = 1.05$, $SD = .61$, minimum = 0, maximum = 3.88).
Additionally, we tested our expectations with an alternative measure for exposure to economic consequence framing, where the share of economic consequence framing was multiplied by the visibility of economic news. This was done because it can be expected that the effect of exposure to economic consequence framing on economic sophistication is stronger when economic news is more visible (see Jebril et al., 2013 for a similar argument). Using this alternative exposure measure leads to the same conclusions.

8 Domesticated Economic News and Attribution of Responsibility

It has always been a challenge for citizens to decide whether to hold their government accountable for their nation's problems, and this challenge has only grown in light of globalization and the transnationalization of political and economic arrangements. Many political challenges—such as climate change, refugees, and terrorism—are transnational issues with manifold causes (Olausson, 2014). This makes it difficult to assess if and to which degree the national government should be held accountable. In addition, multilevel governance structures, like the EU, make it even harder for voters to determine which level of government should be credited or blamed. Thus, "attributing responsibility correctly in multi-level systems is a daunting task" (Hobolt and Tilley, 2014, p. 156).

This is certainly true for the Great Recession, which started as a banking crisis in 2008 and affected the global economy for much longer than a normal recession. Due to globalization and the integration of economic systems, international developments have a strong impact on national economies. Worldwide, the Great Recession has affected all aspects of daily life, including the public, political, and media agendas (Hollanders and Vliegenthart, 2011; Kleinnijenhuis et al., 2013).

Given the difficulty of assigning responsibility for economic developments, this chapter studies an important antecedent of the attribution of responsibility for the economic crisis that started in 2008: information cues in media coverage. As we argue, the degree of *domestication* (which is an important element of mainstreamed economic news) serves as a cue which audiences rely on to assess whether national politicians should be held responsible for economic developments. This mechanism is the third of three by which mainstreamed economic news informs inattentive audiences, next to the alarm bell function (Chapter 4) and the elaboration-inducing elements (Chapters 5, 6, and 7).

Previous research has shown that attribution of responsibility is affected by system-level factors, such as the political system and the openness of the economy (Duch and Stevenson, 2008; Lewis-Beck and Stegmaier, 2013), and individual level factors, such as personal attitudes and predispositions (Vries and Giger, 2014). Information cues in the media are expected to be a third key antecedent of attribution of responsibility for the economy. Experimental studies have shown that information cues shape responsibility attribution (e.g., Hobolt, Tilley, and Wittrock, 2013; Iyengar, 1994). So far, these studies on the effects of information cues on attribution of economic responsibility have largely overlooked one important aspect of the information cues—namely, the geographical focus.

We argue that the geographical focus in media coverage of the economy influences whether national politicians are held responsible. The media make complex, global developments salient for domestic audiences by connecting the coverage to national actors and discussing the impact on home audiences. We argue that such domesticated coverage affects whether people assign responsibility for economic developments to national politicians. The geographical focus of media coverage provides a clue as to whether economic developments are caused by factors internal or external to the country, which, in turn, should affect whether governments are held accountable for economic developments. As we shall see, the inattentive audience is affected the most by these cues.

Attribution of Responsibility Matters

Attribution of responsibility is "the act of deciding who or what can be held accountable" (Hobolt and Tilley, 2014, p. 9). When people assess who should be held responsible for past economic developments, they attribute causal responsibility. Retrospective causal responsibility should be distinguished from prospective treatment responsibility, which is "future-oriented and problem-solving in nature" (Iyengar, 1990, p. 23) and deals with the question how problems can be solved or prevented in the future. Attribution of responsibility is an important link between (economic) perceptions and vote choice or government approval (Gomez and Wilson, 2003; Hobolt and Tilley, 2014; Powell and Whitten, 1993; Togeby, 2007). When the government is perceived to be responsible for economic developments, economic voting is likely to occur (Powell and Whitten, 1993). When economic developments are attributed to external factors, economic perceptions matter less for government approval. To hold the incumbent government accountable for economic developments, voters need to judge which part of economic developments can be attributed to the government and which part is beyond the government's control. Such attributions of responsibilities matter, in particular, in multilevel government structures and policy areas, in which actors and developments at different levels (regional, national, European, global) can influence economic developments (Hobolt and Tilley, 2014). Bellucci (2014) showed that vote choice in Italy was affected by whether voters attributed responsibility for the economic crisis to international or domestic politicians. Similarly, Lobo and Lewis-Beck (2012) showed that the economy has less influence on vote choice when the EU rather than national politicians is seen as responsible for economic developments.

News and Attribution of Responsibility

Given the importance of attribution of responsibility for performance voting, a number of studies have turned to its antecedents (Hobolt and Tilley, 2014; Iyengar, 1994). Hobolt and Tilley (2014) have shown that the way voters attribute responsibility in multilevel government structures reflects not merely the institutional divisions of responsibility but also that individual perceptions play an important role. Citizens do not always get it right and may blame or credit politicians who do not have functional responsibility (Cutler, 2008). Attribution theory gives insight into why people hold certain politicians accountable. Thus, people constantly search for causal explanations (Weiner, 1985, 1986), especially in crisis situations with negative and unexpected events (Coombs, 2007). This causal search is first of all motivated by a desire to avoid making similar mistakes in the future (Weiner, 1985)—for example, reelecting the politicians who are seen as responsible for economic malaise. Causal attribution is also a way to protect one's self-image, assigning responsibility for negative developments to the out-group, while giving credit to the in-group (Hobolt and Tilley, 2014, p. 20). In line with this self-serving bias, predispositions such as partisanship or ideology shape views of which politician should be held accountable (Rudolph, 2003). Strong partisans will blame politicians from opposing parties for economic downturn and attribute responsibility to "their own" politicians when the economy improves.

Media coverage is another key antecedent that shapes how we attribute responsibility (Hobolt et al., 2013; Maestas, Atkeson, Croom, and Bryant, 2008). Informational shortcuts and cues help people attribute responsibility when faced with complex developments (Hobolt et al., 2013, p. 154). Media coverage provides such cues and can play an important role in shaping attribution of responsibility.

Thus, differently framed news can shape attributions of responsibility. A frame is "a central organizing idea or story line that provides meaning to an unfolding strip of events" (Gamson and Modigliani, 1987, p. 143). Research on media framing effects focuses on how different "interpretive schemas" can be invoked by framing the same message in different ways (Scheufele, 1999). Entman (1993) also suggested that frames help individuals make associations between an issue and the interpretive schemas relevant to its definition, causes, implications, and treatment, with attention being mainly focused on treatment and definition (Tewksbury, Scheufele, Bryant, and Oliver, 2009).

In his seminal work, *Is Anyone Responsible?: How Television Frames Political Issues*, Iyengar (1994) showed that exposure to television coverage of political issues that uses episodic framing and focuses on specific events and cases prompts viewers to hold individual actors accountable. When political events are placed in a broader context (so-called thematic framed news), people are more likely to hold national governments accountable.

The main argument of Iyengar's study is that when citizens are exposed to an article that portrays societal level attributions and not individual ones, they are more prone to attribute responsibility at the societal level, too.

Not surprisingly, evidence suggests that the media, when reporting a crisis, tend to use the attribution of responsibility frame more than other generic frames (human interest, conflict, morality, and economic consequences; An and Gower, 2009). When using the attribution of responsibility frame, a news outlet presents an issue or problem in a way that attributes responsibility for its cause or solution to either the government, an individual, or a group (Semetko and Valkenburg, 2000). In an experimental study (Valkenburg et al., 1999), respondents read stories that blamed the government for inadequately handling crime. After reading these stories, the participants in the experiment saw the government as responsible for the problems in crime.[1] When it comes to economic matters, we likewise expect that media framing affects the assignment of responsibility, in particular, when the news is domesticated.

Domesticated Economic News and Attribution of Responsibility

Coverage of global and international developments is often characterized by a high degree of domestication (Cohen, 2013). An example of such a story is the article "This Is Why Petrol Prices Fall Today," which explains to the readers that "due to changes in the world market the price of petrol and diesel oil drop 7 and 14 pennies per liter respectively."[2] The article discusses how international developments affect consumers in Denmark. Domestication is also used in economic news, although the degree of domestication varies between media outlets (Ruigrok and Van Atteveldt, 2007). More broadly, domestication refers to news dealing with economic developments from a national rather than international perspective. The open Danish economy is strongly intertwined with the economy of other European countries, and broader international economic developments strongly affect developments in Denmark. When journalists describe economic developments, the developments in Denmark can be described either as the consequence of international developments or as purely national. An example of a domesticated article about economic developments is "Corydon [the Danish finance minister] in Good Spirits: Denmark Is on the Right Track,"[3] which reports the highest levels of consumer confidence since the start of the economic crisis. In the article, the minister of finance attributes this development to the politics of the government: "Consumers have put the crisis behind them and retail is booming. Construction activity is up, and exports are taking off. In short: The government's policy is working, according to the Minister of Finance." The article makes no reference to similar trends in other countries or the possible influence of the world economy on the reported trends. We expect that the media's focus on national developments in the coverage of the economy will translate into attribution of responsibility for economic development to national political actors.

Following attribution theory, the degree of domestication of complex international developments is expected to influence whether responsibility is attributed to national governments or to other actors (Olausson, 2009, p. 422). In general, the locus of control is an important factor in attributing responsibility (Weiner, 1985). When people see developments as the consequences of internal factors, attribution of responsibility is high. When people see developments as the consequences of external factors, attribution of responsibility is low. Translating this process to the economic context, the degree of domestication of economic news will be a cue for the audience to decide whether or not the national government should be held responsible for economic developments. When audiences are exposed to domesticated economic news, they can be expected to associate the crisis with national political actors and, consequently, to hold national politicians accountable for the economy and to consider the crisis relevant when they evaluate national politicians (Shehata and Falasca, 2014). When the media associate the crisis with foreign actors and locations, the perceived relevance of the economic situation for national politics declines (Althaus and Kim, 2006).

Several studies have shown that the associations that the media make between issues and actors affect how the audience understands these issues and, in turn, whom they hold accountable. Maestas et al. (2008) analysed attribution of responsibility for the problems with providing aid in the aftermath of Hurricane Katrina in 2005. They showed that television news was more likely to blame state officials than federal officials. In turn, the audience was more likely to hold state officials responsible. Similarly, De Bruycker and Walgrave (2014) showed that the Belgian media associated the Great Recession more with government parties than with opposition parties and that audiences, especially those with higher media exposure, consequently saw the crisis as an issue owned by the government. Hobolt and Tilley (2014) found the same mechanism for EU-level actors. People who are exposed to news about the EU are more likely to correctly assign responsibility to it than are people with low exposure.

Key Questions

In sum, we expect that the degree of domestication in coverage of the economy serves as an information cue for who should be held responsible for economic developments. The more one is exposed to domesticated coverage, the more one should see the national government as responsible for economic developments. We test this expectation in two steps. First, we look at the result of an experiment, studying how differently framed news affects attribution of responsibility for the economic crisis. Second, we study the effect of exposure to domesticated economic news on attribution of responsibility using the panel study (see Methodological Appendix).

An Experimental Study of News Exposure and Attribution of Responsibility

Before turning to the results of our panel study, we first report the results of an experiment. In the experiment we test how the use of an attribution of responsibility frame in the news influences the actual attributions of responsibility for the economic crisis. Framing effects have been frequently identified through experiments (Valkenburg et al., 1999). They have two main advantages: the possibility to isolate the content feature of interest and the ability to draw causal inferences. Respondents are randomly assigned to different treatment groups. Differences in attribution of responsibility after exposure can be assigned to the respondents having been exposed to differently framed news items.[4]

Two news articles were constructed for the purposes of the experiment (see Box 8.1). In both experimental groups, respondents are exposed to news that blames an actor for the national economic situation. One article attributes responsibility for the economic crisis to banks, and the other attributes responsibility to the EU.

Box 8.1   Stimulus material for experiment where either the banks or the EU are held responsible for the economic crisis

Common first paragraphs

According to a Statistics Denmark report on growth released yesterday, Denmark's GDP (Gross Domestic Product) shrunk by 0.2 percent during the third quarter of 2013. The numbers for Denmark follow a trend in European countries after the European Sovereign Debt crisis hit the Union in 2010.

Although the recession is quite small, this decrease in GDP follows a rather "moody" fluctuation with small increases and small decreases during the past two years. According to experts, this shows that the economic climate is still keeping up compared to other countries, but is struggling to fully recover from the dip. But who is to blame for this immutability? We have asked Peter Nielsen, an academic economist, to explain it to us:

Last paragraph for the "Banks" Group

The main problem stems from the problems within the banking system. Most countries in the EU have spent millions of their taxpayers' money to rescue problematic banks which were exposed to toxic hedge funds that burst on the other side of the Atlantic. This created holes in the state budget that can only be filled with cuts and higher taxes. And in return, the banks are still not eager to "return" the money to the society by making loans easier for the common people. They proved that they are not to be trusted.

Last paragraph for the "EU" Group

The main problem stems from the problems within the EU. Most northern countries in the EU have spent billions of their taxpayers' money to rescue problematic countries, which offered benefits which are unthinkable in the north like pensions at 55. This created insecurity and fear among investors that can only be filled with financial discipline from these countries. And in return, Greece, Portugal and other countries are still not trying to do the reforms needed in order to restore the economic climate in the Union. They proved that they are not to be trusted.

The choice of actors, the banks and the EU, is made because they have been involved in the public discussion about the economic crisis all over Europe. The role of the EU in the crisis was heavily debated. Both actors have been claimed to be responsible for the crisis. Studies by economists have underlined the importance of "aggressive risk taking in the subprime market" as a primary cause of the financial turmoil which started in 2007 (Borio, 2008). Other studies have focused on the European response to the financial crisis, which was late and uncoordinated (Dabrowski, 2010), and economists have argued that the crisis had contagion effects from some Eurozone countries to other European countries (Arghyrou and Kontonikas, 2012). These academic discussions have been propagated in the media around both actors, the banks and the EU (Kottasz and Bennett, 2014; Mylonas, 2012). Meanwhile, the reputation of the banking sector after the crisis has been harmed (Kottasz and Bennett, 2014), and the decrease in trust in the EU has been dramatic.[5]

The first two paragraphs of the articles are identical, describing a financial problem (the national economy is not growing, naturally following the moody fluctuations the past couple of years). The third and last paragraph are different for the two conditions. News blaming the banks points out that most EU countries have spent billions of dollars to save the banking system over the past years, and the banks themselves do not "return" the money by giving easy loans to people. The other news points out that the problem lies in the EU. Greece and Portugal received billions of taxpayers' money but did not implement the needed reforms. Both articles have similar wordings, with a minimum of different words. In both cases the story includes an academic expert as source, which is part of journalistic routines (Shoemaker and Reese, 1996).[6]

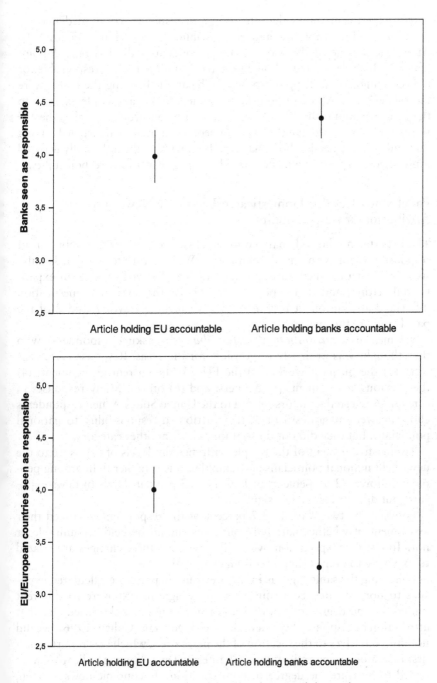

Figure 8.1 Experiment showing that attribution of responsibility in the news impacts attribution of responsibility by the audience

Note: Mean values and 95% confidence intervals. Scales from 1 (not responsible) to 5 (responsible).

Our experiment shows that attribution of responsibility in media coverage influenced to whom the audience attributes responsibility (Figure 8.1). After reading one of the articles, the respondents indicated on a 5-point scale to which degree they thought the bank and the EU are responsible for the economic crisis.[7] People exposed to the article blaming the banks were more likely to attribute responsibility to the banks than people exposed to the article blaming the EU. People exposed to an article blaming the EU were more likely to blame the EU than people exposed to an article blaming the banks. These results show that even for a highly salient, broadly debated topic, media exposure influences to whom people attribute responsibility.

Panel Study Results: Domesticated Economic News and Attribution of Responsibility

The experiment showed that economic coverage can affect attribution of responsibility for economic developments. We now turn to our panel analysis to see whether such an effect can also be observed outside an experimental setting, and more specifically, whether the level of domestication influences attribution of responsibility. We include waves 1 and 2 of the panel study in the analysis.

We measured *attribution of responsibility* by asking respondents who they thought was primarily responsible for the crisis. Response categories were (1) the business world, (2) the EU, (3) the current government, (4) the previous government, (5) bankers, and (6) others. Many responses in category 6 referred to actors related to the United States. When respondents chose answer categories 3 or 4, they attributed responsibility to national politicians, but they did not do so if they chose another category.

Twenty-five percent of the people with medium levels of exposure to the news held national politicians accountable. This is higher than among people with lower (20.8 percent) or higher (23.3 percent) levels of news exposure, but differences are not significant.

Between the two waves, 13.7 percent of the respondents changed their assessment of whether national politicians should be held accountable or not. To test our expectation, we analyse whether these changes are related to exposure to domesticated economic news.

Following the same logic as in the previous chapters, we calculated exposure to domesticated economic news by weighting exposure to different outlets by the degree of domestication in the news. Acknowledging that attribution of responsibility is a multifaceted concept (Cohen, 1996), we did not limit ourselves to the location of the news story, which was reported as a first indicator of domestication in Chapter 3. The following indicators were coded to measure the degree of domestication of economic news (Cohen, 1996, p. 85): (1) the location where the story took place, (2) the affected location, and (3) whether national or international politicians were the main actors of the news story. Following Hobolt and Tilley (2014), we additionally coded (4) whether the story explicitly attributed responsibility to an actor and, if so, whether that actor was a national or international politician. To measure location, coders identified whether the story took place in Denmark or outside of Denmark. Affected location refers to whether Denmark was explicitly mentioned as affected by developments described in the news story. For example, a news story about economic growth in China may have Denmark as the affected location if it addresses how it will affect Danish export to China. Coders furthermore identified whether the first mentioned actor in the story was a Danish or a foreign politician. Finally, they coded whether the story indicates that an individual or a group or some level of government is responsible for a problem. If a person or government entity was held responsible, coders coded whether this person or government was Danish or foreign.[8] Based on the four indicators, we calculate the degree of domestication per outlet. If the location or actor was national, this was seen as an indication of domesticated coverage (see Chapter 3). A foreign location or actor indicates an international perspective. Per outlet, we calculated the degree of domestication according to each of the four indicators by subtracting articles with an international focus from the number of articles with a domestic focus and dividing by the total number of articles. The four domestication scales could potentially range from –1, when all articles had an international outlook, to +1, when each article has a domestic perspective. After calculating the degree of domestication for each indicator separately, the overall degree of domestication per outlet was calculated by taking the average of the four indicators. To measure exposure to domesticated economic news, we combined the self-reported exposure to 16 outlets at time 2 of the survey with the degree of domestication in economic news in these outlets, using the following formula:

Exposure to domesticated economic news = ((Exposure to outlet 1 × domestication score in outlet 1) + (exposure to outlet 2 × domestication score in outlet 2) + (. . .) + (exposure medium 16 × domestication score in outlet 16))/16 outlets.[9]

Figure 8.2 shows that exposure to domesticated economic news does affect attribution of responsibility. Attribution of responsibility at time 2 is

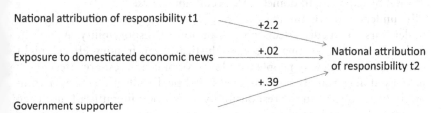

Figure 8.2 Explaining attribution of responsibility t2

Note: Unstandardized beta-coefficients. Significant at $p < .1$ (two-sided t-tests). See Appendix table 8.1.

primarily explained by the lagged dependent variable. Government supporters are more likely to attribute responsibility to national politicians than are
supporters of the opposition.[10] As expected, exposure to domesticated news
makes it more likely that national politicians are held accountable. The predicted probability of attributing responsibility to national politicians is .21
at exposure to domesticated news one standard deviation below the mean,
and .25 one standard deviation above the mean.

Robustness tests were conducted to test whether other content characteristics might have affected attribution of responsibility. When the same model
was run with an unweighted media exposure measure, the effect of exposure
was not significant. In an additional test, we weighted exposure by the visibility of economic news and regressed this weighted domesticated exposure measure on attribution of responsibility. Again, no significant effect on
attribution of responsibility was found. Similarly, exposure weighted by the
tone of economic news or the tone towards national actors did not have a
significant effect on attribution of responsibility. The results of these tests
strengthen our conclusion that the degree of domestication is the content
feature that leads news consumers to hold national politicians accountable. Finally, we tested a regression model where treatment responsibility,
rather than causal responsibility, was the dependent variable.[11] This analysis
showed that exposure to domesticated economic news did not make people
more likely to believe that national politicians rather than foreign or international actors should solve the crisis.

Domesticated Economic News and the Inattentive Audience

The inattentive audience is affected the most by exposure to domesticated
news. We tested the effect of exposure to domesticated economic news for
people with low, medium, and high levels of economic interest. Table 8.1 compares the effect of exposure to domesticated news on attribution of responsibility to national politicians for groups with different levels of economic interest.

For the group with low levels of economic interest, exposure to domesticated economic news makes it significantly more likely that responsibility is
attributed to national politicians. For the attentive audience, this result does
not hold: people with medium and high levels of economic interest are not
affected by exposure to domesticated economic news.

To understand this finding, we refer to previous research investigating
moderators for media effects on attribution of responsibility. A look at
studies on the moderating role of sophistication in framing effects might
help us understand why people with low economic interest are affected the
most by domesticated economic news. Political sophistication is a commonly used concept in the responsibility attribution literature. It has been
seen as a direct independent variable; several studies have found that low
sophisticates are more likely to blame certain actors over others (Gomez

Table 8.1 Explaining attribution of responsibility t2 (split for groups with different levels of economic interest)

	Model 1			Model 2			Model 3		
	Low economic interest			Medium economic interest			High economic interest		
	B	SE B	Exp(B)	B	SE B	Exp(B)	B	SE B	Exp(B)
Constant	-2.45	0.31***	0.09	-2.02	0.21***	0.13	-2.51	0.37***	.09
Attribute responsibility to national politicians t1	2.22	0.30***	9.21	2.09	0.18***	8.07	2.39	0.31***	10.89
Exposure to domesticated economic news	0.09	0.03**	1.10	0.00	0.02	1.00	0.02	0.03	1.02
Government supporter	-0.49	0.33	0.61	0.37	0.18*	1.45	1.25	0.31***	3.50
N	34			977			341		
-2 log likelihood	316.42			872			286.78		
Percentage correctly classified	79.6			80.1			82.7		
Nagelkerke R^2	.27			.24			.36		

Note: ***$p < .001$, **$p < .01$, *$p < .05$ (two-sided t-tests).

and Wilson, 2003; Hellwig, 2007; Hellwig and Coffey, 2011; Hellwig, Ringsmuth, and Freeman, 2008) and that high sophisticates attribute more responsibility for economic issues to the EU than low sophisticates (Hobolt et al., 2013). However, Maestas et al. (2008) found no differences in levels of sophistication when examining attributions of responsibility.

Framing effects are built upon pre-existing schemas. Previous studies investigating the effectiveness of frames for sophisticated and less sophisticated individuals have shown contradictory results. Some studies argue that high sophisticates are more susceptible to framing effects because they are already familiar with the argument (McGuire, 1964) or they have the mental capacity to process a framing mechanism (Krosnick and Brannon, 1993a). Others have argued that low sophisticates are more susceptible to framing effects because they cannot counterargue a frame (Kinder and Sanders, 1990; Schuck and de Vreese, 2006).

The finding that people with low economic interest are most affected by domesticated economic news might have to do with to the nature of the message. Previous studies have shown that the nature of the message plays a role in how effective it is. For example, it was found that for the politically aware, the more effective media messages supported their predispositions, while conflicting messages were more effective among less politically aware respondents (Hansen, 2007).

Lee and Chang (2010) also made an inference that resonates with our study: they found that framing effects were stronger for less sophisticated individuals when the issue was portrayed as easy, whereas the effects were stronger for high sophisticates when the issue was portrayed as hard. The argument is that "harder issues require greater cognitive skills and efforts to be used in making choices" (Lee and Chang, 2010, p. 74). Domesticating economic news is a way of simplifying complex economic matters for the inattentive audience, who do not have to think about responsibility for the economy in the framework of multilevel governance but instead can relate it to familiar distinctions, such as the current and previous government or left- and right-wing parties.

Domestication, Attribution, and Economic Development

In this chapter we used various methods to show that domestication of economic news makes audiences attribute responsibility for the economy to national politicians. This finding is an important one given that attribution of responsibility is "a core component of the study of representative democracy" (Hobolt and Tilley, 2014, p. 10). In the sanctional version of the competitive model of democracy, voters hold politicians accountable for past developments, including economic developments. To do so, they need to be able to correctly attribute responsibility to the right level of government, in particular in multilevel government structures. As Hobolt and Tilley (2014) argue, psychological processes, such as self-serving attribution biases, can have a strong effect on the attribution of blame or credit to politicians. In this chapter we have argued that another psychological process also plays an important role—following cues from media coverage to determine the locus of control and, in turn (and in line with attribution theory), to assign responsibility to internal or external factors. Exposure to domesticated economic news had an effect only on perceived retrospective function responsibility for the crisis and not on prospective treatment responsibility. This result is also in line with attribution theory because it shows that cues on locus of control chiefly affect causal assessments about *previous* developments.

In a broader perspective, domestication is also likely to be an important antecedent of attributing responsibility for global developments and crises, including refugee crises, climate change, and international terrorism. This likely connection raises the question whether the degree of domestication in the media is related to real-world developments. The content analysis presented in Chapter 3 generally showed high degrees of domestication in all economic coverage. Nienstedt et al. (2015) came to similar conclusions about coverage of the Euro crisis in 11 European countries. At the same time, we found large variation among different types of outlets, with higher degrees of domestication in online news outlets, television news, and tabloid newspapers. Broadsheet newspapers had a more international outlook. This variation underlines the importance of studying individual-level media exposure rather than media coverage in general when researching the media's role in attribution of responsibility. The results support our general argument that the domestication of economic news is an integral part of the mainstreaming of economic news because it is present across the board and is most pronounced in the outlets that are most read and watched by the mainstream audience. Other studies suggest that the degree of domestication of economic news varies over time and that economic developments and politicians' rhetoric influence shifts in domestication from one year to the next. In 2008 and 2009, at the start of the economic crisis in Denmark, it was mainly treated as a foreign crisis in the Danish news (Goul Andersen, 2010). In another study, we confirmed this finding by Goul Andersen and additionally observed that in 2008, the financial and economic crisis was mainly regarded as an American event—58 percent of articles explicitly referring to the term "crisis" also mentioned the United States or America (van Dalen and de Vreese, 2014). References to this country were therefore almost double those made to Denmark. In subsequent years the crisis became less associated with the United States and more with Denmark. Since 2010, the crisis was more often framed as a Danish than an American event. This change in framing reflects economic developments and a change in the rhetoric of politicians. In 2008, the economic crisis was mainly a banking crisis, but later, it turned into a more general economic and political crisis (Kleinnijenhuis et al., 2015). This shift of *policy venue* is likely to have led to a more domestic focus. Finally, Danish politicians may also have actively tried to frame the crisis as either an international or a national one. In the literature of frame building, the government is generally seen as the *primary definer* (Hall, Critcher, Jefferson, Clarke, and Roberts, 1978)—in other words, the political actor that is most likely to have its frame copied in the media. In the beginning of the recession, when the economic decline was strongest, the Danish government clearly had an incentive to frame the crisis as something caused by foreign developments. Goul Andersen (2010) relates the domestic focus to successful blame avoidance strategies by the sitting government and to the opposition's failure to politicize the issue. Later, when the end of the recession was in sight, it was in the interest of the Danish government to take ownership of the recovery. Together, these economic and political factors explain the shift in the framing of the crisis from being associated mainly with American politicians to being associated increasingly with Danish politicians.

This example shows that although domestication is a general feature of mainstreamed economic news, it varies depending on economic and political developments. The fluctuating degree of domestication suggests that it truly is a heuristic or cue that helps the inattentive audience correctly attribute responsibility. Here we need to stress that based on our data, we cannot determine whether this is indeed the case. We would need to study the relation between the degree of domestication and attribution of responsibility at different points of time. Alternatively, experts could be asked about their views on the degree to which national politicians should be held accountable. Following Hobolt and Tilley (2014), data such as these could serve as a baseline to assess whether exposure to domesticated news helps "getting it right."

In any case, the results underline the media's responsibility to carefully choose between a domesticated or international focus and to be aware of the consequences of these different discourses in regard to responsibility attribution. Journalists might even have to choose between two evils when they cover transnational developments or crises. On the one hand, journalists could choose to domesticate transnational coverage, thereby making the news more attractive for the inattentive audience at home. However, their choice might run the risk of the audience mistakenly believing that the national government should be held accountable for developments over which it has little control. In such a situation, domesticated coverage could ultimately affect government support. On the other hand, transnational developments might be covered from a global, cosmopolitan perspective (Olausson, 2014). This type of reporting may more accurately reflect the nature of the events but may also be difficult for inattentive audiences to relate to. A global perspective and low levels of domestication may give the impression that the responsibility for international developments lies with abstract entities, such as global organizations or the international political system. Ultimately, the audience may be left with the impression that everybody, and thus nobody, is responsible.

Notes

1 In the experiment, respondents also read an article blaming the government in relation to the introduction of the euro. However, this did not affect attribution of responsibility.

2 Rasmussen, Rikke J., Derfor falder benzinpriserne fra i dag. *Ekstrabladet.dk*, 16 April 2013.

3 Ritzau, Corydon I højt humør: Det går den rigtige vej I Danmark, *Børsen*, 20 June 2014.

4 The survey experiment was conducted as an integrated part of wave 3 in the panel survey that was fielded between 18 November 2013 and 1 December 2013. The respondents who participated in the survey experiment were newly recruited. The experiment was conducted by TNS/Gallup between 18 November 2013 and 1 December 2013, and it included 130 respondents. Sixty-four respondents were randomly assigned to the "banks" group and 66 to the "EU" group. The response rate was 47.2 percent. Randomization tests showed that the two groups were similar on the main variables (age, gender, education).

5 European Commission, Directorate-General for Communication, Strategy, Corporate Communication Actions and Eurobarometer Unit. Standard Eurobarometer 80: Public opinion in the European Union; First results. 2013. http://ec.europa.eu/public_opinion/archives/eb/eb80/eb80_first_en.pdf.

6 In a pre-study, 49 individuals were asked how believable these two arguments are and how often they have they heard the two arguments. The differences between the two articles were not significant. This test strengthens us in our conviction that the arguments have similar strength and that they are both equally present in the public sphere.

7 "Who do you think is responsible for the economic crisis?" The banks (scale from 1 [not at all] to 5 [very]); Who do you think is responsible for the economic crisis? The EU/EU countries (scale from 1 [not at all] to 5 [very]).

8 Coding was done by four native Danish speakers. Inter-coder reliability tests showed satisfactory levels of coder agreement for location (Krippendorff's alpha = .83), affected location (.85), and actor identification (.86). The actors to whom responsibility could be attributed are the same as for the variable "actor identification." However, inter-coder agreement was lower for the coding decision whether or not responsibility was attributed (.63, percent agreement 81 percent). The attribution of responsibility indicator is still included as an indicator of domestication because exploratory factor analysis suggests that this indicator loads on the same dimension as the other three indicators.

9 The following formula was used:

Exposure to domesticated economic news = Exposure to EkstraBladet*.37 + exposure to ekstrabladet.dk*.33 + exposure to BT*.59 + exposure to BT.dk*.54 + exposure to TV2 nyheder*.55 + exposure to TV2.dk*.55 + exposure to DR TV avisen*.56 + exposure to DR.dk*.41+ exposure to Politiken*.21 + exposure to Politiken.dk*.44 + exposure to Berlingske*.01 + exposure to Berlingske.dk*0.2 + exposure to JyllandsPosten*(−.01) + exposure to JyllandsPosten.dk*(−.04) + exposure to Børsen*.22 + exposure to Borsen.dk*.03.

To make the results better interpretable, we calculated z-scores of the weighted domesticated exposure measure (minimum = −1.86, maximum = 4.28).

10 Government supporter was measured with the following question: "Which party would you vote for if elections were held today?" (a) Socialdemokratiet, (b) Radikale Venstre, (c) Det Konservative Folkeparti, (d) Socialistisk Folkeparti, (e) Liberal Alliance, (f) Kristendemokraterne, (g) Dansk Folkeparti, (h) Venstre, (i) Enhedslisten, (j) A candidate outside a party, (k) Would vote blank, (l) Would not vote, (m) Don't know, (n) Do not want to answer.

Respondents choosing Socialdemokratiet, Radikale Venstre, or Socialistisk Folkeparti are coded as government supporters.

11 Treatment responsibility was measured as follows: "Who do you think is primarily capable of solving the economic crisis?" (1) the business world, (2) the EU, (3) the current government, (4) the previous government, (5) bankers, (6) others (open answers), (7) nobody. Respondents choosing the current government or the previous government are coded as attributing treatment responsibility to national politicians. Additionally, we tested whether exposure to domesticated news has a significant effect on holding the current government rather than national politicians more broadly accountable.

9 Economic News and Government Approval

In the previous chapters, we have seen that mainstreamed economic news informs citizens about the economy through three mechanisms: the alarm bell function (Chapter 4), induced elaboration (Chapters 5, 6, and 7), and heuristics (Chapter 8). In the coming two chapters, we explore the *effects* of economic news that go beyond helping citizens perform their democratic duties. We show that economic news affects government approval and consumer expectations. The chapters emphasize how relevant economic news is because it has real-world consequences. In this chapter we show that during times of positive economic change after a long period of economic downturn, economic news influences how the audience evaluate the way the government handles the economy. Their evaluations, in turn, have an impact on overall approval of the government. Before presenting our argument why exposure to economic news affects government evaluations, we first review the literature on the relation between economic evaluations and government approval.

Economic Evaluations and Government Approval

In examining the relationship between evaluations of the government's handling of the economy and overall government approval, this chapter builds upon a long tradition of research on economic voting. In a nutshell, research on economic voting studies how trends in evaluations of the economy affect incumbents' popularity and electoral support for governments (Lewis-Beck and Stegmaier, 2013; Stubager, Lewis-Beck, and Nadeau, 2013). Numerous studies have shown that the propensity to vote for the incumbent government fluctuates according to economic assessments (MacKuen et al., 1992; Nannestad and Paldam, 1994; Whitten and Palmer, 1999). When people are positive about the economy, they will evaluate the government positively. Government approval is even more sensitive to the deterioration of the economy than to its improvement (Nannestad and Paldam, 1997). When the electorate perceives a downward economic trend, it is less likely to support the incumbents. Economic conditions and perceptions do not only matter for vote choice during elections but also for the popularity of the government during non-election times (Lewis-Beck and Paldam, 2000). Sanders (2000) showed, for example, that economic conditions matter for the popularity of the British government. Wlezien, Franklin, and Twiggs (1997) showed that the economy matters for citizens' approval of the way the government handles the economy. In Scandinavia, the state of the economy affects support for the prime minister's party (Larsen, 2016).

Although there is large support for the economic voting thesis, the strength of the relation between economic perceptions and government approval varies over time. Economic voting is conditioned by different factors, such as perceived and actual levels of political responsibility (see Chapter 8) and the political context (Powell and Whitten, 1993). For example, Bill Clinton's famous campaign slogan in 1992, "It's the economy, stupid," marked the political context of the immediate post–Cold War era, in which the economy was considered the most important factor when evaluating incumbents.

Like the political context, the economic context also matters. The Great Recession led to a renewed interest in economic voting (e.g., Magalhães, 2014; Shehata and Falasca, 2014). Since the 1990s, when many economic voting studies were conducted, worldwide economies have become increasingly global and interconnected (Almunia, Benetrix, Eichengreen, O'Rourke, and Rua, 2010). This change has affected the dynamic relation between economic evaluations and government evaluations (Hellwig, 2007; Magalhães, 2014; Shehata, 2014). Several scholars have discussed the possibility that economic voting may be limited in the future (Lewis-Beck and Stegmaier, 2007). Due to the complex context of modern economics, in which many actors are involved, the relation between government policy and economic developments is becoming increasingly hard to discern (Anderson, 2007; Lewis-Beck and Stegmaier, 2007). As Hellwig (2007, p. 772) puts it, "globalization increases the volatility and hence the uncertainty of public assessments of government performance."

Studies conducted at the start of the Great Recession in countries both mildly and severely affected by economic crisis confirm this statement. Shehata and Falasca (2014) argued that citizens in Sweden did not "attach greater weight to economic considerations in their government approval assessments following the outbreak of economic crisis." Similar results were found in a study of the Portuguese and Italian elections. "Noneconomic issues made somewhat of a resurgence" (Magalhães, 2014, p. 198) because many Portuguese voters partly blamed other actors for their economic condition. In Italian elections during the crisis, economic voting did occur but was mediated by attributions of responsibility (Bellucci, 2014).

These studies raise the question whether, post-2008, assessments of the economy still matter for government approval. We expect that they do, especially in the recovery phase after the crisis. We think that the non-findings of economic voting during the start of the crisis should be understood in the context of the rapid global economic turmoil and complex developments.

Even financial journalists had problems understanding the complicated economic developments (Davis, 2007; Doyle, 2006), so it is no surprise that citizens had difficulties attributing responsibility and connecting economic developments to government evaluations.

As mentioned earlier, the importance of the economy when predicting votes or government evaluations fluctuates over time (Powell and Whitten, 1993). We argue that it is relevant to examine how strong the relationship between economic evaluations and overall government approval is at a time when the economy is *recovering* from a long crisis. A long period of economic decline should make people more susceptible to a sudden positive change (Soroka, 2014). We expect that in such a context, evaluations of the way the government handles the economy are an important antecedent of overall government approval (Magalhães, 2014; Miller and Krosnick, 1996). Media coverage is expected to be an important driver of this relation. We expect the government to be more visible in economic news in times of economic recovery. Building on priming literature and research into media effects on vote choice, we argue that greater government visibility in the news should, in turn, affect government approval.

Media Exposure and Economic Government Evaluations

Several scholars have found that media exposure influences evaluations of the national economic climate, which consequently influences vote choice (e.g., Nadeau, Niemi, and Amato, 2000). For instance, Hetherington (1996) found that the news that voters consumed played an important role in predicting their retrospective economic evaluations. In this chapter we look, in particular, at the *visibility* of economic news as an antecedent of evaluations of the way the government handles the economy. It is well known from priming literature that the attention paid to an issue affects its salience when people are making voting decision (de Vreese, 2004; Iyengar and Kinder, 1987; Pan and Kosicki, 1997). Although the priming thesis is not uncontested (Lenz, 2009; Malhotra and Krosnick, 2007), most research on priming has argued that news media's emphasis on an issue enhances the accessibility of thoughts and evaluations about the issue. An example of priming is the media attention to Reagan's handling of the Iran-Contra affair, which subsequently affected his popularity (Krosnick and Kinder, 1990). Priming theory has also been used in other contexts outside voting and the evaluation of politicians—for example, in testing the effect of crime news on racial attitudes (Valentino, 1999) and how violent representations in media prime aggressive cognitive associations (Bushman, 1998).

According to the priming thesis apropos of the economy, people should be more likely to base their assessment of the government on economic performance when the economy dominates the public and media agenda. The topic's visibility in the public domain and in the media makes the economy more accessible when people are forming opinions about the government (Shehata, 2014).

We assume that the government is well aware of this relationship and will try to push the economy to the top of the media agenda during times of positive change in the economy. Governments try to take credit when the economy is performing well and to avoid blame during crises (Weaver, 1986). As economic conditions improve, not only do we expect that the government wants media attention to the economy; we also expect that the government itself wants to be visible in economic news. Due to their position as primary definers of news, government sources are in a good position to affect the media agenda (Hall et al., 1978). A study that looked at the state of the economy and the visibility of actors showed that during periods of economic prosperity, incumbents gain not only more positive coverage than opponents but also significantly more economic coverage (Shah, Watts, Domke, Fan, and Fibison, 1999).

Previous research has shown that the visibility of political actors influences political support (Hopmann, Vliegenthart, de Vreese, and Albæk, 2010). In congruence with agenda-setting theory—which suggests that the visibility that the media dedicate to an issue affects the importance that news users attach to the issue (McCombs and Shaw, 1972)—these studies have shown that the salience of political actors in the news affects vote choice for these actors. Hopmann et al. (2010) showed that the parties' visibility in the news media has an impact on vote choice for undecided voters. Two other studies have found similar results. Semetko and Schönbach (1994) found that even slight changes in the visibility of political actors can affect party evaluations, while Oegema and Kleinnijenhuis (2000) showed that the greater a party leader's visibility in the news, the higher the probability that people will vote for that particular party. Likewise, we expect that it is beneficial to government actors to appear in economic news at times of economic recovery.

Key Questions

Based on previous research on economic voting and media effects on political evaluations, we expect that exposure to news about the economy is an important antecedent of economic and overall government approval. We expect that when the economy is improving, exposure to economic news will lead to positive evaluations of the government handling the economy. After years of negative economic developments, at a time of positive change in the economic situation and a more positive tone of economic news, media exposure is expected to lead to more positive views on the economic situation (Soroka, 2014). We expect that increased media attention for the economy will also positively affect evaluations of the way the government handles the economy because government actors will be visible in economic coverage (Shah et al., 1999). Positive evaluations of the government's handling of the economy are, in turn, expected to affect overall government evaluations (see Figure 9.1).

We test our expectations with data from our panel study (see Methodological Appendix). As we have seen in Chapter 2, the Danish economy improved during our panel study. The improvement was also visible in the tone of economic news, especially between wave 2 and wave 3. Between waves 1 and 2, the average tone of economic news was –.29 on a scale from –1 to +1.[1] Between waves 2 and 3 the average tone improved to –.17, after which it levelled out and remained at the same level between waves 3 and 4.

Thus, a change in the reporting of the economy occurred between waves 2 and 3. During this period, people became more positive towards the government, in general, and in their evaluation of how the government handles the economy. Overall government approval was measured by asking the respondents to indicate on a scale from 1 (very poorly) to 5 (very well) "how well or poorly they think the current Danish government is performing in general." To measure evaluations of the way the government handles the economy, we asked "how well or poorly do you think the current Danish government is performing when it comes to the economy?" For both questions, the evaluations of the government improved significantly between the two waves.

Given that we expect to find a strong influence of economic evaluations on overall government evaluations as the economy changes for the better, we test our expectations by analysing change between waves 2 and 3, when the economy, economic news, and government evaluations change in a positive direction.

We will test our expectations in three steps. First, we test whether evaluations of the way the government handles the economy (still) affect overall government approval. Second, we study whether exposure to economic news leads to positive evaluations of the way the government handles the economy. We compare the influence of exposure to economic news on economic evaluations of governments to the influence of exposure to economic news on other issue-specific government evaluations (e.g., the environment

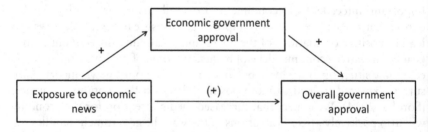

Figure 9.1 Anticipated relationship between exposure to economic news, evaluations of the way the government handles the economy, and overall government evaluations

or the EU). If our argument holds true, economic news affects evaluations of the government's handling of the economy but not evaluations of the government's handling of other issues. Third, we study whether evaluations of the government's handling of the economy lead to an indirect effect of exposure to economic news on overall government approval.

Exposure to Economic News and Government Evaluations

Before analysing the relation between exposure to economic news and government evaluations with our panel design, we first look at the relation between general news exposure and government evaluations. Overall, evaluations were slightly on the left of the neutral middle point of the scale, meaning that respondents were somewhat more negative than positive towards the government. Differences between the groups with low, medium, and high levels of news exposure were small and not significant.[2] When we look at the evaluations of the way the government handles the economy, we see a similar pattern and no significant difference between the groups with different levels of news exposure.[3] These results show that at the start of the period of economic improvement, media exposure and government evaluations were not related. We will see whether this changes over the period of economic improvement after we analyse whether evaluations of the government's handling of the economy—despite predictions to the contrary—still matter today for overall government evaluations.

Do Economic Evaluations (Still) Affect Overall Government Approval?

As mentioned, research at the start of the Great Recession often found no relation between economic perceptions and government approval, raising questions about the possible demise of economic voting. However, during the period of economic recovery, we found a clear relation between evaluations of the government's handling of the economy and overall government evaluations. After controlling for the lagged dependent variables, evaluations of the government's handling of the economy had a significant and strong effect on overall government approval (Table 9.1). Just how important these evaluations are for overall government approval becomes even clearer when we compare their impact to the impact of other issue-specific evaluations. Following de Vreese (2004), we also asked respondents to evaluate how the government handles the topics of welfare, immigration, economy, the EU, climate, and crime. Each of these evaluations had a positive and significant relation with overall government approval, even after controlling for overall approval at time 1. However, there is a striking difference in strength of the effects. Economic evaluations were by far the largest predictor of overall government approval.[4] This finding shows that the economic voting thesis remains relevant.

Table 9.1 Explaining overall government approval t2

	Model 1			Model 2		
	B	SE B	β	B	SE B	β
Constant	0.51	0.05***		−0.03	0.06	
Government approval t1	0.33	0.02***	.35	0.25	0.02***	.26
Approval of government's handling of the economy	0.48	0.02***	.50	0.33	0.02***	.34
Approval of government's handling of welfare				0.18	0.02***	.17
Approval of government's handling of immigration				0.06	0.02**	.06
Approval of government's handling of the EU				0.07	0.02**	.06
Approval of government's handling of the environment				0.08	0.02***	.07
Approval of government's handling of crime				0.05	0.02*	.05
Government supporter	0.24	0.04***	.11	0.16	0.04***	.07
N	1,286			1,286		
Adj. R^2	.70			.74		

Note: ***$p < .001$, **$p < .01$, *$p < .05$ (two-sided t-tests).

Economic News and Economic Government Evaluations

Now that we have seen that economic government evaluations matter for overall economic evaluations, we test whether exposure to economic news is indeed an antecedent of these evaluations. To do so, we conducted a regression analysis with evaluations of the government's handling of the economy at time 2 as the dependent variable and exposure to economic news as the independent variable (Table 9.2). Exposure to economic news was measured with the following formula:

Exposure to economic news = ((Exposure to outlet 1 × share of articles which deal with the economy in outlet 1) + (exposure to outlet 2 × share of articles which deal with the economy in outlet 2) + (. . .) + (exposure medium 16 × share of articles which deal with the economy in outlet 16))/16 outlets.[5]

We included the lagged dependent variable as a control variable to the model. We also controlled for whether the respondents previously voted for the government, because previous voting is strongly related to evaluations of the government's handling of the economy. After controlling for these

Table 9.2 Effect of media exposure on evaluation of the government's handling of the economy t2

	B	SE B	β
Constant	1.23	0.06***	
Approval of government's handling of the economy t1	0.52	0.02***	.55
Government supporter	0.58	0.05**	.25
Exposure to economic news	0.23	0.11*	.04
N	1,286		
Adj. R^2	.49		

Note: ***$p < .001$, **$p < .01$, *$p < .05$ (two-sided t-tests).

variables, exposure to economic news had a significant effect. The more one is exposed to economic news, the more positively one evaluates the government's handling of the economy.

Now that we have seen that evaluations of the government's economic management influence government approval and that exposure to economic news influences economic evaluations, we turn our attention to the combined effects of these two relations as depicted in Figure 9.1. Is there an indirect influence of exposure to economic news on the one hand, and of government approval on the other, through evaluations of the government's handling of the economy? We tested this question following the same bootstrap procedure as in Chapters 5 and 6. The results are illustrated in Figure 9.2. The figure shows a positive relation between exposure to economic news and government approval, and this relation is mediated by economic government evaluations. In addition, we conducted the same mediation analysis with exposure to economic news where government actors are visible as independent variables.[6] This analysis showed similar result. The results are in line with our explanation that the visibility of government actors in economic news is the reason why exposure to economic news during times of positive change in economic conditions leads to more positive economic government evaluations and, ultimately, to higher levels of government approval.

Economic News, Government Approval, and the Inattentive Audience

Similar to what we did in the previous chapters, we tested whether the relation between exposure to economic news and government approval in the inattentive audience is different from this relation in the attentive audience. Previous research on the role of issue-specific interest in media effects on government evaluations has shown mixed results. Krosnick and Brannon

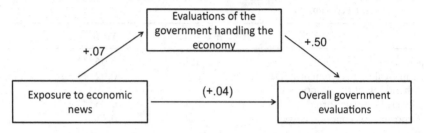

Figure 9.2 The mediating effect of economic government evaluations on the relationship between exposure to economic news and overall evaluations

Note: Standardized beta-coefficients. Significant at $p < .05$ (two-sided t-tests).

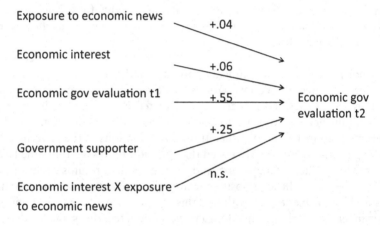

Figure 9.3 Moderating effect of economic interest on the effect of economic news
exposure on evaluation of the government's handling of the economy

Note: Standardized beta-coefficients. Significant at $p < .1$ (two-sided t-tests). See Appendix
table 9.1.

(1993b) and Valenzuela (2009) showed that media exposure had less effect
on government evaluations by those with high levels of political interest.
Van der Brug, Semetko, and Valkenburg (2007), however, showed that
attentiveness to political affairs (a measure of interest, discussion, and news
use) was not related to news media priming effects in the context of a summit meeting of the EU. This finding suggests that the role of interest varies
across issues.

In our study, the relation between exposure to economic news and evaluations of the government's economic handling was not moderated by economic interest (see Figure 9.3). Economic interest was positively related to
approval of the government's handling of the economy, but there was no

significant interaction with exposure to economic news. Thus, media exposure affected economic evaluations of the inattentive and attentive audiences in the same way.

Economic Perceptions Still Matter

This chapter showed that economic perceptions are still relevant when individuals form overall government evaluations and that exposure to economic news is an important antecedent of this relation. The results contradict predictions that in increasingly globalized economies, citizens no longer attach particular weight to economic conditions when evaluating the government (Hellwig, 2007; Magalhães, 2014). In our study, which was conducted during a time of positive change in the tone of economic news and in economic government evaluations, we see that the government is rewarded. This finding highlights the importance of the economic context in which economic voting is studied. Although previous studies have shown that the economy influences evaluations more during downturns (Nannestad and Paldam, 1997), our findings point in the other direction. We think that they are the result of the long period of negative economic news that preceded the positive economic turn at the time of our study. Soroka (2014) argues that the relative impact of negative or positive developments depends on the context in which they occur. In a "more negative environment, we react somewhat less to negative change and somewhat more to positive change" (Soroka, 2014, p. 71). Our reaction has to do with the discrepancy between our expectations and actual developments. After years of negative economic developments during the Great Recession, a change in the economy for the better goes against our expectations. This situation explains why we found a positive relation between exposure to economic news and economic government evaluations. In the years before the Great Recession, when the economy grew and the overall tone of economic coverage was more positive, the opposite effect was observed. During this time negative developments went against general expectations and had a strong effect.

Our data suggest that a positive change in tone rather than the absolute level of negativity affects the strength of the relation between economic perceptions and government approval. The results of the content analysis of news media coverage between waves 2 and 3 of the study showed that the tone of economic news was negative. However, it was less negative than during the previous period in the study. Hence, the audience was able to pick up the differences from other periods with more negative news. Other studies have also suggested that changes in economic indicators have a larger influence on people's economic expectations than the actual levels of these indicators (Soroka, 2014). We observe the same for the tone of economic news. Further analysis showed that the relation between media exposure and government evaluations was not present between waves 1 and 2 when the news was more negative (see Table 9.3). More surprising, neither did

Table 9.3 Explaining approval of the government's handling of the economy (t2), at different time points

	Model 1 between waves 1 and 2			Model 2 between waves 3 and 4		
	B	SE B	β	B	SE B	β
Constant	0.98	0.07***		1.17	0.07***	
Approval of government's handling of the economy t1	0.58	0.02***	.53	0.62	0.02***	0.65
Government supporter	0.43	0.06***	.16	0.18	0.06**	0.08
Exposure to economic news	0.15	0.12	.02	0.02	0.12	.00
N	1,665			1,042		
Adj. R^2	.38			.48		

Note: ***$p < .001$, **$p < .01$ (two-sided t-tests).

exposure to economic news have a significant effect on government evaluations between waves 3 and 4. In this period, the tone of economic news was similar to the tone between waves 2 and 3.

The change in economic conditions after a long period of negative economic developments might also explain why economic interest did not moderate the relation between exposure to economic news and government evaluations. After a long period of negativity in economic coverage, somewhat less negative economic news might be noticed by all readers and viewers, and affect their evaluations of the government, regardless of their level of interest in the economy. This effect is in line with Soroka's (2014, p. 119) observation that negativity can be self-limiting when it is persistent and all-encompassing. In such a context, we are most likely to find an effect of positive developments across the whole population.

Like Chapter 8, this chapter highlights the role of economic news in electoral evaluations. Further research is needed to study the combined influence of exposure to economic news on attribution of responsibility, economic government evaluations, and government approval. Regardless of whether national governments should actually take the blame or credit for economic affairs, perceptions are what matter, and economic news shapes these perceptions. This places a large responsibility on economic journalists. In the next chapter, we will look at another real-world effect of economic news: the influence of uncertainty in economic news on consumer expectations.

Notes

1 The tone is calculated as (the number of positive news items – the number of negative news)/all news items.
2 Evaluation of overall government approval was measured on a scale from 1 (disapprove) to 5 (approve). Group with low news exposure: $M = 2.69$, $SD = .99$;

medium exposure group: M = 2.79, SD = .94; high news exposure group: M = 2.72, SD = 1.01).

3 Evaluation of the way the government handles the economy was measured on a scale from 1 (disapprove) to 5 (approve). Group with low news exposure: M = 2.72, SD = 1.02; medium exposure group: M = 2.79, SD = .98; high news exposure group: M = 2.87, SD = 1.05).

4 Partial F-tests showed that the effect of economic evaluations is significantly higher than the effect of other evaluations: economy and welfare: $F(1, 1,279)$ 18.7, p < .01; economy and immigration: $F(1, 1,279)$ 72.5, p < .01; economy and EU: $F(1, 1,279)$ 79.24, p < .01; economy and climate: $F(1, 1,279)$ 77.3, p < .0001; economy and crime: $F(1, 1,279)$ 77.8, p < .01.

5 We weighted exposure to the different outlets measured at wave 3 by the share of news items that deals with the economy measured between wave 2 and wave 3. We use the visibility of the offline edition of each outlet as proxy for the visibility of the online edition.

Exposure to economic news = (Exposure to EkstraBladet*.11 + exposure to ekstrabladet.dk*.11 + exposure to BT*.12 + exposure to BT.dk*.12 + exposure to TV2 nyheder*.22 + exposure to TV2.dk*.22 + exposure to DR TV avisen*.25 + exposure to DR.dk*.25 + exposure to Politiken*.21 + exposure to Politiken. dk*.21 + exposure to Berlingske*.33 + exposure to Berlingske.dk*.33 + exposure to JyllandsPosten*.28 + exposure to JyllandsPosten.dk*.28 + exposure to Børsen*.52 + exposure to Borsen.dk*.52)/16. (M = .27, SD = .19, minimum = 0, maximum = 1.48.)

6 Governmental actor visibility was accessed via a manual content analysis.

10 Mediated Uncertainty and Consumer Expectations

In the previous chapters, we have shown that mainstreamed economic news helps people get the economy right. The mass media function as an alarm bell and magnifying glass, and help the audience form correct perceptions of the state of the economy. Mainstreamed economic news—with its focus on negativity and its use of human-interest and consequence framing—leads to more elaboration and, consequently, greater interest in the economy, higher economic efficacy, and increased knowledge. Furthermore, the level of domestication in economic news serves as a cue for whether national governments should be held responsible for economic developments.

In this chapter we turn the focus away from the impact of mainstreamed economic news on assessments and on knowledge about the *current* state of the economy. Instead, we turn our attention to optimism or pessimism about where the economy is heading (consumer expectations). We argue that as economic news becomes more mainstream, it also becomes more *future* oriented. This future-oriented news is accompanied by uncertainty, which breeds pessimism about where the economy is heading. With few exceptions, previous research on the effects of economic news on consumer expectations has largely ignored uncertainty. Previous research in other areas, however, has shown that subjective feelings of uncertainty negatively affect people's perceptions (Alvarez and Franklin, 1994; McGraw, Hasecke, and Conger, 2003). As we show in this chapter, uncertainty in mainstreamed economic news lowers economic expectations.

Consumer Expectations

Consumer expectations refers to the optimism or pessimism with which people think about the future state of their personal finances and the overall economy. While consumer confidence or consumer sentiment can refer to confidence in the current as well as the future state of the economy, we use the term consumer expectations to refer to confidence in the *future state* of the economy.

Few indicators of public opinion have as much real-world impact as monthly measures of consumer expectation. Started as a measure of income expectations in 1952 by George Katona, it was the "first widely used subjective indicator" (Bechtel, 2003, p. 325). Graber (1982) highlights consumer confidence as an important aspect of public opinion because it shows that public perceptions are consequential and can impact people's behaviour. Consumer confidence predicts macro-economic developments and has therefore become one of the most important economic indicators. Politicians, economists, and journalists wait for the monthly consumer expectation data with great anticipation. The influence of consumer expectations goes beyond the economic domain because it can also affect politicians' popularity (MacKuen et al., 1992) and even election outcomes (Hetherington, 1996).

Numerous studies have looked at the antecedents of consumer expectations, showing that they reflect real-world economic conditions to a large extent but that the economy alone also leaves a lot of variance unexplained (Doms and Morin, 2004). Next to political conditions (De Boef and Kellstedt, 2004), the mass media are an important antecedent. Economic news is not a one-on-one reflection of the state of the economy but rather emphasizes change, negativity, and extended periods of boom or burst. This mediated tone in economic news can affect economic expectations (Boomgaarden et al., 2011; Goidel and Langley, 1995; Hollanders and Vliegenthart, 2011). While the tone of economic news is an important aspect of economic coverage, other aspects, such as framing and emotions, can be expected to have effects as well. However, studies explaining consumer confidence hardly look at other aspects of coverage, apart from the tone of economic news. One element of economic news that has received limited attention as an antecedent is the degree of uncertainty (see Goidel and Langley, 1995, p. 326 for an exception).

Mainstreamed Economic News and Uncertainty

We believe that it is important to study the influence of uncertainty in economic news on economic expectations because we see it as an element of mainstreamed economic news. Uncertainty can be defined as "the absence of definite expectations" (Katona, 1960, p. 56). Uncertainty can be a subjective feeling, but it can also be present in the information one is confronted with. Uncertainty of information implies a certain degree of incompleteness of information (Smithson, 2008), and more specifically, limited knowledge or no knowledge about the probability of certain outcomes (Bracha and Weber, 2012, p. 5). In a similar vein, Ellsberg (1961, p. 657) speaks of the ambiguity of information, which he describes as the "nature of one's information concerning the relative likelihood of events." Uncertainty should be distinguished from the related concept of risk (Knight, 1948). Risk refers to negative outcomes with known probability. For risky situations one can forecast the likelihood of a negative outcome, whereas for uncertain situations, there is little or no basis for predictions.

Journalists actively introduce uncertainty in their news reports by using words like "may" or "suggests" (Hansen, 2015; Stocking and Holstein, 2009), by using an uncertainty frame (Olausson, 2009), by highlighting controversies (Zehr, 2000, p. 98), or by presenting conflicting information (Svensson, Albæk, van Dalen, and de Vreese, 2017b). Research on science journalism has shown not only that media report the uncertainty and controversies among scholars and experts but also that they *manufacture uncertainty* (Stocking and Holstein, 2009) through overemphasis (Ashe, 2013; Friedman, Dunwoody, and Rogers, 1999). At the level of the individual journalist, education in and experience with the topic that the journalist is covering may lead him or her either to accentuate or limit uncertainty in the news. Additionally, the journalists' role conceptions and the audience's views may play a role in how they represent uncertainty (Stocking and Holstein, 2009). At the level of the journalistic profession, organizational routines and news values may have a similar influence. The goal of explaining complex issues to non-expert audiences and presenting novel perspectives has to be balanced with accurately representing scientific debate and guarding oneself against criticism (Stocking and Holstein, 1993, p. 199). According to Friedman et al. (1999, p. xii), journalists "are very active in uncertainty coverage" because controversy and debate have news value (see also Jaworski, Fitzgerald, and Morris, 2003). These individual- and professional-level influences are likely at play in the reporting of economic news as well; economic news has become like mainstream news, and therefore there is reason to expect that uncertainty is becoming more present in economic news.

Economic journalism seems to follow a more and more future-oriented journalistic trend (Hyde, 2006), with increasing speculation about forthcoming developments (Neiger, 2007). Over time journalists themselves have become more active in speculation and forecasting future events rather than leaving such undertakings to their sources (Hansen, 2015). When journalists speculate about the future, they often introduce uncertainty in the news in their desire to present a balanced account of events and highlight both sides of a story.

Our content analysis supports the relation between the future-oriented nature of economic news and uncertainty. Figure 10.1 shows the share of economic news items that include expectations, assumptions, or predictions for the macro-economic situation in the country, based on the year-long content analysis of the 16 outlets (see Methodological Appendix).[1] This was the case in almost one-fourth of the news items, which indicates that uncertainty is an important feature of economic news. One indicator of uncertainty in economic news is the presentation of conflicting information about the economic climate. When an article presents a mixed evaluation of the general economic climate, simultaneously reporting that the economy is both thriving and deteriorating, it triggers uncertainty among the audience (Svensson et al., 2017b). Further analysis showed that 12 percent of future-oriented news presented mixed evaluations of economic developments,

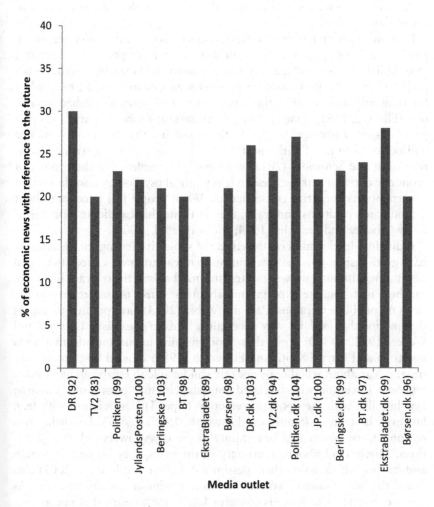

Figure 10.1 Future-oriented economic news

Note: Number of articles in brackets. See Methodological Appendix for details.

which is significantly more than news that was not future oriented (6 percent, $\chi^2 = 13.206$, $df = 1$, $p < .01$).

Consumer Expectations and Uncertainty

Macro-economic studies have shown that uncertainty about the future negatively affects the economy and delays economic recovery during a recession (Dixit and Pindyck, 1994; Haddow, Hare, Hooley, and Shakir, 2013). Uncertainty can negatively affect investments, raise the cost of finance, and cause labour market distortions (Haddow et al., 2013). Similarly, we expect uncertainty in news about the national economy to decrease confidence in the economic future.

Previous research has shown that feelings of uncertainty foster pessimism (Smithson, 2008, p. 208). Although some people are prone to ambiguity, most individuals are ambiguity averse (Einhorn and Hogarth, 1986). People prefer a bet with known odds over a bet with unknown odds, even when the odds are unfavourable; this has come to be known as Ellsberg's paradox (Ellsberg, 1961). One of the explanations for Ellsberg's paradox is that people assign additional weight to the possibility that the worst outcome will occur when faced with uncertainty. Thus, uncertainty lowers expectations. Ilut and Schneider (2012) confirmed this tendency in the context of economic decision making. Research in political psychology also shows that uncertainty has negative consequences. When people feel uncertain about a candidate's positions and traits, they evaluate that candidate more negatively (Alvarez and Franklin, 1994; McGraw et al., 2003).

Individual-level studies on the effects of subjective feelings of uncertainty have given insight into the mechanisms that lead to lower expectations and pessimism. Although we will not test this mechanism, the relevant literature can help us formulate expectations about the effect of uncertainty in the news on public perceptions. Patt and Weber (2014) have pointed to fear as the emotion that explains why uncertainty leads to pessimism. Camerer and Weber (1992, p. 330) argue that "not knowing important information is upsetting and scary." Smith and Ellsworth (1985) showed that uncertainty triggers fear about whether or not one will be able to escape an unpleasant outcome. Uncertainty is associated not only with the "pessimistic" emotion fear but also with the optimistic emotion hope. The association with fear, however, is stronger (Smith and Ellsworth, 1985, p. 827). Following this reasoning, we expect that uncertainty in the news lowers public expectations. People read about uncertainty in the news, they become uncertain and fearful, which makes them pessimistic. Lerner and Keltner (2001) also found that fear causes individuals to make pessimistic risk assessments. As far as consumer confidence is concerned, this result means that uncertainty may make individuals *more* pessimistic about the future and make them adopt more risk-averse behaviour.

Following this argument, we expect that uncertainty in economic news lowers optimism about the economy's future. Similar to our line of reasoning, Goidel and Langley (1995, p. 326) suggested that negative news lowers economic evaluations when "economic signals are mixed and subsequently, subject to a variety of interpretations." Elsewhere, we have shown that individuals who are exposed to television news that includes conflicting information about the economy's state become uncertain. Uncertainty, in turn, lowers consumer expectations (Svensson et al., 2017b). We will search for evidence of a relation between the presence of uncertainty in economic news and national consumer expectations at the aggregate country level.

Key Questions

In this chapter we return to the time-series data from Chapters 2 and 4 to study the relation between uncertainty in economic news and national levels of consumer expectations over a 17-year period. We first study how the degree of uncertainty in economic news develops over time and see how this development relates to real economic development and negativity in economic news. Then we study whether mediated uncertainty negatively influences consumer expectations *above and beyond* the influence of the real economic developments and the tone of economic news. To deepen our understanding of the effects of uncertainty in economic news, we test whether uncertainty affects sociotropic as well as egotropic expectations. Finally, we study whether uncertainty in economic news can trigger asymmetric responses by increasing the salience of negative information.

Mediated Uncertainty and Consumer Expectations

We measure uncertainty in economic news articles between 1996 and 2012 in the three broadsheet newspapers which were included in the time-series analysis (*Politiken, Berlingske,* and *Jyllands-Posten*; see Methodological Appendix). *Uncertainty in economic news* was measured with dictionary-based, automated content analysis, similar to the approach used to measure the tone of economic news in Chapter 4 (Loughran and McDonald, 2011; see Methodological Appendix).

The main aim of our analysis is to find out whether uncertainty in economic news affects consumer confidence rather than to explain how real-world developments and journalistic routines shape the level of uncertainty in the news. Nevertheless, it is insightful to see when uncertainty makes it into the news, especially in relation to the economic boom and bust periods between 2003 and 2012 (see Figure 10.2). At the beginning of 2004, at the start of the economic boom, uncertainty in the news increased sharply. An op-ed in *Berlingske*, for example, stated that "uncertainty requires caution."[2] After a brief period, the level of uncertainty dropped again. At the peak of economic growth in 2007, uncertainty was at its lowest, with an average of three words indicating uncertainty per article. In 2008, when Denmark entered a recession, uncertainty sharply increased again, with headlines like "Uncertainty: Large Uncertainty About Property Values."[3] In 2009, although the Danish economy had still not improved, uncertainty decreased again. Uncertainty in the news fluctuated heavily between 2009 and 2011. During these years, the tone of economic news remained negative (see Chapter 4). These observations seem to suggest that uncertainty in the news is more volatile than the tone of the news and increases when the economy is undergoing change, even when change is positive. In times of change, journalists might inject uncertainty into the news as a way of attracting

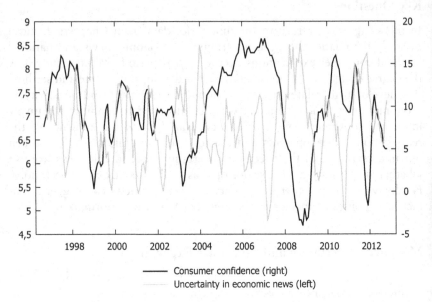

Figure 10.2 Uncertainty in economic news (grey line) and consumer confidence
(black line) (August 1996–December 2012)

Note: The scale for consumer confidence can be found on the right. The scale for uncertainty
in economic news can be found on the left. Monthly data. The three-month moving average of
uncertainty is displayed.

audience interest or of voicing reservations about the economy's direction,
with headlines such as "The Economy Is Improving—Maybe."[4] Claims
about uncertainty in the economy are often attributed to external sources—
for example, "Investment Organization: Be Prepared for an Uncertainty
Fall"[5] or "OECD Report: Uncertainty About Danish Growth."[6] Mediated
uncertainty, however, does not necessarily reflect real-world uncertainty;
after all, journalists might select these sources in order to introduce uncertainty into the news.

Consumer expectations are inversely related to uncertainty in the news
($r = -.22$, $p < .05$). Figure 10.2 also shows the development of consumer
expectations during the same period.[7] This measure is based on four questions: (1) How do you think the national economic situation will be in a year
compared with today? (2) How do you think the level of unemployment will
be in a year compared with today? (3) How do you think your household's
financial situation will be in a year compared with today? (4) Do you expect
to save any money during the coming 12 months? The monthly score for
each question is a weighted aggregate of all respondents' answers and can,
in theory, range from –100 to +100.[8]

Between 2003 and 2007, when the economy grew, consumer confidence kept rising, peaking in July 2007. After November 2007, at the start of several years of economic contraction and stagnation, consumer expectations dropped sharply. Despite several upturns, consumer confidence never recovered to the same levels experienced just prior to the economic downturn. While the development of consumer expectations is clearly related to the development of the real-world economy, it diverges from the general economic climate at times. In 2008 and 2011, when uncertainty was high in the news, consumer confidence was significantly lower than the economic climate would predict. A Granger causality test showed that uncertainty Granger-causes consumer confidence ($F(2, 190) = 3.44$, $p < .05$). This result means that the development of consumer confidence can be better explained when uncertainty in the previous month is taken into account than when only the previous level of consumer confidence is considered (Granger, 1969). The reversed effect is weaker and not significant ($F(2, 190) = 2.98$, $p < .1$).[9] These results give initial support to the idea that uncertainty influences consumer expectations.

Figure 10.3 shows stronger support for the predicted influence of uncertainty in macro-economic news on consumer expectations.[10] We test whether uncertainty in macro-economic news affects consumer expectations after controlling for the influence of consumer expectations in the previous months (the lagged dependent variable), the actual economy, and tone of economic news. These controls were included because previous research has shown that tone and real-world economic developments

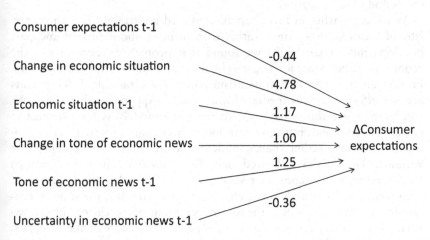

Figure 10.3 Explaining change in consumer expectations (August 1996–December 2012)

Note: Unstandardized beta-coefficients. Significant at $p < .05$ (two-sided t-tests). See Appendix table 10.1.

affect consumer confidence (e.g., Damstra, Boukes, and Vliegenthart, 2018; Soroka et al., 2015). Consumer expectations are primarily explained by their past and by real-world economic developments. The actual state of the economy was controlled for by including Composite Leading Indicators (CLI) (see Chapter 4). The tone of economic news in the previous month and the change in tone in the current month have a significant influence on consumer confidence, in line with previous research (Soroka et al., 2015).[11] Likewise, the level of uncertainty in economic news during the previous month has a significant effect on consumer expectations in the current month.[12]

In addition, we tested uncertainty's effect when negative and positive tones are included in the model separately instead of being combined into a one-tone measure. Consumer expectations are lower when the tone of economic news was negative in the previous month and becomes more negative in the current month (see Appendix table 10.1). Neither positive tone nor change in positive tone has a significant effect, and they are therefore both excluded from the model. These findings confirm that the response to economic news is asymmetric. Again, we find that the degree of uncertainty in the previous month makes people more pessimistic about the future state of the economy, in line with our expectations.[13] If journalists include, on average, one more term indicating uncertainty per news article, economic expectations will drop by one-third of a point in the month after. The long-run multiplier for uncertainty is −.79. Thus, a one standard-deviation increase in uncertainty will, in the long run, decrease consumer confidence by one point, which is about 3.5 percent of the range of consumer expectations in the period of investigation.

As we saw earlier in this chapter, mediated uncertainty is a characteristic of future-oriented news rather than of news about current and past developments. Accordingly, we found that people's expectations of the economy's *future* state are negatively affected by uncertainty in the news. Further analysis shows that assessments of past economic developments are not affected by this mediated uncertainty (Appendix table 10.4). We conducted regression analyses with the same models as for prospective consumer sentiment, but now with monthly changes in retrospective economic sentiment rather than confidence in the future as the dependent variable. This analysis showed that, like confidence in the economy's future, retrospective consumer sentiment is explained by the consumers' own past, the economy's state, changes in the economy, the tone of economic news, and changes in the tone of economic news. Uncertainty, however, did not affect retrospective assessments of the state of the economy. This is confirmed in a regression model where positive tone and negative tone in economic news are included separately in the model. Again, we found no significant effect of uncertainty.[14]

Table 10.1 Explaining change in consumer expectations (August 1996–December 2012)

| | Egotropic | | | | Sociotropic | | | |
| | Model 1 Consumer expectations: savings | | Model 2 Consumer expectations: personal finance | | Model 3 Consumer expectations: national economy | | Model 4 Consumer expectations: unemployment | |
	B	SE B	B	SE B	B	SE B	B	SE B
Constant	1.71	25.05	-9.12	20.55	39.53	41.42	210.23	55.18***
Consumer expectations t-1	-0.63	0.07***	-0.71	0.07***	-0.48	0.07***	-0.24	0.05***
Consumer expectations t-2	0.28	0.07***	0.18	0.07*	0.21	0.07***		
Consumer expectations t-3			0.17	0.07*				
Economic indicators t-1	0.15	0.25	0.14	0.20	-0.31	0.40	-2.20	0.54***
Δ Economic indicators	1.56	1.50	2.25	1.24#	9.12	2.66***	-5.70	2.16***
Negativity t-1	-1.65	0.80*	-0.94	0.66	-1.36	1.26	2.04	1.09#
Δ Negativity	0.22	0.73	-1.49	0.59*	-2.74	1.14*	1.41	1.01
Uncertainty t-1	-0.27	0.23	0.38	0.19#	-0.56	0.37	-0.71	0.33*
Adj. R²	.30		.35		.24		.21	
AIC	1,067.32		989.11		1,254.64		1,219.39	
HQC	1,077.93		1,001.02		1,265.24		1,219.39	
SBC	1,093.51		1,018.52		1,280.83		1,233.04	
N	195		194		195		196	
Breusch-Godfrey	1.64	(p = .20)	2.02	(p = .16)	0.72	(p = .40)	2.15	(p = .14)
Ljung Box Q	0.20	(p = .66)	0.10	(p = .75)	0.06	(p = .81)	1.36	(p = .24)

Note: Unstandardized beta-coefficients with standard error. ***$p < .01$, *$p < .05$, #$p < .1$ (two-sided t-tests).

The Impersonal Effect of Mediated Uncertainty

To further understand the influence of mediated uncertainty, we look at its effect on egotropic and sociotropic consumer expectations separately. Due to direct experiences of their economic situations combined with interpersonal communication, citizens do not depend totally on the media to form expectations about their own economic futures. Individual-level research has shown no or limited media effects on confidence about one's own economic situation (egotropic consumer expectations), which are shaped more by personal experiences (Mutz, 1998). Two of the questions that we used to measure consumer expectations deal with expectations about the individual's personal economic future: How do you think your household's financial situation will be in a year compared with today? Do you expect to save any money during the coming 12 months? We analysed the impact of mediated uncertainty on these two indicators of egotropic consumer expectations (Table 10.1). In each model, changes in consumer confidence are first explained by past levels of consumer confidence.[15] Expected savings decrease when news is negative but are not affected by uncertainty. The population does not expect to save less money when journalists report uncertainty about the macro-economy. The effect of uncertainty on personal finances is significant at $p < .1$, but the effect is in the opposite direction than expected. Both analyses show that mediated uncertainty does not decrease egotropic consumer expectations.

This finding is in line with what referred to as the "impersonal impact" of the media in Chapter 2. People rely on media information to form opinions about the national economy but depend less on this information to form expectations about their personal economy. Mass media have an effect on "perceptions of the frequency or severity of a problem, but not on personal judgments of concern or importance" (Mutz, 1992, p. 490). Media coverage matters more for perceptions of the macro-economy (sociotropic evaluations), such as state-level or national-level unemployment (Mutz, 1998). Boomgaarden et al. (2011) found support for the impersonal impact of media coverage on consumer sentiment during the 2008–2009 economic crisis. During this crisis, when the economy was a highly salient issue, media coverage affected sociotropic consumer sentiment but had only a weak effect on assessments of the personal economic situation.

Similarly, we found that although uncertainty in economic news did not affect egotropic consumer expectations, it did affect sociotropic consumer expectations (see Table 10.1). Our consumer expectations measure includes two questions that deal with sociotropic consumer confidence: How do you think the national economic situation will be in a year compared with today? How do you think the level of unemployment will be in a year compared with today? Mediated uncertainty has a negative effect on expectations about the national economy, which is close to significant (p = .13). When economic news features more uncertainty, this leads to a significant increase in concerns about national levels of unemployment.

These findings confirm the impersonal nature of the effects of economic news. Mediated uncertainty increases sociotropic concerns about national unemployment but does not decrease egotropic consumer expectations.

Does Uncertainty Trigger Asymmetric Responses?

Previously in this chapter, we argued that the negative effect of mediated uncertainty on consumer confidence is the result of people becoming fearful when they are confronted with uncertain information. Unfortunately, no time-series data are available on emotions about the economy among the national population. Therefore, we cannot test this explanation. An alternative explanation for lowered expectations due to uncertainty would be that people place more weight on negative outcomes versus positive outcomes when they feel uncertain. This is in line with prospect theory (Kahneman and Tversky, 1979), according to which people are averse to loss when they have to make decisions *under uncertain circumstances* (Soroka, 2014). According to Ellsberg (1961), the extra weight given to worst-case scenarios is the result of deliberate decision making (Tiedens and Linton, 2001). This deliberation and reasoning may be triggered by the uncertainty of the situation. People put more effort into assessing the validity of information under uncertain conditions (Baas, De Dreu, and Nijstad, 2012). Following this reasoning, it could be expected that uncertainty in the news lowers public expectations because people place more weight on negative information when they are exposed to uncertain information. This explanation could be tested with our data.

To test whether uncertainty in economic news triggers an asymmetric response to economic news, we ran two additional regression models explaining consumer expectations. The first model includes an interaction between uncertainty and tone (see Table 10.2).[16] If uncertainty in the news indeed makes negative information more salient, the effect of tone should be stronger when uncertainty in the news is high. In line with this asymmetric response explanation, the interaction term between tone and uncertainty is positive. However, the coefficient is not statistically (p = .82) or substantially significant.[17] This result was confirmed in a regression model in which we looked at the moderating effect of positive and negative news separately. If uncertainty indeed makes negative information more salient than positive information, the interaction effect between uncertainty and negative news should be larger than the interaction with positive news. However, there is no interaction effect of uncertainty and positive news. The interaction between uncertainty and negative news is negative but not statistically (p = .78) or substantially significant.[18] An *F*-test showed that the difference

Table 10.2 Consumer confidence explained by uncertainty in economic news (August 1996–December 2012)

	Model 1		Model 2	
	B	SE B	B	SE B
Constant	−112.29	24.83***	−109.22	25.07***
Consumer confidence t-1	0.56	0.06***	0.56	0.06***
Economic indicators t-1	1.17	0.25***	1.13	0.25***
Δ Economic indicators	4.72	1.18***	4.69	1.18***
Tone t-1	1.26	0.42**		
Δ Tone	1.00	0.39*		
Positive news t-1			0.60	0.82
Negative news t-1			−1.62	0.64*
Δ Negative news t-1			−1.55	0.54***
Uncertainty t-1	−0.36	0.17*	−0.32	0.18#
Tone t-1 × uncertainty t-1	0.05	0.27		
Positive news t-1 × uncertainty t-1			0.00	0.56
Negative news t-1 × uncertainty t-1			−0.12	0.45
Adj. R^2	.75		0.75	
AIC	961.24		963.31	
HQC	971.85		976.59	
SBC	987.46		996.09	
N	196		196	
Breusch-Godfrey	1.17	($p = 0.28$)	0.93	($p = .34$)
Ljung Box Q	0.46	($p = 0.50$)	0.37	($p = .54$)

Note: Unstandardized beta-coefficients with standard error. ***$p < .01$, *$p < .05$, #$p < .1$ (two-sided t-tests).

in effect size of the positive and negative interaction term was not significant ($F(1, 188) = 1.42$, n.s.). Thus, our analysis does not show that uncertainty in economic news increases the effect of negative information.

Uncertainty and Economic Perceptions

The analysis of the impact of uncertainty on public opinion formation shows that uncertainty in the news makes people pessimistic. Research on the individual level previously showed that people are generally averse to uncertainty and that uncertainty and ambiguity lead to fear and negative expectations. This chapter shows that media reports about economic uncertainty have a similar effect on aggregated levels of consumer expectations.

We found that consumer confidence reflects lagged levels of uncertainty but not concurrent changes in uncertainty. This effect is different from the effect of tone, in particular, negativity. On the one hand, corroborating previous research, our study shows that consumer confidence reflects both levels of, and changes in, negativity. People react to shifting levels of negativity, perhaps resulting from evolutionary advantages of noting new information and changes in the environment (Soroka et al., 2015). On the other hand, people react to the mere existence of uncertainty. This result implies that exposure to uncertain information makes people feel uncertain, which triggers fear and pessimism, independently of whether uncertainty increased or decreased. The different effects of change in uncertainty versus change in tone underline that uncertainty is not merely an aspect of negativity. Not only were uncertainty and negativity weakly correlated, but uncertainty had an independent effect on consumer confidence, which was not due to making negative information more salient. Thus, uncertainty's negative effect cannot be explained as an asymmetric response to ambiguous information. This does not mean that there is no asymmetric responsiveness. The study did confirm that public opinion reacts more to negative than to positive news. However, contrary to our expectation, the strength of asymmetric responsiveness did not increase with higher levels of uncertainty in the news. Perhaps uncertainty does trigger asymmetric responses in some individuals—for example, those with high levels of sophistication (McGraw et al., 2003). This should be the subject of future research, preferably in controlled experiments. Such experiments could include measures of subjective uncertainty and emotions like fear or sadness to understand the mechanisms linking exposure to uncertain information and pessimism, and to study the moderating role of sophistication. Our macro-level study offers limited possibilities to test these mechanisms.

Content analysis of uncertainty in economic news at a lower level of aggregation could tell us more about how much uncertainty is due to journalistic intervention and how much reflects uncertainties in the real economy, such as uncertainty on financial markets or in policy decisions. Such a content analysis could also show whether uncertainty is more present in specific outlets, such as tabloid newspapers or television news. Ideally, some measure of real-world economic uncertainty would have been included in the regression analysis predicting consumer confidence. When we use economic policy uncertainty in Europe as a proxy for uncertainty in the Danish economy (Baker, Bloom, and Davis, 2015), mediated uncertainty remains significant. Independently of how much uncertainty in economic news is manufactured by journalists and how much is a reflection of uncertainty in the economy, it is the mass media that make citizens aware of uncertainty about the future of the economy, which makes it relevant to study the effect of news content. Thus, the results presented in this chapter provide a note of caution to our rather optimistic story about the effect of mainstreamed economic news. Although mainstreamed economic news might help people understand and navigate the current economy, when accompanied with considerable levels of uncertainty, it can also make people more pessimistic about the economic future.

Notes

1 The coding instruction for this measure was the following: Does the article provide or suggest an expectation, assumption or prediction for the economic situation either in Denmark or for the Danish people/the Danish economy regarding the future period. Krippendorff's alpha for the inter-coder reliability test was .68.
2 Leder Usikkerhed fordrer forsigtighed. *Berlingske*, 6 December 2003, p. 16.
3 Peter Hartung. Usikkerhed: stor usikkerhed om værdien af ejendomme. *Berlingske*, 19 November 2008, p. 28.
4 Lone Anderse. Økonomien lysner—måske. *Jyllands-Posten*, 2 April 2009, p. 2.
5 Las Olsen, Investeringsforeninger: Gør klar til et usikkert efterår, *Jyllands-Posten*, 19 August 2006, p. 6.
6 Jørgen Ullerup, OECD-rapport: Usikkerhed om dansk opsving, *Jyllands-Posten*, 12 May 2004, p. 1.
7 The dependent variable *consumer expectations* is operationalized as the non-seasonally adjusted monthly Consumer Confidence Indicator. Each month, Statistics Denmark asks a random selection of the Danish population about their perceptions and expectations of the national and personal economies. In the first two weeks of each month, a representative sample of about 1,500 people is interviewed by telephone (response rate around 63 percent). These people are randomly selected from the population, are between 16 and 74 years old, and reside in Denmark. After the data are collected, they are weighted by age group representativeness and by family size.
 Statistics Denmark is a Danish state institution under the Ministry of Social Affairs and the Interior. The data were downloaded from the website of the European Commission. Accessed 25 September 2013. http://ec.europa.eu/economy_finance/db_indicators/surveys/time_series/index_en.htm.
8 The four questions are combined into the Consumer Confidence Indicator using the following formula: (question1 – question 2 + question3 + question 4)/4. The confidence interval is 2–3 percent.
9 Two lags of both variables were included in the Granger causality test because this is the minimum number of lags for models without autocorrelation.
10 Breusch-Godfrey and Ling Box Q statistics show that all regression models are free of autocorrelation.
11 Granger causality test revealed bidirectional causality between Composite Leading Indicators and consumer expectations. Therefore, we do not conclude that concurrent changes in CLI influence consumer expectations. Consumer expectations do not Granger-cause tone, thus we are more confident in the effect of concurrent changes in tone on consumer confidence. The same applies to negativity in Appendix table 10.1.
12 We also tested whether concurrent changes in uncertainty had an effect on consumer expectations. When both lagged uncertainty in economic news and concurrent change in uncertainty are included, neither variable is significant. The model in which only lagged uncertainty is included has a better fit (AIC, HQC, and SBC) than the model in which both change and lagged uncertainty are included. Excluding lagged uncertainty from the model and keeping change in uncertainty improve the model less, and change in uncertainty is only significant at $p < .1$.
13 Additional tests were done to check the robustness of this result. First, we included the visibility of economic news as an extra control variable in the models. Visibility of economic news was operationalized as the monthly number of articles about the Danish macro-economy. Visibility did not change the impact of uncertainty on consumer confidence. Second, we included the unemployment

rate, price index, and production index to control for the current state of the economy. After including these indicators, the effect of lagged uncertainty remained significant. Finally, following Doms and Morin (2004), we tested the model with differently specified months, which also confirmed that consumer confidence is explained by uncertainty in the previous month. Consumer confidence data are collected in the first two weeks of each month, whereas the content analysis is done for the whole month. Thus, when we include concurrent changes, consumer confidence is partly explained by news that is presented after consumer data are collected. The results are confirmed in a model with several lags of uncertainty and with a model in which a month is defined as running from the 16th of the month until the 15th of the following month.

14 In line with the analysis explaining consumer expectations, we found an effect of change in negative tone but not in positive tone. Interestingly, however, a positive tone does influence retrospective assessments on the economy, where we found no effect on confidence in the future of the economy.

15 The number of past levels of consumer confidence included in the model is the minimal number of lags for a model without autocorrelation.

16 Uncertainty, tone, negativity, and positivity have been mean centred, otherwise the models testing interactions would suffer from multicollinearity.

17 The marginal effect of tone was positive for the whole range of mean-centered uncertainty and significant for mean-centered uncertainty values between –1.57 and 1.52 (79.6 percent of the months, Johnson-Neyman significance test). The change in effect size of tone from the low end to the high end of the mean-uncertainty scale was only marginal.

18 The marginal effect of negative tone on consumer confidence was negative for the whole range of mean-centered uncertainty and significant for mean-centered uncertainty values between –1.02 and 1.31 (64.8 percent of the months, Johnson-Neyman significance test). The increase in effect size was not substantially significant.

11 Getting the Good Message Through
Against All Odds?

The economy is complex. Economic news deals with interest rates, major currency exchange rates, unemployment rates, the stock market, housing market developments, consumer confidence, and costs of energy resources, among many others. These areas can either be interlinked and aligned, such as housing markets, interest rates, and mortgages; or they can develop independently, such as the stock market and debt rates. What is potentially good news in one area of the world or the economy can be bad in another. Processes of transnationalization and globalization have augmented this complexity and interdependence. Citizens might seem at a loss as to how to manoeuvre in this environment. For most economic developments, they have to rely on sources other than their own experiences to get an impression of how things are developing. At times, the economy is a real "doorstep issue," such as when salaries are negotiated or employment situations change. But for many decisions, both big and small—whether putting a house up for sale, booking a foreign vacation, or selling off stock—citizens are highly dependent on information provided by the news media.

Taking this media dependency as a starting point, our book shows that we might be on to some good news here. News about the economy has become more like mainstream news, and we are now witnessing an abundant flow of economic information. The media have become better at fulfilling their role of providing cues about the economy to a majority of citizens. Throughout this book we have challenged an overt and largely pessimistic view on the state and effects of economic news. We argue that the mainstreaming of economic news in actual fact often sufficiently informs people in accordance with the normative requirements of the competitive model of democracy. Economic news helps people correctly assess the direction in which the economy is heading, increases economic knowledge and economic efficacy, and helps the audience hold powerholders accountable for economic developments. In particular, and perhaps surprisingly, the *inattentive audience* benefits disproportionately from exposure to economic news coverage.

Such a bold conclusion may seem counterintuitive and, of course, is much more nuanced than we have stated here. In this chapter we first summarize our key findings. We then move on to challenge these results. What are the boundary conditions to our findings? Which standards should we apply when assessing the performance of economic news? Does the increased use of social media as information source challenge our findings?

Our Key Findings

We started by asking if people have a baseline understanding of the economy. Again, because the economy is a mixed bag of various topics, many linked and many unclear, it is interesting to see if people have an accurate perception, by and large, of developments in the *general* economic climate. We find that despite the topic's complex nature, the answer is that citizens generally *do* have a good sense of the direction in which the economy is heading. This is even the case for the inattentive audience. We found that across more than two dozen European countries (Chapter 2), people generally make accurate assessments of economic developments. Moreover, and importantly for this book's focus, citizens' correct economic assessments go hand in hand with media usage. The more news is consumed, the better the assessments. Of course, this correlation tells us little about the relationship's direction or causality, but it is an initial indication that economic knowledge and economic news are not in as bad a state as some suggest.

Moving beyond this positive, albeit tip-of-the-iceberg finding, we developed our argument (in Chapter 3) about *which* type of economic news helps inattentive audiences, in particular, make sense of economic developments and *why* this is the case. Our argument is built around recent research on the nature and composition of the inattentive audience and around a broader argument about the monitorial citizen, for whom learning can occur as an incidental by-product of media consumption. We identified and elaborated on three mechanisms by which the media help people not intrinsically interested in economic news make sense of the economy. These mechanisms were then related to five key aspects of economic news coverage: visibility, negativity, human interest, consequence framing, and domestication. Each of these news content features is central in the empirical chapters, in which we unpack how these features benefit the inattentive audience. In Chapters 4 to 8, we demonstrated how mainstreamed economic news informs the audience through the three identified mechanisms. Table 11.1 gives an overview of the findings from these chapters.

We first looked at visibility in the news and how it helps shape citizens' perceptions of economic developments. Using a time-series design, we demonstrated the basic *alarm bell* function of economic news (Chapter 4). Economic journalism alerts the inattentive audience with extensive negative economic coverage when it really matters—that is, when the economy declines and especially in times of prolonged recession. This ringing of the alarm bell and increased media attention help audiences perceive economic developments more accurately. We consider the alarm bell function a

Table 11.1 Overview of mechanisms and empirical findings of mainstream economic news helping the understanding of economic news

Mechanism	Characteristic of mainstreamed economic news	Informed about the economy	Conclusion	For whom?
1. Alarm bell	Hyped coverage during crisis (visibility and negativity)	Accurate perceptions of economic developments	Supported (Chapter 4)	(not tested)*
2a. Induced elaboration	Human interest framing	Interest in the economy	Supported (Chapter 5)	People with low economic interest most affected
2b. Induced elaboration	Negativity	Economic efficacy	Supported (Chapter 6)	People with low economic interest most affected
2c. Induced elaboration	Consequence framing	Economic sophistication	Supported (Chapter 7)	People with low economic interest most affected
3. Heuristics	Domestication	Attribution of responsibility for the economy	Supported (Chapter 8)	People with low economic interest most affected

Note: *The alarm bell function was only studied at the aggregate level. Therefore we cannot draw any conclusions about whether people with low economic interest are most affected.

foundational finding for the argument that news media do meet a minimum expected standard in the realm of the economy.

Chapters 5, 6, and 7 focus on the notion of *elaboration-inducing* elements of economic news: content characteristics that make the news engaging for the audience, in general, and the inattentive audience, in particular. Engaging news, in turn, makes the inattentive audience more interested, more economically efficacious, and more knowledgeable. Exposure to human-interest framing makes people relate the news more to their own lives, which raises interest in economic developments (Chapter 5). Chapter 6 shows that people pay more attention to negative news, which, in turn, raises confidence in their own capability to understand the economy (economic efficacy). In addition, exposure to economic news using consequence framing leads to knowledge gains (Chapter 7). In each of these chapters, we show that the people who benefit the most from this type of news are people with low interest in the news.

In Chapter 8 we looked at the effect of domestication of economic news. Media make global economic developments relevant to domestic audiences by connecting the coverage to national actors and discussing the impact at home. We showed that exposure to such domesticated economic news makes people attribute responsibility for economic developments to national (political) actors. This effect demonstrates that mainstreamed economic news provides *cues* or *mental shortcuts* on which audiences rely when they hold politicians accountable. This finding puts a heavy responsibility on the shoulders of economic journalists; such shortcuts and cues are beneficial only if they help people attribute responsibility where it is due. Again, the inattentive audience, in particular, was affected.

Although the key focus of the book was on people's knowledge and interest in the economy, in the final chapters we turned to additional *consequences* that economic news may have. We show that economic news affects government evaluations (Chapter 9). This finding is not novel, and popular wisdom often points to the economy as an essential cue for citizens who are making political evaluations. What *is* new, however, is that even in today's globalized economies—which led some scholars to announce the end of economic voting—we show that economic information is still an important source for citizens making evaluations. This finding holds for all individuals, regardless of their level of economic interest. Moreover, in Chapter 10 we show that economic news may also influence expectations about the economic *future*. We argue that economic news is becoming more and more future oriented and is accompanied by a large degree of uncertainty in economic coverage. Economic coverage that highlights uncertainty about the state and development of the economy makes people pessimistic and lowers expectations about the nation's economic future. The study of uncertainty's impact is a novel addition to extant research on economic news and its implications. Our findings show that mainstreamed economic news may also have negative side effects, which are not immediately apparent.

So where does that leave us at the end of the day? In most of the empirical analyses, we demonstrate mechanisms and effects, which, other things equal, can only be seen as good: news makes citizens better able to judge the direction in which the economy is heading; it makes them more interested, more economically efficacious, and more economically knowledgeable; and it provides a mental shortcut for holding powerholders accountable. These effects are seen particularly in the inattentive audience.

A Virtuous Circle Everywhere?

The preceding conclusion would clearly be a convenient place to end our account. But we feel that these findings offer ample food for reflection. One of the most fundamental points of reflection is that the dynamics we observe presuppose, of course, some level of exposure to news and information about the economy. In an environment with an abundance of supply and choice of content, this assumption is ironically also one of the most contentious prerequisites because many citizens may shy away from traditional news sources. Whereas evidence from the United States has mostly pointed towards divides across partisan lines in news consumption—such that citizens self-select exposure to like-minded media content (e.g., Iyengar and Hahn, 2009)—concern is also growing about citizens tuning out of the news flow all together. Patterson (2003, p. 97) puts it this way: "There is something worse than exposure to persistently negative news, and that is no news exposure at all."

A supply of economic and political information is a necessary, but not sufficient, condition for citizens to learn from the news. Other research has shown that the more political information is available in a certain environment, the higher the average level of political knowledge among citizens living in that environment (Curran et al., 2009). The implicit underlying mechanism is that the more information is available, the higher the chance that people will consume it. In that sense, supply sets a boundary condition for *demand*, but evidence from several locations in Europe has indeed highlighted the increasing divide between news consumers and news avoiders (Bos et al., 2016; Skovsgaard, Shehata, and Strömbäck, 2016). It is thus not sufficient that the news is available; it must also be consumed. To challenge our "optimistic" findings, which assume some level of news consumption, we investigate the differential situation for those who avoid the news and those who consume it.

In Table 11.2 we return to our data to compare news avoiders and news consumers. We operationalize news avoiders as people who do not watch or read any news outlet more than once a week. Fifty-eight respondents (3.5 percent) fit this criterion. Twenty-two of these indicated that they do not even watch or read any of the 16 news outlets included in our study. We compare these news avoiders' backgrounds and their level of knowledge of and interest in the economy with the rest of the respondents. To see whether a little news exposure can make a difference, we compare the 58

Table 11.2 Comparing news avoiders to occasional and regular news users

	News avoiders*	Occasional news users**	Regular news users
Female	67.2%$_a$	57.9%$_{ab}$	47.7%$_b$
Age (*M* with *SD*)	38.67$_a$ (15.62)	46.21$_b$ (16.21)	54.46$_c$ (16.20)
Highly educated	15.5%$_a$	21.5%$_a$	26.3%$_a$
Economic interest	3.48$_a$	3.70$_a$	3.97$_b$
Economic knowledge	1.0$_a$	1.64$_b$	2.18$_c$
Economic efficacy	2.43$_a$	2.76$_b$	3.02$_b$
Correct perception of Economy (wave 4)	19%$_a$	41%$_b$	45%$_b$
N	58	107	1501

Note: *News avoiders: reading or viewing no news outlet more than once a week. ** Occasional news users: reading or viewing one news outlet more than once a week. Rowwise: different subscripts indicate that differences are significant at *p* < .05.

news avoiders to 107 respondents who watch or read only one news outlet more than once a week.

News avoiders are younger than people who do not avoid news, are more likely to be female, and have lower economic interest. The share of highly educated people is not significantly lower among news avoiders than among news users. There is no significant difference between news users and news avoiders as regards holding national government accountable for the economic crisis and correct perceptions of macro-economic developments during waves 1, 2, and 3. However, as we can see in Table 11.2, following the other indicators, news avoiders are less knowledgeable of the economy than the rest of the population: news avoiders are significantly less knowledgeable than people who consume news, feel less efficacious, and are half as likely to correctly perceive the positive macro-economic developments during the last wave of the survey. This finding is interesting in light of the debate on news avoidance. Generally, people are said to avoid news because they do not wish to be confronted with all the trouble in the world. Our analysis shows that as a consequence of wishing to avoid negative news, they also miss positive developments.

When we compare the news avoiders to the people who expose themselves to a minimum amount of news, we see some remarkable differences. These differences are not due to different levels of economic interest or to the degree of education because these two aspects are not significantly different from the news avoiders. People who expose themselves to one media outlet more than once a week have significantly higher levels of economic knowledge and feel more efficacious than news avoiders. They are also significantly more likely to correctly perceive the economic improvement during the last wave of the survey, which came after a long period of economic decline. These results are especially remarkable when we compare the people who expose themselves to a minimum level of news with the rest of the respondents who follow more news. The degree of economic knowledge and of economic interest is significantly lower, but their economic efficacy and correct perceptions of the economic situation at wave 4 of the survey are not significantly different to the rest of the population. This result suggests that not much exposure to mainstreamed economic news is required for it to have a positive effect. In practical terms, the minimal level of news exposure that is required for the positive mechanisms to kick in and for the creation of a virtuous circle is probably one outlet more than once a week.

Acknowledging that a minimal level of news consumption is a prerequisite obviously raises the comparative question of what this situation might be like in other countries. Table 11.3 shows that the share of news avoiders in our country of investigation (Denmark) is comparable to other countries within and outside Europe. Across the countries included in the table, on average 5 percent of the population indicate that they did not consume any news in the past month (Newman et al., 2015, p. 6). In most countries the share of news avoiders is within 2 percentage points of this average,

Table 11.3 Share of news avoiders in selected developed
countries around the world

Country	News avoiders
United States	11%
United Kingdom	7%
Germany	3%
Spain	5%
Italy	3%
France	7%
Ireland	5%
Denmark	4%
Finland	1%
Japan	6%
Australia	6%
Urban Brazil	3%

Source: Reuters Institute Digital News Report 2015 (Newman et al.,
2015, p. 6).

including Denmark (4 percent). Thus, in terms of news avoidance, our case
country is comparable to other developed countries. The only exception is
the United States, where 11 percent avoid the news. We have little reason
to believe that the *mechanisms* explored in this book differ in other countries once a baseline of exposure is in place. Moreover, our comparative
analyses in Chapter 2 showed that Denmark was, comparatively speaking,
a "normal" case when it comes to the relation between news exposure and
economic assessments. We therefore emphasize that this book is not a case
study of Denmark as such but rather a case where we had exceptionally
good data over time.

Good News for All?

Throughout the book we have demonstrated that most relationships per-
tain, in particular, to those who are less interested in the economy to start
with. On the one hand, it is encouraging that those with less resources tend
to benefit more. On the other hand, this finding might also point to certain
limitations of the virtuous circle. Given that the inattentive group benefit-
ted from news coverage at a time of heightened attention to the economy,
we could possibly be detecting a peak caused by the prolonged economic
crisis; perhaps the observed beneficial effects were more pronounced in this
special period than during other times. Undoubtedly, these qualifications are
speculative in nature, and even if some were correct, we would nonetheless
consider it important to demonstrate that in a period of economic crisis and
heightened attention to the economy, the citizens who may not be in the
most comfortable and resourceful position do not seem to lose out more—
on the contrary.

On a more general level, our findings speak to the two-edged role of interest. In a high-choice news environment, *motivation* and resources, such as existing interest, are of key importance for understanding news use (Elenbaas et al., 2014; Prior, 2010). Here, we know that we are looking at something that is distributed unevenly. At the same time, we have shown that interest not only functions as a *predictor* of news media choice and avoidance but can also be *affected* by news use (see Chapter 5). This finding speaks in more general terms to an increased interest in reciprocal models of media effects, where concepts may function as predictors of news media effects but are also influenced by them (e.g., Moeller and de Vreese, 2015; Slater, 2007; Valkenburg and Peter, 2013).

An important part of our endeavour was to explicate the mechanisms through which the observed effects occur. We developed our theoretical expectations based on extant research and showed that "alarm bell ringing," inducing elaboration, and heuristics are core mechanisms for understanding the effects. Each of these mechanisms was related to specific news content features and relevant outcome variables. In current research, and also in our work, these mechanisms have been developed and tested separately. We believe that future research would be well served by considering the relationship between these mechanisms. For example, if sudden changes in visibility and tone of economic news cause alarm bells to ring, other mechanisms could possibly simultaneously become salient, too. This variation and interplay of mechanisms might affect, in turn, the importance of prior levels of economic interest and lead to relatively larger or smaller gains in knowledge in the inattentive audience. While we were able to explicate and further develop extant research in the realm of the economy, we believe that future research would benefit by considering such simultaneous and potentially reinforcing processes.

The Need for Critical (Economic) Journalism

We started out with an interest in disentangling the impact of economic news on citizens' understanding of the economy. From the outset we had our eyes peeled for more positive effects than have been noted in much of the extant discussions. We mostly uncovered relationships indicating that exposure to news was beneficial rather than detrimental and that mainstreamed economic news is beneficial to democratic citizenship in various ways. That said, some effects are less positive or straightforward—such as the finding that uncertainty in economic news dampened consumer expectations (Chapter 10). Other research has demonstrated that economic news is not a reflection of actual economic developments per se and that this inexact representation can have ramifications for citizens' economic expectations (Soroka, 2014). Specifically, we consider it important for future research to identify content features that might negatively affect understanding and obstruct citizens in expressing interest and efficacious sentiments. Different pages of a newspaper and different segments of a television news programme will expose readers and viewers to a variety of stories about economic developments—some positive and some negative (e.g., rising stock markets and problematic interest rates). This subject area was not included in the context of our study, but conceivably, such a blend of stories may ultimately confuse news consumers unless connections and context are provided for them to make sense of seemingly contradictory economic developments in the news. The need for journalism to connect the dots and provide context and connection between different types of economic news points to a larger observation about developments in economic journalism. The inter-relatedness of the global economy has also meant that "explaining" "the economy" has, if anything, only become more daunting for experts and journalists.

A lesson from this book is that economic journalists should not be afraid of using their general journalistic toolbox when covering the economy. Human-interest stories help to spark economic interest. Highlighting consequences in news frames is good for generating economic knowledge. At the same time, it is important to be aware that if news is domesticated—which can help "bring home" a story—it can leave citizens de facto with the idea that *domestic* actors might be mainly responsible. This is sometimes obviously the case, but oftentimes, it is probably not, or only in part. This negative effect of domestication, like the negative effect of uncertainty, needs to be taken to heart by journalists and media.

In any event, many journalists might be encouraged that their coverage of complex matters is actually helpful, especially to the inattentive audience. The magnification of economic news in visibility and tone since the start of the Great Recession is positive and confirms the burglar alarm function of the news (Zaller, 2003). The elaboration-inducing and engaging features of mainstreamed economic news, and subsequent effects on knowledge, are a valuable contribution of journalism—which fits in with a normative notion of journalism's role in society according to the competitive democracy model. Arguably, this concept of the media's role is more limited than, for example, the full news standard (Zaller, 2003) because, unlike the latter, the monitorial model does not imply that the media must educate the audience to become economic experts. It is enough to create a baseline level of sufficiently informed citizens who respond when journalists ring the alarm bells. In other words, to be an informed citizen, one need not maximize news consumption. Satisficing is sufficient (Simon, 2013).

Media organizations and journalists received a lot of criticism during and after the last economic crisis for failing to live up to their role as watchdog vis-à-vis business and finance (Starkman, 2014). The debate is still ongoing about reconstructing the events that caused the crisis and any role played by the media (Roush, 2014; Usher, 2013) Looking forward, it is too early to know if the crisis had a "quality lifting" effect on economic journalism. Having been blamed for missing many signs in the economy leading up to the crisis, perhaps journalists are now more aware of the importance not only of mainstreamed economic news but also of critical, investigative reporting. Still, at least some observations suggest that, several years into the Great Recession, more critical attention is paid to the financial sector than before the start of the crisis (Picard, 2015). Some have argued that such critical coverage is hindered by the fact that it is often hard for economic and business reporters to independently access relevant information. However, the International Consortium of Investigative Journalists documenting large-scale tax evasion (e.g., the Panama Papers) shows that cross-national collaboration on complex topics by investigative reporters can lead to actual and broadly consumed news. Whether these examples are exceptions or indicative of a new, post-crisis economic journalism remains to be seen.

Economic News in a Changing Information Environment

Throughout the book we have analysed and discussed the media and the impact of their coverage on citizens. While being more inclusive than most extant research in terms of looking at different types of media (newspapers and television, online and offline) and outlets (broadsheets and tabloid papers, public service broadcasting and commercial news broadcasts), we are still confined to traditional, mainstream media stemming from legacy media organizations. We could have encompassed the more specialized and dedicated financial press. Internationally, the *Financial Times* has obtained a unique position, but many countries today have dedicated, specialized financial newspapers and daytime or 24-hour financial and economic news channels. Similarly, a wealth of background analyses, stock market advice, and financial analyses exist, all aimed at a more specific, expert audience. Although we include the specialist newspaper *Børsen* in our analysis, we were mostly interested in the general dynamics of how broadly consumed news and information contributes to general knowledge about the economy. Of course, we acknowledge that specialized outlets can play an important role in overall news provision about the economy. They most likely serve as a starting point for much of the general economic news, and these outlets have contributed to the mainstreaming of economic news in regular papers and news shows.

We largely discard the role of social media. While undoubtedly the nature of social media is changing economic news (Thøis Madsen, 2018) and Facebook is increasingly becoming a key news portal, we had several reasons for not putting social media centre stage in this investigation. First, the key position of social media as a news broker was simply less prevalent at the time of designing the research. Second, a pertinent but unanswered question is whether economy-related news provided through Facebook and other platforms extends beyond the sharing/liking of regular news stories, which we readily include with our current approach. This question should be answered but was beyond the scope of our endeavour. A third consideration is the nature of social media platforms such as Twitter. Because a key finding in our research is that a certain amount of information and context are necessary to see positive effects, we were unconvinced that any appreciable effects would be achieved on a platform known for its brevity and its limited elite audience.

Social media platforms were beyond the scope of this study, but looking ahead, we do see that they could potentially play an interesting role. If something is rapidly changing, the legacy media *and* social media can help alert citizens to this event. We would expect social media to typically function as an alert and a pointer to other news platforms that provide more in-depth information. To put it bluntly, following news on social media does not seem to be the best way to *learn* about the economy. But being directed to important news on traditional media outlets and encouraged to do additional information seeking could be a possible positive role for social media. Social media could, in fact, augment some of the dynamics that we have uncovered in this book on the positive role of the media, particularly regarding the inattentive audience. Conversely, the risk exists that social media speed up the news cycle to such a degree that even relevant developments requiring people's attention drop off the agenda as quickly as they appear (Chadwick, 2011). The social media's alarm bell could ring more intensely than the mass media's, but too briefly to grab the attention of the inattentive audience.

Both the role of specialized news and information and the role of social media are key features of the changing information environment that we consider pertinent in future investigations of the media and the economy.

New Questions Raised

Our book has covered a lot of ground in rediscovering how the media may help some citizens. Yet our studies also raised several questions. We would like to underscore at least four relevant questions in this concluding chapter: (1) the role of personal experience, media, and "network communication," (2) broader notions of economic knowledge, (3) the economy as politics, and (4) the changing nature of the economy.

First, this book is about the impact of economic news. The subject matter does not imply that we take an exclusively media-centric approach to our work, and we are the first to acknowledge that the media are not all that matters. In Chapter 2 we broadly introduce the media as *one* influence alongside several others—for example, personal experiences and interpersonal communication. Other scholars have cautioned not to overemphasize the media's role in forming economic perceptions (Haller and Norpoth, 1997). Nonetheless, we argued *why* we believe that it is important to focus on the media; the media are a key source of information on topics that are frequently distant, abstract, and of varying utility. We reiterate this argument here but also call for even more comprehensive and inclusive studies that situate media effects in a broader range of influences (see Mutz,

1992). We view such research as an especially interesting avenue to further unpack the role of interpersonal and network communication, whether it involves the composition and conversations in physical networks or the impact of online and social media networks—which may play into some of the dynamics that we investigated. We point to the notion of network communication as a good place to start. Network communication considers the composition of the network (in terms of homogeneity or heterogeneity) and the role of interpersonal and social media—based communication (how often a topic is discussed and whether the discussion takes place between like-minded people). Network communication is likely to provide a piece of the puzzle about the influence of very personal experience and of "impersonal" mediated perceptions.

Second, we believe that more work is needed to explore the impact of economic news on other types of economic knowledge. We have studied the positive effects of mainstreamed economic news by looking at accurate perceptions of economic developments; interest in, and knowledge about, the economy; and feeling efficacious vis-à-vis the economy. These indicators are arguably *not* proxies for a deep and detailed comprehension of central bank interest policies, new bank products, or insights in stock trades. While we believe that our indicators are sufficient for executing the role of citizen according to the competitive democracy ideal, digging deeper into the multifaceted notion of understanding would allow us to elucidate how it influences common economic decisions (e.g., mortgage, car purchase finance, and pension choices). These decisions are not made daily, but at least they are made by most citizens a number of times during their lifespans. We think it questionable that the positive influence of mainstreamed economic news can be found if we raise the bar on what understanding means and what is considered to be sufficient knowledge. Our analysis did not address the question whether the mainstreaming of economic news favours a particular economic outlook, like neoliberalism. This could in turn affect the public's understanding of the economy that the media provide. At the same time, we need to pay attention to the increasing questioning of shared facts and knowledge (Van Aelst et al., 2017). The questioning and debating of many facts has relevance for economic reporting. If unemployment and public spending figures are no longer shared and established facts in the public discussion, we can hardly expect the media to report effectively on these developments and citizens to acquire baseline knowledge.

Third, future investigations would be well advised to look at the relationship between the economic and the political arenas. Obviously, boundary conditions for economic developments are set politically. The implication is that political developments matter greatly for the economy. As we observe polarizing developments in politics, perhaps most notably in the United States (Prior, 2013), all kinds of questions arise about the undisputed nature of "economic facts" and whether or not filter bubbles are conceivable in the realms of the economy (for an overview see Zuiderveen Borgesius et al.,

2016). Discussions about information quality, trustworthiness, and accuracy that are entrenched in the fake news discourse are obviously also relevant for the economy. Partisan divisions affect how citizens apprehend elite cues and media coverage of the economy, thus creating partisan-driven differences in economic perceptions. Bisgaard (2015) suggests that, during times of economic crisis, partisanship does not influence actual perceptions of economic conditions, but people polarize along partisan lines over the question of who is responsible for the state of the economy.

Fourth, future research might do well to consider changes in the nature of the economy and to further delineate the concept of the economy. The arrival of the "sharing economy" has prompted all kinds of new economic relations. The level of trust in such new developments, as well as their viability and success, might hinge, among others, on the role of the media, with all the concomitant qualifications that we have outlined throughout this book. Moreover, changing attitudes about new "currencies" like Bitcoin and new economic players like Uber and Airbnb are also intriguing. Initially, the latter were seen as pioneers breaking old monopolies and encouraging a sharing economy. Now, such players and platforms are also seen as commercial endeavours that try to avoid contributions, such as taxation, to the conventional economic system. Future research should consider the involvement of news and information in these dynamics.

Some Final Words

The Great Recession generated an unprecedented amount of attention and was a defining event of the past decade. Although the media were initially blamed as the culprit, our research suggests that in actual fact they ultimately helped citizens during the crisis—in particular, the inattentive audience. Our conclusions extend well beyond the Great Recession, which is, thankfully, an extraordinary event. We now know what kinds of news content can generally help citizens, even when topics are abstract and complex. If citizens become better at judging the direction of the economy, become more interested, more economically efficacious, and more economically knowledgeable, this is good news—even more so if these improvements are demonstrated by those people who have a low interest in the economy to start with. We have not assessed how short or long lasting these effects are, and the global economy inspires many follow-up questions that are as yet unanswered. But if mainstreamed news can indeed help the information poor get richer, then that is a good place to start.

References

Albæk, E. (2011). The interaction between experts and journalists in news journalism. *Journalism, 12*(3), 335–348.

Albæk, E., Christiansen, P.M., and Togeby, L. (2003). Experts in the mass media: Researchers as sources in Danish daily newspapers, 1961–2001. *Journalism and Mass Communication Quarterly, 80*(4), 937–948.

Albæk, E., van Dalen, A., Jebril, N., and de Vreese, C. (2014). *Political journalism in comparative perspective*. Cambridge: Cambridge University Press.

Almunia, M., Benetrix, A.S., Eichengreen, B., O'Rourke, K.H., and Rua, G. (2010). From great depression to great credit crisis: Similarities, differences and lessons. *Economic Policy, 25*, 219–265.

Alsem, K.J., Brakman, S., Hoogduin, L., and Kuper, G. (2008). The impact of newspapers on consumer confidence: Does spin bias exist? *Applied Economics, 40*, 531–539.

Althaus, S.L., and Kim, Y.M. (2006). Priming effects in complex information environments: Reassessing the impact of news discourse on presidential approval. *Journal of Politics, 68*(4), 960–976.

Alvarez, M.R., and Franklin, C.H. (1994). Uncertainty and political perceptions. *Journal of Politics, 56*, 671–688.

An, S.K., and Gower, K.K. (2009). How do the news media frame crises? A content analysis of crisis news coverage. *Public Relations Review, 35*(2), 107–112.

Anderson, C.J. (2007). The end of economic voting? Contingency dilemmas and the limits of democratic accountability. *Annual Review of Political Science, 10*, 271–296.

Arghyrou, M.G., and Kontonikas, A. (2012). The EMU sovereign-debt crisis: Fundamentals, expectations and contagion. *Journal of International Financial Markets, Institutions and Money, 22*(4), 658–677.

Arrese, Á., and Vara, A. (2015). Divergent perspectives? Financial newspapers and the general interest press. In R.G. Picard (Ed.), *The Euro crisis in the media: Journalistic coverage of economic crisis and European Institutions* (pp. 149–176). London: I.B. Tauris.

Ashe, T. (2013). *How the media report scientific risk and uncertainty: A review of the literature*. Oxford: Reuters Institute for the Study of Journalism.

Atkin, C.K., Galloway, J., and Nayman, O.B. (1976). News media exposure, political knowledge and campaign interest. *Journalism Quarterly, 53*(2), 231–237.

Baker, S.R., Bloom, N., & Davis, S.J. (2016). *Measuring economic policy uncertainty*. The Quarterly Journal of Economics, *131*(4), 1593–1636.

Bandura, A. (1986). *Social foundations of thought and action: A social cognitive theory*. London: Prentice-Hall Inc.

Barabas, J., and Jerit, J. (2005). *Surveillance knowledge and the mass media*. Paper presented at the Annual Meeting of the American Political Science Association, Washington, DC.

Bartsch, A., Oliver, M.B., Nitsch, C., and Scherr, S. (2016). Inspired by the Paralympics: Effects of empathy on audience interest in para-sports and on the destigmatization of persons with disabilities. *Communication Research*, 45(4), 525–553. https://doi.org/10.1177/0093650215626984

Baum, M.A. (2003). Soft news and political knowledge: Evidence of absence or absence of evidence? *Political Communication*, 20(2), 173–190.

Bauman, Z. (2000). *Liquid modernity*. Cambridge: Polity.

Baumgartner, J., and Morris, J.S. (2006). The daily show effect: Candidate evaluations, efficacy, and American youth. *American Politics Research*, 34(3), 341–367.

Bechtel, G.G. (2003). One voice for consumer confidence: Case 9/11. *International Journal of Public Opinion Research*, 15(3), 325–334.

Becker, A.B. (2011). Political humor as democratic relief? The effects of exposure to comedy and straight news on trust and efficacy. *Atlantic Journal of Communication*, 19(5), 235–250.

Bellucci, P. (2014). The political consequences of blame attribution for the economic crisis in the 2013 Italian national election. *Journal of Elections, Public Opinion and Parties*, 24(2), 243–263.

Bennett, S.E., Flickinger, R.S., and Rhine, S.L. (2000). Political talk over here, over there, over time. *British Journal of Political Science*, 30(01), 99–119.

Bennett, W.L. (2003). The burglar alarm that just keeps ringing: A response to Zaller. *Political Communication*, 20, 131–138.

Bennett, W.L., and Iyengar, S. (2008). A new era of minimal effects? The changing foundations of political communication. *Journal of communication*, 58(4), 707–731.

Berent, M., and Krosnick, J.A. (1995). The Relation between political attitude importance and knowledge structure. In M. Lodge and K.M. McGraw (Eds.), *Political judgment* (pp. 91–109). Ann Arbor: University of Michigan Press.

Bisgaard, M. (2015). Bias will find a way: Economic perceptions, attributions of blame, and partisan-motivated reasoning during crisis. *The Journal of Politics*, 77(3), 849–860.

Blendon, R.J., Benson, J.M., Brodie, M., Morin, R., Altman, D.E., Gitterman, D., . . . James, M. (1997). Bridging the gap between the public's and economists' views of the economy. *The Journal of Economic Perspectives*, 11(3), 105–118.

Blood, D., and Philips, P.C.B. (1995). Recession headline news, consumer sentiment, the state of the economy and presidential popularity: A time series analysis 1989–1993. *International Journal of Public Opinion Research*, 7(1), 2–22.

Blumler, J.G. (1979). The role of theory in uses and gratifications studies. *Communication Research*, 6(1), 9–36.

Blumler, J.G., and Kavanagh, D. (1999). The third age of political communication: Influences and features. *Political Communication*, 16(3), 209–230.

Bobrow, S.A., and Bower, G.H. (1969). Comprehension and recall of sentences. *Journal of Experimental Psychology*, 80, 455–461.

Boczkowski, P.J., and Mitchelstein, E. (2013). *The news gap: When the information preferences of the media and the public diverge*. Cambridge, MA: MIT press.

Boomgaarden, H.G., van Spanje, J., Vliegenthart, R., and de Vreese, C.H. (2011). Covering the crisis: Media coverage of the economic crisis and citizens' economic expectations. *Acta Politica, 46*(4), 353–379.

Borio, C.E. (2008). The financial turmoil of 2007-? A preliminary assessment and some policy considerations. BIS Working Paper, No. 251.

Bos, L., Kruikemeier, S., and de Vreese, C. (2016). Nation binding: How public service broadcasting mitigates political selective exposure. *PloS One, 11*(5), e0155112.

Bosch, B. (2014). Beyond vox pop: The role of news sourcing and political beliefs in exemplification effects. *Mass Communication and Society, 17*(2), 217–235.

Boukes, M., Boomgaarden, H.G., Moorman, M., and de Vreese, C.H. (2015). Political news with a personal touch: How human interest framing indirectly affects policy attitudes. *Journalism and Mass Communication Quarterly, 92*(1), 121–141.

Boukes, M., and Vliegenthart, R. (2017). A general pattern of newsworthiness? Analyzing news factors in tabloid, broadsheet, financial, and regional newspapers. *Journalism.* https://doi.org/10.1177/1464884917725989

Boulianne, S. (2011). Stimulating or reinforcing political interest: Using panel data to examine reciprocal effects between news media and political interest. *Political Communication, 28*(2), 147–162. https://doi.org/10.1080/10584609.2010.540305

Bracha, A., and Weber, E.U. (2012). *A psychological perspective of financial panic.* FRB of Boston Public Policy Discussion Paper No. 12–7.

Brader, T. (2006). *Campaigning for hearts and minds: How emotional appeals in political ads work.* Chicago, IL: University of Chicago Press.

Brants, K. (1998). Who's Afraid of Infotainment? *European Journal of Communication, 13*(3), 315–335.

Brants, K., and Van Praag, P. (2006). Signs of media logic half a century of political communication in the Netherlands. *Javnost-The Public, 13*(1), 25–40.

Bushman, B.J. (1998). Priming effects of media violence on the accessibility of aggressive constructs in memory. *Personality and Social Psychology Bulletin, 24*, 537–545.

Baas, M., De Dreu, C., and Nijstad, B.A. (2012). Emotions that associate with uncertainty lead to structured ideation. *Emotion, 12*(5), 1004–1014.

Camerer, C., and Weber, M. (1992). Recent developments in modeling preferences: Uncertainty and ambiguity. *Journal of Risk and Uncertainty, 5*, 325–370.

Carpini, M.X.D., and Keeter, S. (1993). Measuring political knowledge: Putting first things first. *American Journal of Political Science*, 1179–1206.

Carroll, C.D. (2003). Macroeconomic expectations of households and professional forecasters. *The Quarterly Journal of Economics*, 269–298.

Casey, G.P., and Owen, A.L. (2013). Good news, bad news, and consumer confidence. *Social Science Quarterly, 94*, 292–315.

Chadwick, A. (2011). The political information cycle in a hybrid news system: The British prime minister and the "Bullygate" affair. *The International Journal of Press/Politics, 16*(1), 3–29.

Chaffee, S.H., and Kanihan, S.F. (1997). Learning about politics from mass media. *Political Communication, 14*(4), 421–430.

Chakravartty, P., and Schiller, D. (2010). Neoliberal newspeak and digital capitalism in crisis. *International Journal of Communication, 4*, 670–692.

Chang, L., and Krosnick, J.A. (2003). Measuring the frequency of regular behaviors: Comparing the "typical week" to the "past week." *Sociological Methodology, 33*(1), 55–80.

Cohen, A.A. (1996). *Global newsrooms, local audiences: A study of the Eurovision news exchange* (Vol. 12). New Barnet, Herts: John Libbey and Company.

Cohen, A.A. (2013). *Foreign news on television: Where in the world is the global village?* New York: Peter Lang.

Conover, P.J., and Feldman, S. (1986). Emotional reactions to the economy: I'm mad as hell and I'm not going to take it anymore. *American Journal of Political Science, 30*(1), 50–79.

Converse, P.E. (1964). The nature of belief systems in mass publics. *Critical Review, 18*(3), 1–74.

Coombs, W.T. (2007). Attribution theory as a guide for post-crisis communication research. *Public Relations Review, 33*(2), 135–139.

Curran, J., Iyengar, S., Lund, A.B., and Salovaara-Moring, I. (2009). Media system, public knowledge and democracy: A comparative study. *European Journal of Communication, 24*(1), 5–26.

Curtin, R. (2009). *What US consumers know about the economy: The impact of economic crisis on knowledge.* Paper presented at the III OECD World Forum on "Measuring the Progress of Societies", Busan, Republic of Korea, October.

Cutler, F. (2008). Whodunnit? Voters and responsibility in Canadian federalism. *Canadian Journal of Political Science, 41*(03), 627–654.

Dabrowski, M. (2010). The global financial crisis: Lessons for European integration. *Economic Systems, 34*(1), 38–54.

Damstra, A., and Boukes, M. (2018). The economy, the news, and the public: A longitudinal study of the impact of economic news on economic evaluations and expectations. *Communication Research.* https://doi.org/0093650217750971

Damstra, A., Boukes, M., and Vliegenthart, R. (2018). The economy. How do the media cover it and what are the effects? A literature review. *Sociology Compass, 12*(5), e12579.

Davis, A. (2005). Media effects and the active elite audience: A study of communications in the London Stock Exchange. *European Journal of Communication, 20*(3), 303–326.

Davis, A. (2006). Media effects and the question of the rational audience: Lessons from the financial markets. *Media, Culture and Society, 28*(4), 603–625.

Davis, A. (2007). The economic inefficiencies of market liberalization: The case of financial information in the London Stock Exchange. *Global Media and Communication, 3,* 157–178.

Davis, A. (2018). Whose economy, whose news? In L. Basu, S. Schifferes, and S. Knowles (Eds.), *The media and austerity: Comparative perspectives.* London: Routledge.

De Boef, S., and Keele, L. (2008). Taking time seriously. *American Journal of Political Science, 52*(1), 184–200.

De Boef, S., and Kellstedt, P.M. (2004). The political (and economic) origins of consumer confidence. *American Journal of Political Science, 48*(4), 633–649.

De Bruycker, I., and Walgrave, S. (2014). How a new issue becomes an owned issue: Media coverage and the Financial Crisis in Belgium (2008–2009). *International Journal of Public Opinion Research, 26*(1), 86–97.

de Vreese, C.H., Peter, J. & Semetko, H.A. (2001). Framing politics at the launch of the Euro: A cross-national comparative study of frames in the news. *Political Communication, 18*(2), 107–122.

de Vreese, C.H. (2004). Primed by the Euro: The impact of a referendum campaign on public opinion and evaluations of government and political leaders. *Scandinavian Political Studies, 27,* 45–64.

de Vreese, C. H. (2005). News framing: Theory and typology. *Information Design Journal+ Document Design, 13*(1), 51–62.

de Vreese, C. H., and Boomgaarden, H. (2006). News, political knowledge and participation: The differential effects of news media exposure on political knowledge and participation. *Acta Politica, 41*(4), 317–341.

Delli Carpini, M. X. (2004). Mediating democratic engagement: The impact of communications on citizens' involvement in political and civic life. In L. L. Kaid (Ed.), *Handbook of political communication research* (pp. 357–394). Hillsdale, NJ: Lawrence Erlbaum Associates.

Delli Carpini, M. X., and Keeter, S. (1997). *What Americans know about politics and why it matters.* New Haven, CT: Yale University Press.

Dixit, A. K., and Pindyck, R. S. (1994). *Investment under uncertainty.* Princeton, NJ: Princeton University Press.

Doms, M. E., and Morin, N. J. (2004). Consumer sentiment, the economy, and the news media. *FRB of San Francisco Working Paper* (2004–09).

Downs, A. (1957). An economic theory of political action in a democracy. *The Journal of Political Economy,* 135–150.

Doyle, G. (2006). Financial News Journalism: A post-Enron analysis of approaches towards economic and financial news production in the UK. *Journalism, 7*(4), 433–452.

Duch, R. M., and Stevenson, R. T. (2008). *The economic vote: How political and economic institutions condition election results.* Cambridge: Cambridge University Press.

Dunn, L. F., and Mirzaie, I. A. (2006). Turns in consumer confidence: An information advantage linked to manufacturing. *Economic Inquiry, 44*(2), 343–351.

Eide, M., and Knight, G. (1999). Public/private service: Service journalism and the problems of everyday life. *European Journal of Communication, 14*(4), 525–547.

Einhorn, H. J., and Hogarth, R. M. (1986). Decision making under ambiguity. *Journal of Business, 59,* 225–250.

Elenbaas, M., de Vreese, C., Schuck, A., and Boomgaarden, H. (2014). Reconciling passive and motivated learning: The saturation-conditional impact of media coverage and motivation on political information. *Communication Research, 41*(4), 481–504.

Ellsberg, D. (1961). Risk, ambiguity, and the savage axioms. *Quarterly Journal of Economics, 75,* 643–669.

Entman, R. M. (1993). Framing: Towards clarification of a fractured paradigm. *Journal of Communication, 43*(4), 51–58.

Ettema, J. S., and Kline, F. G. (1977). Deficits, differences, and ceilings contingent conditions for understanding the knowledge gap. *Communication Research, 4*(2), 179–202.

Eveland, W. P., Jr. (2001). The cognitive mediation model of learning from the news: Evidence from nonelection, off-year election, and presidential election contexts. *Communication Research, 28*(5), 571–601.

Eveland, W. P., Jr. (2002). News information processing as mediator of the relationship between motivations and political knowledge. *Journalism and Mass Communication Quarterly, 79*(1), 26–40.

Eveland, W. P., Jr. (2004). The effect of political discussion in producing informed citizens: The roles of information, motivation, and elaboration. *Political Communication, 21*(2), 177–193.

Eveland, W.P., Jr., and Scheufele, D.A. (2000). Connecting news media use with gaps in knowledge and participation. *Political Communication, 17*(3), 215–237.

Eveland, W.P., Jr., Shah, D.V., and Kwak, N. (2003). Assessing causality in the cognitive mediation model a panel study of motivations, information processing, and learning during campaign 2000. *Communication Research, 30*(4), 359–386.

Fan, D.P. (1993). *Predictions of consumer confidence/sentiment from the press.* Paper presented at the Section on survey research methods. American Statistical Association, Alexandria, VA.

Fishman, M. (1978). Crime waves as ideology. *Social Problems, 25,* 531–543.

Fiske, S.T., and Taylor, S.E. (1991). *Social cognition* (2nd ed.). New York: McGraw-Hill Book Company, Inc.

Fogarty, B.J. (2005). Determining economic news coverage. *International Journal of Public Opinion Research, 17*(2), 149–172.

Fraile, M. (2011). Widening or reducing the knowledge gap? Testing the media effects on political knowledge in Spain (2004–2006). *The International Journal of Press/Politics, 16*(2), 163–184.

Frank, R. (2003). 'These crowded circumstances'; When pack journalists bash pack journalists. *Journalism, 4*(4), 441–458.

Friedman, S.M., Dunwoody, S., and Rogers, C.L. (1999). *Communicating uncertainty: Media coverage of new and controversial science.* London: Routledge.

Galston, W.A. (2001). Political knowledge, political engagement, and civic education. *Annual Review of Political Science, 4*(1), 217–234.

Galston, W.A. (2004). Civic education and political participation. *Political Science and Politics, 37*(2), 263–266.

Galtung, J., and Ruge, M.H. (1965). The structure of foreign news: The presentation of the Congo, Cuba and Cyprus Crises in four Norwegian newspapers. *Journal of Peace Research, 2*(1), 64–90.

Gamson, W.A., and Modigliani, A. (1987). The changing culture of affirmative action. In R.D. Braungart (Ed.), *Research in political sociology* (Vol. 3, pp. 137–177). Greenwich, CT: JAI Press.

Gastil, J., and Dillard, J.P. (1999). Increasing political sophistication through public deliberation. *Political Communication, 16*(1), 3–23.

Genova, B.K., and Greenberg, B.S. (1979). Interests in news and the knowledge gap. *Public Opinion Quarterly, 43*(1), 79–91.

Gist, M.E., and Mitchell, T.R. (1992). Self-efficacy: A theoretical analysis of its determinants and malleability. *Academy of Management Review, 17*(2), 183–211.

Gnisci, A., van Dalen, A., and Di Conza, A. (2014). Interviews in a polarized television market: The Anglo-American watchdog model put to the test. *Political Communication, 31*(1), 112–130.

Goidel, R.K., and Langley, R.E. (1995). Media coverage of the economy and aggregate economic evaluations: Uncovering evidence of indirect media effects. *Political Research Quarterly, 48*(2), 313–328.

Gomez, B.T., and Wilson, J.M. (2003). Causal attribution and economic voting in American congressional elections. *Political Research Quarterly, 56*(3), 271–282.

Gordon, S.B., and Segura, G.M. (1997). Cross—national variation in the political sophistication of individuals: Capability or choice? *The Journal of Politics, 59*(1), 126–147.

Goul Andersen, J. (2010). "It's the economy, stupid!" eller "crisis? What crisis?" ["It's the economy, stupid!" or "crisis? What crisis?"]. *Tidskrift Politik, 13*(1), 18–35.

Grabe, M. E., Zhou, S., Lang, A., and Bolls, P. D. (2000). Packaging television news: The effects of tabloid on information processing and evaluative responses. *Journal of Broadcasting and Electronic Media, 44*(4), 581–598.

Graber, D. A. (1980). *Mass media and American politics.* Washington, DC: Congressional Quarterly Press.

Graber, D. A. (1982). Reading between the lines of consumer confidence measures. *Public Opinion Quarterly, 46*(3), 336–339.

Graber, D. A. (1988). *Processing the news: How people tame the information tide.* New York: Longman.

Graber, D. A. (1994). Why voters fail information tests: Can the hurdles be overcome? *Political Communication, 11*(4), 331–346.

Graber, D. A. (2001). *Processing politics: Learning from television in the internet age.* Chicago, IL: University of Chicago Press.

Graber, D. A. (2009). *Mass media and American politics.* London: Sage.

Granger, C. W. (1969). Investigating causal relations by econometric models and cross-spectral methods. *Econometrica: Journal of the Econometric Society*, 424–438.

Green-Pedersen, C., and Bjerre Mortensen, P. (2013). *Danish policy agenda project: Radio news. Data (1984–2003).* Retrieved April 27, 2013, from www.agenda setting.dk

Guerrera, F. (2009). Why generalists were not equipped to cover the complexities of the crisis. *Ethical Space: The International Journal of Communication Ethics, 6*(3/4), 44–49.

Guo, Z., and Moy, P. (1998). Medium or message? Predicting dimensions of political sophistication. *International Journal of Public Opinion Research, 10*(1), 25–50.

Gurevitch, M., Levy, M. R., and Roeh, I. (1991). The global newsroom: Convergences and diversities in the globalization of television news. In P. Dahlgren and C. Sparks (Eds.), *Communication and citizenship: Journalism and the public sphere* (pp. 195–216). London: Routledge.

Haddow, A., Hare, C., Hooley, J., and Shakir, T. (2013). Macroeconomic uncertainty: What is it, how can we measure it and why does it matter? *Bank of England Quarterly Bulletin, 53*(2), 100–109.

Hall, S., Critcher, C., Jefferson, T., Clarke, J., and Roberts, B. (1978). *Policing the crisis.* London: Macmillan.

Haller, H. B., and Norpoth, H. (1997). Reality bites: News exposure and economic opinion. *Public Opinion Quarterly*, 555–575.

Hansen, K. M. (2007). The sophisticated public: The effect of competing frames on public opinion. *Scandinavian Political Studies, 30*(3), 377–396.

Hansen, K. R. (2015). News from the future: A corpus linguistic analysis of future-oriented, unreal and counterfactual news discourse. *Discourse and Communication, 10*, 115–136.

Harcup, T., and O'Neill, D. (2001). What is news? Galtung and Ruge revisited. *Journalism Studies, 2*(2), 261–280.

Harrington, D. E. (1989). Economic news on television: The determinants of coverage. *Public Opinion Quarterly, 53*(1), 17–40.

Hayes, A. F. (2013). *Introduction to mediation, moderation, and conditional process analysis.* London: The Guildford Press.

Helleiner, E. (2011). Understanding the 2007–2008 global financial crisis: Lessons for scholars of international political economy. *Annual Review of Political Science, 14*, 67–87.

Hellwig, T. T. (2007). Economic openness, policy uncertainty, and the dynamics of government support. *Electoral Studies*, 26, 772–786.

Hellwig, T. T., and Coffey, E. (2011). Public opinion, party messages, and responsibility for the financial crisis in Britain. *Electoral Studies*, 30(3), 417–426.

Hellwig, T. T., Ringsmuth, E. M., and Freeman, J. R. (2008). The American public and the room to maneuver: Responsibility attributions and policy efficacy in an era of globalization. *International Studies Quarterly*, 52(4), 855–880.

Hester, J. B., and Gibson, R. (2003). The economy and second-level agenda setting: A time-series analysis of economic news and public opinion about the economy. *Journalism and Mass Communication Quarterly*, 80, 73–90.

Hetherington, M. J. (1996). The media's role in forming voters' national economic evaluations in 1992. *American Journal of Political Science*, 40(2), 372–395.

Hetsroni, A., Sheaffer, Z., Ben Zion, U., and Rosenboim, M. (2014). Economic expectations, optimistic bias, and television viewing during economic recession: A cultivation study. *Communication Research*, 41(2), 180–207.

Hobolt, S. B., and Tilley, J. (2014). *Blaming Europe? Responsibility without accountability in the European union.* Oxford: Oxford University Press.

Hobolt, S. B., Tilley, J., and Wittrock, J. (2013). Listening to the government: How information shapes responsibility attributions. *Political Behavior*, 35(1), 153–174.

Holbert, R. L., Benoit, W., Hansen, G., and Wen, W. C. (2002). The role of communication in the formation of an issue-based citizenry. *Communication Monographs*, 69(4), 296–310.

Hollander, B. A. (1995). The new news and the 1992 presidential campaign: Perceived vs. actual political knowledge. *Journalism and Mass Communication Quarterly*, 72(4), 786–798.

Hollanders, D., and Vliegenthart, R. (2011). The influence of negative newspaper coverage on consumer confidence: The Dutch case. *Journal of Economic Psychology*, 32(3), 367–373.

Holt, K., Shehata, A., Strömbäck, J., and Ljungberg, E. (2013). Age and the effects of news media attention and social media use on political interest and participation: Do social media function as leveller? *European Journal of Communication*, 28(1), 19–34.

Hopmann, D. N., Vliegenthart, R., de Vreese, C., and Albæk, E. (2010). Effects of election news coverage: How visibility and tone influence party choice. *Political Communication*, 27(4), 389–405.

Hopmann, D. N., Wonneberger, A., Shehata, A., and Höijer, J. (2015). Selective media exposure and increasing knowledge gaps in Swiss referendum campaigns. *International Journal of Public Opinion Research*, 28(1), 73–95.

Huxford, J. (2012). Reporting on recession: Journalism, prediction, and the economy. *International Business and Economics Research Journal (IBER)*, 11(3), 343–356.

Hyde, J. (2006). News coverage of genetic cloning: When science journalism becomes future-oriented speculation. *Journal of Communication Inquire*, 30, 229–250.

Ilut, C., and Schneider, M. (2012). Ambiguous business cycles. *American Economic Review*, 8, 2368–2399.

Ito, T. A., Larsen, J. T., Smith, K. N., and Cacioppo, J. T. (1998). Negative information weights more heavily on the brain: The negativity bias in evaluative categorizations. *Journal of Personality and Social Psychology*, 75(4), 887–900.

Iyengar, S. (1990). Framing responsibility for political issues: The case of poverty. *Political Behavior*, 12(1), 19–40.

Iyengar, S. (1994). *Is anyone responsible? How television frames political issues.* Chicago, IL: University of Chicago Press.

Iyengar, S., Curran, J., Lund, A. B., Salovaara-Moring, I., Hahn, K. S., and Coen, S. (2010). Cross-National versus individual-level differences in political information: A media systems perspective. *Journal of Elections, Public Opinion and Parties, 20*(3), 291–309.

Iyengar, S., and Hahn, K. S. (2009). Red media, blue media: Evidence of ideological selectivity in media use. *Journal of Communication, 59*(1), 19–39.

Iyengar, S., Hahn, K. S., Bonfadelli, H., and Marr, M. (2009). "Dark areas of ignorance" revisited. Comparing international affairs knowledge in Switzerland and the United States. *Communication Research, 36*(3), 341–358.

Iyengar, S., and Kinder, D. (1987). *News that matters: Television and American opinion.* Chicago, IL: University of Chicago Press.

Jaworski, A., Fitzgerald, R., and Morris, D. (2003). Certainty and speculation in news reporting of the future: The execution of Timothy McVeigh. *Discourse Studies, 5*(1), 33–48.

Jebril, N., de Vreese, C. H., van Dalen, A., and Albæk, E. (2013). The effects of human interest and conflict news frames on the dynamics of political knowledge gains: Evidence from a cross-national study. *Scandinavian Political Studies, 36*(3), 201–226.

Jerit, J., Barabas, J., and Bolsen, T. (2006). Citizens, knowledge, and the information environment. *American Journal of Political Science, 50*(2), 266–282.

Johnston, C. D., and Wronski, J. (2015). Personality dispositions and political preferences across hard and easy issues. *Political Psychology, 36*(1), 35–53.

Ju, Y. (2008). The asymmetry in economic news coverage and its impact on public perception in South Korea. *International Journal of Public Opinion Research, 20*(2), 237–249.

Ju, Y. (2011). *Obtrusiveness and negative bias: Issue attribute's influence on the asymmetric news coverage of the economy.* Paper presented at the Annual conference of the International Communication Association, Boston, MA.

Kahneman, D., and Tversky, A. (1979). Prospect theory: An analysis of decision under risk. *Econometrica: Journal of the Econometric Society, 47*(2), 263–291.

Kaid, L. L., McKinney, M. S., and Tedesco, J. C. (2007). Introduction: Political information efficacy and young voters. *American Behavioral Scientist, 50*(9), 1093–1111.

Katona, G. (1960). *The powerful consumer: Psychological studies of the American economy.* New York: McGraw-Hill Book Company, Inc.

Katz, I., Assor, A., Kanat-Maymon, Y., and Bereby-Meyer, Y. (2006). Interest as a motivational resource: Feedback and gender matter, but interest makes the difference. *Social Psychology of Education, 9*(1), 27–42.

Kenski, K., and Stroud, N. J. (2006). Connections between internet use and political efficacy, knowledge, and participation. *Journal of Broadcasting and Electronic Media, 50*(2), 173–192.

Kidwell, B., Hardesty, D. M., and Childers, T. L. (2008). Emotional calibration effects on consumer choice. *Journal of Consumer Research, 35*(4), 611–621.

Kier, C., and van Dalen, A. (2014). Har finanskrisen sparket liv i kritisk erhvervsjournalistik? [Has the financial crisis revived critical business journalism?]. In R. Buch and M. Verner (Eds.), *Krisen I Økonomi and Journalistik* (pp. 227–242). Ajour.

Kinder, D.R., and Kiewiet, D.R. (1979). Economic discontent and political behavior: The role of personal grievances and collective economic judgments in congressional voting. *American Journal of Political Science*, 23(3), 495–527.

Kinder, D.R., and Sanders, L.M. (1990). Mimicking political debate with survey questions: The case of white opinion on affirmative action for blacks. *Social Cognition*, 8(1), 73.

Kjær, P., and Langer, R. (2005). Infused with news value: Management, managerial knowledge and the institutionalization of business news. *Scandinavian Journal of Management*, 21(2), 209–233.

Kleinnijenhuis, J., Schultz, F., and Oegema, D. (2015). Frame complexity and the financial crisis: A comparison of the United States, the United Kingdom, and Germany in the period 2007–2012. *Journal of Communication*, 65(1), 1–23.

Kleinnijenhuis, J., Schultz, F., Oegema, D., and van Atteveldt, W. (2013). Financial news and market panics in the age of high-frequency sentiment trading algorithms. *Journalism*, 14(2), 271–291.

Knight, F.H. (1948). *Risk, uncertainty and profit*. Boston, MA: Houghton-Mifflin.

Kostadinova, P., and Dimitrova, D.V. (2012). Communicating policy change: Media framing of economic news in post-communist Bulgaria. *European Journal of Communication*, 27(2), 171–186.

Kottasz, R., and Bennett, R. (2014). Managing the reputation of the banking industry after the global financial crisis: Implications of public anger, processing depth and retroactive memory interference for public recall of events. *Journal of Marketing Communications*, 22(3), 248–306.

Kriesi, H., and Pappas, T.S. (2015). *European populism in the shadow of the great recession*. Colchester: ECPR Press.

Krosnick, J.A., and Brannon, L.A. (1993a). The impact of the Gulf War on the ingredients of presidential evaluations: Multidimensional effects of political involvement. *American Political Science Review*, 87(4), 963–975.

Krosnick, J.A., and Brannon, L.A. (1993b). The media and the foundations of presidential support: George Bush and the Persian Gulf conflict. *Journal of Social Issues*, 49(4), 167–182.

Krosnick, J.A., and Kinder, D.R. (1990). Altering the foundations of support for the president through priming. *The American Political Science Review*, 84, 497–512.

Kuklinski, J.H., Quirk, P.J., Jerit, J., Schwieder, D., and Rich, R.F. (2000). Misinformation and the currency of democratic citizenship. *The Journal of Politics*, 62(3), 790–816.

Lang, A. (2000). The limited capacity model of mediated message processing. *Journal of Communication*, 50(1), 46–70.

Lang, A. (2009). The limited capacity model of motivated mediated message processing. In R.L. Nabi and M.B. Oliver (Eds.), *Media processes and effects* (pp. 193–204). Thousand Oaks, CA: Sage.

Larcinese, V., Puglisi, R., and Snyder, J.M. (2011). Partisan bias in economic news: Evidence on the agenda-setting behavior of U.S. newspapers. *Journal of Public Economics*, 95, 1178–1189.

Larsen, M.V. (2016). Economic conditions affect support for Prime Minister parties in Scandinavia. *Scandinavian Political Studies*, 39(3), 226–241.

Lasswell, H.D. (1948). The structure and function of communication in society. *The Communication of Ideas*, 37, 215–228.

Lau, R. R., and Redlawsk, D. P. (2001). Advantages and disadvantages of cognitive heuristics in political decision making. *American Journal of Political Science*, 45(4), 951–971.

Lazarsfeld, P. F., Berelson, B., and Gaudet, H. (1944). *The people's choice: How the voter makes up his mind in a presidential campaign.* New York: Columbia University Press.

Lecheler, S., and de Vreese, C. H. (2013). What a difference a day makes? The effects of repetitive and competitive news framing over time. *Communication Research*, 40(2), 147–175.

Lee, M. (2014). A review of communication scholarship on the financial markets and the financial media. *International Journal of Communication*, 8, 715–736.

Lee, Y. K., and Chang, C. T. (2010). Framing public policy: The impacts of political sophistication and nature of public policy. *The Social Science Journal*, 47(1), 69–89.

Lengauer, G., Esser, F., and Berganza, R. (2012). Negativity in political news: A review of concepts, operationalizations and key findings. *Journalism*, 13(2), 179–202.

Lenz, G. S. (2009). Learning and opinion change, not priming: Reconsidering the priming hypothesis. *American Journal of Political Science*, 53(4), 821–837.

Lerner, J. S., and Keltner, D. (2001). Fear, anger and risk. *Journal of Personality and Social Psychology*, 81(1), 146–159.

Lewis, A., and Scott, A. J. (2000). The economic awareness, knowledge and pocket money practices of a sample of UK adolescents: A study of economic socialisation and economic psychology. *Citizenship, Social and Economics Education*, 4(1), 34–46.

Lewis-Beck, M. S., and Paldam, M. (2000). Economic voting: An introduction. *Electoral Studies*, 19(2), 113–121.

Lewis-Beck, M. S., and Stegmaier, M. (2007). Economic models of the vote. In R. J. Dalton and H. D. Klingemann (Eds.), *The oxford handbook of political behavior* (pp. 518–537). Oxford: Oxford University Press.

Lewis-Beck, M. S., and Stegmaier, M. (2013). The VP-function revisited: A survey of the literature on vote and popularity functions after over 40 years. *Public Choice*, 157(3–4), 367–385.

Lischka, J. A. (2014). Different revenue incentives, different content? Comparing economic news before and during the financial crisis in German public and commercial news outlets over time. *European Journal of Communication*, 29(5), 549–566.

Lischka, J. A. (2015). What follows what? Relations between economic indicators, economic expectations of the public, and news on the general economy and unemployment in Germany, 2002–2011. *Journalism and Mass Communication Quarterly*, 92(2), 374–398.

Lobo, M. C., and Lewis-Beck, M. S. (2012). The integration hypothesis: How the European Union shapes economic voting. *Electoral Studies*, 31(3), 522–528.

Loughran, T., and McDonald, B. (2011). When is a liability not a liability? Textual analysis, dictionaries, and 10-Ks. *The Journal of Finance*, 66(1), 35–65.

Lupia, A. (1994). Shortcuts versus encyclopedias: Information and voting behavior in California insurance reform elections. *American Political Science Review*, 88(1), 63–76.

Lupia, A. (2016). *Uninformed: Why people seem to know so little about politics and what we can do about it.* New York: Oxford University Press.

Lusardi, A. (2008). *Financial literacy: An essential tool for informed consumer choice?* NBER Working Paper No. 14084.

Lusardi, A., and Mitchell, O.S. (2008). Planning and financial literacy: How do women fare? *American Economic Review, 98*(2), 413–417.

Lusardi, A., and Mitchell, O.S. (2011). *Financial literacy and planning: Implications for retirement wellbeing.* NBER Working Paper No. 17078.

Luskin, R.C. (1990). Explaining political sophistication. *Political Behavior, 12*(4), 331–361.

Luskin, R.C., and Bullock, J.G. (2011). "Don't know" means "don't know": DK responses and the public's level of political knowledge. *The Journal of Politics, 73*(2), 547–557.

MacDonald, S.E., Rabinowitz, G., and Listhaug, O. (1995). Political sophistication and models of issue voting. *British Journal of Political Science, 25*(4), 453–483.

MacKuen, M.B., and Coombs, S.L. (1981). *More than news: Media power in public affairs.* Beverly Hills, CA: Sage.

MacKuen, M.B., Erikson, R.S., and Stimson, J.A. (1992). Peasants or bankers? The American electorate and the US economy. *American Political Science Review, 86*(3), 597–611.

Maestas, C.D., Atkeson, L.R., Croom, T., and Bryant, L.A. (2008). Shifting the blame: Federalism, media, and public assignment of blame following Hurricane Katrina. *Publius: The Journal of Federalism, 38*(4), 609–632.

Magalhães, P.C. (2014). The elections of the great recession in Portugal: Performance voting under a blurred responsibility for the economy. *Journal of Elections, Public Opinion and Parties, 24*(2), 180–202.

Malhotra, N., and Krosnick, J.A. (2007). Retrospective and prospective performance assessments during the 2004 election campaign: Tests of mediation and news media priming. *Political Behavior, 29*(2), 249–278.

Manning, P. (2013). Financial journalism, news sources and the banking crisis. *Journalism, 14*(2), 173–189.

Marcus, E.G., Neuman, W.R.N., and Mackuen, M. (2000). *Affective intelligence and political judgment.* Chicago, IL: University of Chicago Press.

Markus, G.B. (1979). *Analyzing panel data: Quantitative applications in the social sciences* (No. 18, Vol. 18). Beverly Hills, CA: Sage.

Martenson, B. (1998). Between state and market: The economy in Swedish television news. In N. Gavin (Ed.), *The economy, media and public knowledge* (pp. 112–133). London and New York: Leicester University Press.

Mayer, R.E. (1980). Elaboration techniques that increase the meaningfulness of technical text: An experimental test of the learning strategy hypothesis. *Journal of Educational Psychology, 72*(6), 770–784.

McCarthy, K.J., and Dolfsma, W. (2009). What's in a name? Understanding the language of the Credit Crunch. *Journal of Economic Issues, 43*(2), 531–548.

McCombs, M.E., and Shaw, D.L. (1972). The agenda-setting function of mass media. *Public Opinion Quarterly, 36*(2), 176–187.

McGraw, K.M., Hasecke, E., and Conger, K. (2003). Ambivalence, uncertainty, and processes of candidate evaluations. *Political Psychology, 24*(3), 421–448.

McGuire, W.J. (1964). Some contemporary approaches. *Advances in Experimental Social Psychology, 1*, 191–229.

McLeod, D.M., Kosicki, G.M., and McLeod, J.M. (2009). Political communication effects. In J. Bryant and M.B. Oliver (Eds.), *Media effects: Advances in theory and research* (3rd ed., pp. 225–278). London: Routledge.

Meffert, M. F., Chung, S., Joiner, A. J., Waks, L., and Garst, J. (2006). The effects of negativity and motivated information processing during a political campaign. *Journal of Communication*, 56(1), 27–51.

Mercille, J. (2014). The role of the media in sustaining Ireland's housing bubble. *New Political Economy*, 19(2), 282–301.

Millburn, M., and McGrail, A. (1992). The dramatic presentation of news and its effect on cognitive complexity. *Political Psychology*, 13(4), 613–632.

Miller, J. M., and Krosnick, J. A. (1996). News media impact on the ingredients of presidential evaluations: A program of research on the priming hypothesis. In D. C. Mutz, P. Sniderman, and R. A. Brody (Eds.), *Political persuasion and attitude change* (pp. 79–100). Ann Arbor: University of Michigan Press.

Moeller, J., and de Vreese, C. (2015). Spiral of political learning: The reciprocal relationship of news media use and political knowledge among adolescents. *Communication Research*, 1–17. https://doi.org/10.1177/0093650215605148

Möller, J., de Vreese, C., Esser, F., and Kunz, R. (2014). Pathway to political participation: The influence of online and offline news media on internal efficacy and turnout of first time voters. *American Behavioral Scientist*, 58(5), 689–700.

Mondak, J. J. (1999). Reconsidering the measurement of political knowledge. *Political Analysis*, 8(1), 57–82.

Mondak, J. J. (2001). Developing valid knowledge scales. *American Journal of Political Science*, 45(1), 224–238.

Morrell, M. (2005). Deliberation, democratic decision-making and internal political efficacy. *Political Behavior*, 27(1), 49–69.

Mujica, C., and Bachmann, I. (2018). The impact of melodramatic news coverage on information recall and comprehension. *Journalism Studies*, 19(3), 334–352.

Mutz, D. C. (1992). Mass media and the depoliticization of personal experience. *American Journal of Political Science*, 36(2), 483–508.

Mutz, D. C. (1998). *Impersonal influence: How perceptions of mass collectives affect political attitudes*. Cambridge: Cambridge University Press.

Mylonas, Y. (2012). Media and the economic crisis of the EU: The 'culturalization' of a systemic crisis and Bild-Zeitung's framing of Greece. *TripleC: Communication, Capitalism and Critique. Open Access Journal for a Global Sustainable Information Society*, 10(2), 646–671.

Nadeau, R., Niemi, R. G., and Amato, T. (2000). Elite economic forecasts, economic news, mass economic expectations, and voting intentions in Great Britain. *European Journal of Political Research*, 38(1), 135–170.

Nannestad, P., and Paldam, M. (1994). The VP-function: A survey of the literature on vote and popularity functions after 25 years. *Public Choice*, 79(3–4), 213–245.

Nannestad, P., and Paldam, M. (1995). It's the government's fault! A cross-section study of economic voting in Denmark, 1990/93. *European Journal of Political Research*, 28(1), 33–62.

Nannestad, P., and Paldam, M. (1997). The grievance asymmetry revisited: A micro study of economic voting in Denmark, 1986–1992. *European Journal of Political Economy*, 13(1), 81–99.

Neiger, M. (2007). Media oracles: The cultural significance and political import of news referring to future events. *Journalism*, 8(3), 309–321.

Neimi, R. G., Graig, S. C., and Mattei, F. (1991). Measuring internal political efficacy in the 1988 national election study. *American Political Science Review*, 85(4), 1407–1413.

Neuman, W. R. (1986). *The paradox of mass politics: Knowledge and opinion in the American electorate*. Cambridge, MA: Harvard University Press.

Neuman, W. R. (1992). *Common knowledge: News and the construction of political meaning*. Chicago, IL: University of Chicago Press.

Neuman, W. R., Marcus, G. E., Grigler, A. N., and MacKuen, M. (2007). *The affect effect: Dynamics of emotion in political thinking and behavior*. Chicago, IL: University of Chicago Press.

Newman, N., Fletcher, R., Levy, D.A.L., and Kleis Nielsen, R. (2016). *Reuters institute digital news report 2016*. Oxford.

Newman, N., Levy, D. A., and Nielsen, R. K. (2015). Reuters Institute digital news report 2015.

Nguyen, V. H., and Claus, E. (2013). Good news, bad news, consumer sentiment and consumption behavior. *Journal of Economic Psychology, 39*, 426–438.

Nielsen, F. A. (2011). A new ANEW. Evaluation of a word list for sentiment analysis in microblogs. Proceedings of the ESWC2011 Workshop on 'Making Sense of Microposts': Big things come in small packages, 93–98.

Nienstedt, H. W., Kepplinger, H. M., and Quiring, O. (2015). What went wrong and why? Roots, responsibility, and solutions of the Euro crisis in European newspapers. In R. G. Picard (Ed.), *The Euro crisis in the media: Journalistic coverage of economic crisis and European institutions* (pp. 19–44). London: I. B. Tauris.

Norris, P. (2000). *A virtuous circle: Political communications in postindustrial societies*. New York: Cambridge University Press.

Oegema, D., and Kleinnijenhuis, J. (2000). Personalization in political television news: A 13-wave survey study to assess effects of text and footage. *Communications, 25*(1), 43–60.

Ohme, J. (2017). *New media, new citizens?* Odense: University of Southern Denmark.

Olausson, U. (2009). Global warming—global responsibility? Media frames of collective action and scientific certainty. *Public Understanding of Science, 18*(4), 421–436.

Olausson, U. (2014). The diversified nature of "Domesticated" news discourse: The case of climate change in national news media. *Journalism Studies, 15*(6), 711–725.

Otto, L., Glogger, I., and Boukes, M. (2016). The softening of journalistic political communication: A critical review of sensationalism, soft news, infotainment, and tabloidization and a comprehensive framework model. *Communication Theory, 27*(2), 136–155.

Pan, Z., and Kosicki, G. M. (1997). Priming and media impact on the evaluations of the president's performance. *Communication Research, 24*(1), 3–30.

Patt, A. G., and Weber, E. U. (2014). Perceptions and communication strategies for the many uncertainties relevant for climate policy. *WIREs Climate Change, 5*, 219–232.

Patterson, T. E. (2003). *The vanishing voter: Public involvement in an age of uncertainty*. New York: Vintage Books.

Pedersen, R. T. (2012). The game frame and political efficacy: Beyond the spiral of cynicism. *European Journal of Communication, 27*(3), 225–240.

Petty, R. E., Brinôl, P., and Priester, J. R. (2009). Mass media attitude change: Implications of the elaboration likelihood model of persuasion. In J. Bryant and M. B. Oliver (Eds.), *Media effects advances in theory and research* (pp. 141–180). New York: Routledge.

Petty, R. E., and Cacioppo, J. T. (1986). *Communication and persuasion: Central and peripheral routes to attitude change*. Berlin: Springer.

Petty, R. E., and Cacioppo, J. T. (1990). Involvement and persuasion: Tradition versus integration. *Pyschological Bulletin, 107*(3), 367–374.

Picard, R. G. (2015). *The Euro crisis in the media: Journalistic coverage of economic crisis and European institutions.* London: I. B. Tauris.

Powell, G. B., Jr., and Whitten, G. D. (1993). A cross-national analysis of economic voting: Taking account of the political context. *American Journal of Political Science, 37*(2), 391–414.

Price, V., Tewksbury, D., and Powers, E. (1997). Switching trains of thought: The impact of news frames on readers' cognitive responses. *Communication Research, 24*(5), 481–506.

Prior, M. (2005). News vs entertainment: How increasing media choice widens gaps in political knowledge and turnout. *American Journal of Political Science, 49*(3), 577–592.

Prior, M. (2010). You've either got it or you don't? The stability of political interest over the life cycle. *The Journal of Politics, 72*(3), 747–766.

Prior, M. (2013). Media and political polarization. *Annual Review of Political Science, 16*, 101–127.

Raju, P. S., Lonial, S. C., and Mangold, W. G. (1995). Differential effects of subjective knowledge, objective knowledge, and usage experience on decision making: An exploratory investigation. *Journal of Consumer Psychology, 4*(2), 153–180.

Rice, R. E., and Atkin, C. K. (2012). *Public communication campaigns.* London: Sage.

Roush, C. (2006). *Profits and losses: Business journalism and its role in society.* Portland, OR: Marion Street Press.

Roush, C. (2014). Why the media got it right. In S. Schifferes and R. Roberts (Eds.), *The media and financial crisis: Comparative and historical perspectives* (pp. 16–27). London: Routledge.

Rudolph, T. J. (2003). Who's responsible for the economy? The formation and consequences of responsibility attributions. *American Journal of Political Science, 47*(4), 698–713.

Rudolph, T. J., Gangl, A., and Stevens, D. (2000). The effects of efficacy and emotions on campaign involvement. *The Journal of Politics, 62*(4), 1189–1197.

Ruigrok, N., and Van Atteveldt, W. (2007). Global angling with a local angle: How US, British, and Dutch newspapers frame global and local terrorist attacks. *The Harvard International Journal of Press/Politics, 12*(1), 68–90.

Sanders, D. (2000). The real economy and the perceived economy in popularity functions: How much do voters need to know? A study of British data, 1974–97. *Electoral Studies, 19*(2), 275–294.

Sanders, D., and Gavin, N. (2004). Television news, economic perceptions and political preferences in Britain, 1997–2001. *Journal of Politics, 66*(4), 1245–1266.

Schäfer, M. S., Ivanova, A., and Schmidt, A. (2013). What drives media attention for climate change? Explaining issue attention in Australian, German and Indian print media from 1996 to 2010. *International Communication Gazette, 78*(2), 156–176.

Schellinck, D.A.T. (1983). Cue choice as a function of time pressure and perceived risk. In R. P. Bagozi and A. M. Tybout (Eds.), *Advances in consumer research* (pp. 410–415). Ann Arbor, MI: Association for Consumer Research.

Scheufele, D. A. (1999). Framing as a theory of media effects. *Journal of Communication, 49*(1), 103–122.

Schmitt, H., Hobolt, S. B., Popa, S. A., and Teperoglou, E. (2015). European parliament election study 2014, voter study. *GESIS Data Archive, Cologne. ZA5160 Data file Version,* 2(0).

Schoenbach, K., and Lauf, E. (2002). The "trap" effect of television and its competitors. *Communication Research,* 29(5), 564–583.

Schuck, A. R. T., and de Vreese, C. H. (2006). Between risk and opportunity news framing and its effects on public support for EU enlargement. *European Journal of Communication,* 21(1), 5–32.

Schuck, A. R. T., Vliegenthart, R., and de Vreese, C. H. (2016). Matching theory and data: Why combining media content with survey data matters. *British Journal of Political Science,* 46(1), 205–213.

Schudson, M. (1998). *The good citizen: A history of civic life.* New York: Martin Kessler Books.

Schweisberger, V., Billinson, J., and Chock, M. K. (2014). Facebook, the third-person effect, and the differential impact hypothesis. *Journal of Computer-Mediated Communication,* 19(3), 403–413.

Semetko, H. A., and Schönbach, K. (1994). *Germany's unity election: Voters and the media.* New York: Hampton Press.

Semetko, H. A., and Valkenburg, P. M. (1998). The impact of attentiveness on political efficacy: Evidence from a three-year German panel study. *International Journal of Public Opinion Research,* 10(3), 195–210.

Semetko, H. A., and Valkenburg, P. M. (2000). Framing European politics: A content analysis of press and television news. *Journal of Communication,* 50(2), 93–109.

Sennov, S. (2014, 28 January). Ny undersøgelse: Er medierne med til at holde økonomien nede? [New study: Do the media keep the economy down?]. *Politiken.*

Shah, D. V., and Scheufele, D. A. (2006). Explicating opinion leadership: Nonpolitical dispositions, information consumption, and civic participation. *Political Communication,* 23(1), 1–22.

Shah, D. V., Watts, M. D., Domke, D., and Fan, D. P. (2002). News framing and cueing of issue regimes: Explaining Clinton's public approval in spite of scandal. *Public Opinion Quarterly,* 66(3), 339–370.

Shah, D. V., Watts, M. D., Domke, D., Fan, D. P., and Fibison, M. (1999). News coverage, economic cues, and the public's presidential preferences, 1984–1996. *The Journal of Politics,* 61(4), 914–943.

Sheafer, T. (2008). The media and economic voting in Israel. *International Journal of Public Opinion Research,* 20(1), 33–51.

Shehata, A. (2014). Game Frames, issue frames, and mobilization: Disentangling the effects of frame exposure and motivated news attention on political cynicism and engagement. *International Journal of Public Opinion Research,* 26(2), 157–177.

Shehata, A., and Falasca, K. (2014). Priming effects during the financial crisis: Accessibility and applicability mechanisms behind government approval. *European Political Science Review,* 6(4), 597–620.

Shehata, A., Hopmann, D. N., Nord, L., and Höijer, J. (2015). Television channel content profiles and differential knowledge growth: A test of the inadvertent learning hypothesis using panel data. *Political Communication,* 32(3), 377–395.

Shoemaker, P. J., and Reese, S. D. (1996). *Mediating the message.* New York: Longman.

Simon, H. A. (2013). *Administrative behavior: A study of decision-making processes in administrative organizations* (4th ed.). New York: The Free Press.

Skovsgaard, M., Shehata, A., and Strömbäck, J. (2016). Opportunity structures for selective exposure: Investigating selective exposure and learning in Swedish election campaigns using panel survey data. *The International Journal of Press/Politics*, 21(4), 527–546.

Slater, M. D. (2007). Reinforcing spirals: The mutual influence of media selectivity and media effects and their impact on individual behavior and social identity. *Communication Theory*, 17(3), 281–303.

Slovic, P., Finucane, M., Peters, E., and MacGregor, D. G. (2002). Rational actors or rational fools: Implications of the affect heuristic for behavioral economics. *The Journal of Socio-Economics*, 31(4), 329–342.

Smith, C. A., and Ellsworth, P. C. (1985). Patterns of cognitive appraisal in emotion. *Journal of Personality and Social Psychology*, 48(4), 813–838.

Smith, K., Cacioppo, J. T., Larsen, J. T., and Chartrand, T. L. (2003). May I have your attention, please: Electrocortical responses to positive and negative stimuli. *Neuropsychologia*, 41(2), 171–183.

Smithson, M. (2008). Psychology's Ambivalent View of Uncertainty. *Uncertainty and Risk: Multidisciplinary Perspectives*, 205–217.

So, J., and Nabi, R. (2013). Reduction of perceived social distance as an explanation for media's influence on personal risk perceptions: A test of the risk convergence model. *Human Communication Research*, 39(3), 317–338.

Soroka, S. N. (2006). Good news and bad news: Asymmetric responses to economic information. *Journal of Politics*, 68(2), 372–385.

Soroka, S. N. (2012). The gatekeeping function: Distributions of information in media and the real world. *The Journal of Politics*, 74(2), 514–528.

Soroka, S. N. (2014). *Negativity in democratic politics: Causes and consequences*. Cambridge: Cambridge University Press.

Soroka, S. N., and McAdams, S. (2015). News, politics, and negativity. *Political Communication*, 32(1), 1–22.

Soroka, S. N., Stecula, D. A., and Wlezien, C. (2015). It's (change) in the (future) economy, stupid: Economic indicators, the media, and public opinion. *American Journal of Political Science*, 59(2), 457–474.

Starkman, D. (2014). *The watchdog that didn't bark: The financial crisis and the disappearance of investigative journalism*. New York: Columbia University Press.

Stocking, S. H., and Holstein, L. W. (1993). Constructing and reconstructing scientific ignorance: Ignorance claims in science and journalism. *Science Communication*, 15(2), 186–210.

Stocking, S. H., and Holstein, L. W. (2009). Manufacturing doubt: Journalists' roles and the construction of ignorance in a scientific controversy. *Public Understanding of Science*, 18(1), 23–42.

Strömbäck, J. (2005). In search of a standard: Four models of democracy and their normative implications for journalism. *Journalism Studies*, 6(3), 331–345.

Strömbäck, J. (2008). Four phases of mediatization: An analysis of the mediatization of politics. *The International Journal of Press/Politics*, 13(3), 228–246.

Strömbäck, J., Djerf-Pierre, M., and Shehata, A. (2013). The dynamics of political interest and news media consumption: A longitudinal perspective. *International Journal of Public Opinion Research*, 25(4), 414–435.

Strömbäck, J., and Shehata, A. (2010). Media malaise or a virtuous circle? Exploring the causal relationships between news media exposure, political news attention and political interest. *European Journal of Political Research*, 49(5), 575–597.

Strömbäck, J., Todal Jenssen, A., and Aalberg, T. (2012). The financial crisis as a global news event: Cross-national media coverage and public knowledge of economic affairs. In T. Aalberg and J. Curran (Eds.), *How media inform democracy: A comparative approach* (pp. 159–175). London: Routledge.

Stryker, J. E., Wray, R. J., Hornik, R. C., and Yanovitzky, I. (2006). Validation of database search terms for content analysis: The case of cancer news coverage. *Journalism and Mass Communication Quarterly, 83*(2), 413–430.

Stubager, R., Lewis-Beck, M. S., and Nadeau, R. (2013). Reaching for profit in the welfare state: Patrimonial economic voting in Denmark. *Electoral Studies, 32*(3), 438–444.

Svensson, H. M., Albæk, E., van Dalen, A., and de Vreese, C. (2017a). Good news in bad news: How negativity enhances economic efficacy. *International Journal of Communication, 11*, 1431–1447.

Svensson, H. M., Albæk, E., van Dalen, A., and de Vreese, C. H. (2017b). The impact of ambiguous economic news on uncertainty and consumer confidence. *European Journal of Communication, 32*(2), 85–99.

Tambini, D. (2010). What are financial journalists for? *Journalism Studies, 11*(2), 158–174.

Temple, M. (2006). Dumbing down is good for you. *British Politics, 1*(2), 257–271.

Tewksbury, D., Hals, M. L., and Bibart, A. (2008). The efficacy of news browsing: The relationship of news consumption style to social and political efficacy. *Journalism and Mass Communication Quarterly, 85*(2), 257–272.

Tewksbury, D., Scheufele, D. A., Bryant, J., and Oliver, M. (2009). News framing theory and research. In J. Bryant and M. B. Oliver (Eds.), *Media effects: Advances in theory and research* (pp. 17–33). New York: Routledge.

Thompson, P. A. (2013). Invested interests? Reflexivity, representation and reporting in financial markets. *Journalism, 14*(2), 208–227.

Thøis Madsen, P. (2018). Økonominyheder på Facebook: Er usikkerhed på arbejdsmarkedet og fordelingen af samfundskagen vigtigere end konjunkturer? [Economic news on Facebook. Are uncertainty on the job market and redistribution more important than economic trends?]. *Journalistica*, (1), 78–94.

Tichenor, P. J., Donohue, G. A., and Olien, C. N. (1970). Mass media flow and differential growth in knowledge. *Public Opinion Quarterly, 34*(2), 159–170.

Tiedens, L. Z., and Linton, S. (2001). Judgment under emotional certainty and uncertainty: The effects of specific emotions on information processing. *Journal of Personality and Social Psychology, 81*(6), 973–988.

Togeby, L. (2007). The context of priming. *Scandinavian Political Studies, 30*(3), 345–376.

Trussler, M., and Soroka, S. (2014). Consumer demand for cynical and negative news frames. *The International Journal of Press/Politics, 19*(3), 360–379.

Usher, N. (2013). Ignored, uninterested, and the blame game: How The New York Times, Marketplace, and TheStreet distanced themselves from preventing the 2007–2009 financial crisis. *Journalism, 14*(2), 190–207.

Valentino, N. A. (1999). Crime news and the priming of racial attitudes during evaluations of the president. *Public Opinion Quarterly, 63*(3), 293–320.

Valentino, N. A., Gregorowicz, K., and Groenendyk, E. (2009). Efficacy, emotions and the habit of participation. *Political Behavior, 31*(3), 307–330.

Valenzuela, S. (2009). Variations in media priming: The moderating role of knowledge, interest, news attention, and discussion. *Journalism and Mass Communication Quarterly, 86*(4), 756–774.

Valkenburg, P. M., and Peter, J. (2013). Five challenges for the future of media-effects research. *International Journal of Communication, 7*, 197–215.

Valkenburg, P. M., Semetko, H. A., and de Vreese, C. H. (1999). The effects of news frames on readers' thoughts and recall. *Communication Research, 37*(1), 42–64.

Van Aelst, P., Strömbäck, J., Aalberg, T., Esser, F., de Vreese, C., Matthes, J., . . . Stępińska, A. (2017). Political communication in a high-choice media environment: A challenge for democracy? *Annals of the International Communication Association, 41*(1), 3–27.

Van Blankenstein, F. M., Dolmans, D. H., Van Der Vleuten, C. P., and Schmidt, H. G. (2008). *The influence of verbal elaboration on subsequent learning: An experimental study in a PBL-setting.* Paper presented at the 8th International Conference for the Learning Sciences.

van Dalen, A., and de Vreese, C. H. (2014). *Economic news and economic voting during the Long Recession: The case of Denmark.* Paper presented at the Nordic Political Science Association, Gothenburg.

van Dalen, A., de Vreese, C. H., and Albæk, E. (2016). Mediated Uncertainty: The negative impact of uncertainty in economic news on consumer confidence. *Public Opinion Quarterly, 81*(1), 111–130.

Van der Brug, W., Semetko, H., and Valkenburg, P. M. (2007). Priming in a multi-party context: The impact of European summit news on evaluations of political leaders. *Political Behavior, 29*(1), 115–141.

Van Deth, J. W. (2000). Interesting but irrelevant: Social capital and the saliency of politics in Western Europe. *European Journal of Political Research, 37*(2), 115–147.

Van Leuven, S., Heinrich, A., and Deprez, A. (2015). Foreign reporting and sourcing practices in the network sphere: A quantitative content analysis of the Arab Spring in Belgian news media. *New Media and Society, 17*(4), 573–591.

Van Oest, R., and Franses, P. H. (2008). Measuring changes in consumer confidence. *Journal of Economic Psychology, 29*(3), 255–275.

Van Raaij, W. F. (1989). Economic news, expectations and macro-economic behaviour. *Journal of Economic Psychology, 10*(4), 473–493.

Vasterman, P.L.M. (2005). Media-hype; Self-reinforcing news waves, journalistic standards and the construction of social problems. *European Journal of Communication, 20*(4), 508–530.

Vliegenthart, R. (2014). Moving up. Applying aggregate level time series analysis in the study of media coverage. *Quality & quantity, 48*(5), 2427–2445.

Vries, C. E., and Giger, N. (2014). Holding governments accountable? Individual heterogeneity in performance voting. *European Journal of Political Research, 53*(2), 345–362.

Walstad, W. B. (1997). The effect of economic knowledge on public opinion of economic issues. *The Journal of Economic Education, 28*(3), 195–205.

Walstad, W. B., and Rebeck, K. (2002). Assessing the economic knowledge and economic opinions of adults. *The Quarterly Review of Economics and Finance, 42*(5), 921–935.

Weaver, D. H. (1980). Audience need for orientation and media effects. *Communication Research, 7*(3), 361–373.

Weaver, R.K. (1986). The politics of blame avoidance. *Journal of Public Policy*, 6(4), 371–398.

Weiner, B. (1985). An attributional theory of achievement motivation and emotion. *Psychological Review*, 92(4), 548–573.

Weiner, B. (1986). *An attributional theory of achievement motivation and emotion.* New York: Springer.

Welles, C. (1973). The bleak wasteland of financial reporting. *Columbia Journalism Review*, 12(2), 40–49.

Whitten, G.D., and Palmer, H.D. (1999). Cross-national analysis of economic voting. *Electoral Studies*, 18(1), 49–67.

Wien, C., and Elmelund-Præstekær, C. (2009). An anatomy of media hypes developing a model for the dynamics and structure of intense media coverage of single issues. *European Journal of Communication*, 24(2), 183–201.

Williams, M.L., Waldauer, C., and Duggal, V.G. (1992). Gender differences in economic knowledge: An extension of the analysis. *The Journal of Economic Education*, 23(3), 219–231.

Wlezien, C., Franklin, M., and Twiggs, D. (1997). Economic perceptions and vote choice: Disentangling the endogeneity. *Political Behavior*, 19(1), 7–17.

Wobker, I., Lehmann-Waffenschmidt, M., Kenning, P., and Gigerenzer, G. (2012). *What do people know about the economy? A test of minimal economic knowledge in Germany.* Dresden Discussion Paper in Economics No. 3/12.

Wojcieszak, M. (2014). Preferences for political decision-making processes and issue publics. *Public Opinion Quarterly*, 78(4), 917–939.

Wonneberger, A., Schoenbach, K., and Van Meurs, L. (2011). Interest in news and politics—or situational determinants? Why people watch the news. *Journal of Broadcasting and Electronic Media*, 55(3), 325–343.

Wooldridge, J.M. (2010). *Econometric analysis of cross section and panel data.* Cambridge, MA: MIT press.

Wu, H.D., and Coleman, R. (2009). Advancing agenda-setting theory: The comparative strength and new contingent conditions of the two levels of agenda-setting effects. *Journalism and Mass Communication Quarterly*, 86(4), 775–789.

Wu, H.D., McCracken, M.W., and Saito, S. (2004). Economic communication in the 'lost decade': News coverage and the Japanese recession. *Gazette*, 66(2), 133–149.

Wu, H.D., Stevenson, R.L., Chen, H.C., and Güner, Z.N. (2002). The conditioned impact of recession news: A time-series analysis of economic communication in the United States, 1987–1996. *International Journal of Public Opinion Research*, 14(1), 19–36.

Yanovitzky, I., and Van Lear, A. (2008). Time series analysis: Traditional and contemporary approaches. In A.F. Hayes, M.D. Slater, and L.B. Snyder (Eds.), *The Sage sourcebook of advanced data analysis methods for communication research* (pp. 89–124). London: Sage.

Young, D.G., and Tisinger, R.M. (2006). Dispelling late-night myths: News consumption among late-night comedy viewers and the predictors of exposure to various late-night shows. *The Harvard International Journal of Press/Politics*, 11(3), 113–134.

Young, L., and Soroka, S.N. (2012). Affective news: The automated coding of sentiment in political texts. *Political Communication*, 29(2), 205–231.

Zaller, J. R. (1992). *The nature and origins of mass opinion*. Cambridge: Cambridge University Press.

Zaller, J. R. (2003). A new standard of news quality: Burglar alarms for the monitorial citizen. *Political Communication, 20*(2), 109–130.

Zehr, S. C. (2000). Public representations of scientific uncertainty about global climate change. *Public Understanding of Science, 9*(2), 85–103.

Zillmann, D. (2006). Exemplification effects in the promotion of safety and health. *Journal of Communication, 56*(suppl_1), S221–S237. https://doi.org/10.1111/j.1460-2466.2006.00291.x

Zuiderveen Borgesius, F. J., Trilling, D., Moeller, J., Bodó, B., de Vreese, C. H., and Helberger, N. (2016). Should we worry about filter bubbles? *Internet Policy Review. Journal on Internet Regulation, 5*(1–16).

Methodological Appendix

The research presented in this book is based on a multi-method design consisting of the following elements:

- A year-long four-wave panel study of media use, economic perceptions, and cognition as well as political attitudes among a sample of the Danish population.
- A year-long content analysis of economic news in 16 outlets during the time of the panel study.
- An automated content analysis of the visibility, tone, and uncertainty in economic news in three Danish broadsheet newspapers between 1996 and 2012.
- A time-series analysis of the relation between economic developments, economic news, and economic perceptions in the same period.
- An experiment looking at the impact of the framing of economic news on attribution of responsibility.

These methods have complementary strengths. The integration of the panel study and content analysis allows us to study the mechanisms behind observed media effects as well as differences in effects across subgroups of the population. The macro-level analysis combining automated content analysis with time-series analysis has high external validity. Internal validity is a strength of experimental designs. In addition, each of these methods goes beyond cross-sectional analysis, allowing us to draw stronger conclusions about direction of causality. In this appendix, the panel study, content analysis, time-series analysis, and automated content analysis are described in depth. The experiment, which plays a less central role in the study, is explained in Chapter 8.

Panel Survey

Over a period of ten months we surveyed the same group of respondents. The major strength of this panel design is that by interviewing the same respondents at different points in time, it is possible to control for the lagged dependent variables in statistical analyses (Markus, 1979; Wooldridge, 2010). Most previous research has examined the effects of economic news in an aggregate setting (De Boef and Kellstedt, 2004; Sanders, 2000; Sheafer, 2008). By employing an individual-level design, it is possible to link specific aspects of news coverage with individual media exposure measures collected in surveys in order to examine the underlying *mechanisms* of media effects. Obtaining panel data is a challenge, especially given the dropout rate between the waves (Wooldridge, 2010), but it allows for a more detailed examination of trends in a period that lasted 10 months.

Table A1 Overview of waves and respondents

Period	Respondents	N	Response rate*/ recontact rate
Wave 1	19 February 2013–4 March 2013	2,480	38%
Wave 2	20 May 2013–2 June 2013	1,666	68%
Wave 3	3 September 2013–16 September 2013	1,287	60%
Wave 4	27 November 2013–9 December 2013	1,043	82%

*AAPOR1.

Table A2 A comparison of the use of three Danish newspapers according to the 2014 European Election Study (EES) and according to the panel study used in this book

Outlet	Source	Less than once a week/ never (%)	Once a week (%)	Every day/ almost every day (%)*
Politiken	EES	79.7	4.5	10.3
Politiken	Panel study w1	83.9	3.6	7.8
Politiken	Panel study w2	84.4	3.9	7.8
Politiken	Panel study w4	83.9	3.7	8.9
Politiken	Panel study w2	87.5	2.5	6.9
Jyllands-Posten	EES	79.5	4.6	9.2
Jyllands-Posten	Panel study w1	83.3	4.5	6.7
Jyllands-Posten	Panel study w2	83.3	3.5	7.1
Jyllands-Posten	Panel study w3	83.2	3.7	7.8
Jyllands-Posten	Panel study w4	82.1	4.2	7.8
Ekstra Bladet	EES	82.5	6.1	6.9
Ekstra Bladet	Panel study w1	83.0	5.9	5.7
Ekstra Bladet	Panel study w2	85.4	5.2	3.9
Ekstra Bladet	Panel study w3	86.7	4.1	4.3
Ekstra Bladet	Panel study w4	88.3	5	2.6

Note: *For the panel study we report the percent of respondents who answered that they use the medium 5–7 days.

The panel survey data were collected online by TNS Gallup. The complete panel survey consisted of four waves, all fielded in 2013 (see Table A1). The polling company drew a stratified sample from their Internet panel G@llup-Forum. The sample is stratified along the variables gender, education, age, and region to make sure that the survey was sent to a group that was representative for the Danish population on these parameters. The respondents who took part in all four waves of the survey (1,043 respondents) were representative of the Danish population on the parameters education and region. Thirty-one percent of the population lives in the capital area compared to 29 percent in the sample; there was a representative distribution in the other regions as well. There was an underrepresentation of young people in the sample (16 percent in the sample versus 35 percent in the population for ages 18–40) and an overrepresentation of older citizens (53 percent in the sample compared to 29 percent in the population for the ages above 60). The group in between (40–60 years) was better represented (32 percent in the sample compared to 36 percent in the population).

Apart from checking the representativeness for demographic background variables, we also assessed whether news use and political interest among the respondents corresponded with what previous studies have found. Participating in four survey waves over a ten-month period is quite demanding for the respondents. A potential concern is that people with limited interested in the topic might not want to participate. Therefore, we checked whether people with high news use and high political interest are overrepresented among the respondents, especially among the people who took part in the final wave.

The 2014 European Election Study (Schmitt et al., 2015) includes questions that are phrased in such a way that they can serve as a baseline to which our data can be compared. For Denmark, the EES asked respondents how often they read three newspapers, which are also in our panel study: *Politiken, Jyllands-Posten*, and *Ekstra Bladet*. Similar to our panel study, the EES asked about news use in general, rather than during a specific week.[1] Table A2 shows large similarities between the EES and our panel survey.[2] According to both the EES and our panel study, around 80 percent of the respondents use each medium less than once a week or never. The percentage of respondents who use the medium every day or almost every day is slightly higher according to the EES data than our panel study. There are no large differences between the first wave and fourth wave of the panel study. Thus, at least according to this comparison, we need not worry that news-savvy respondents are overrepresented in our survey.

As a final step in our assessment of the representativeness of our sample, we compared interest in politics according to the EES survey and the panel study. Despite the differences in answer categories, the results are again rather similar. According to the EES, 26 percent of the Danish population is very interested in politics; according to the panel study, 20 percent (in wave 1) and 21 percent (in wave 4) are very interested. We conclude that the relatively high interest in politics among the respondents is a characteristic of the Danish population and not an indication that our sample is skewed.

Year-Long Content Analysis

The content analysis covered a sample of the economic news content that was published in the periods leading up to the first wave of the survey, and between the four waves of the panel survey, beginning with 22 January and ending on 26 November 2013. The media outlets that were included in the content analysis were the same media outlets that were used in the panel survey to measure a respondent's news consumption. These media outlets were DR1 and TV2 (television), *Politiken, Berlingske, Børsen, Jyllands-Posten* and *Politiken* (broadsheet newspapers), and *Ekstra Bladet* and *BT* (tabloid newspapers), including their websites. These outlets were chosen because of their popularity among the Danish news consumers (high circulation and audience share) and because of their different outlet characteristics as either tabloid or broadsheet newspapers, or public service or semiprivate broadcasters, which ensures a broad variety of news content. To identify economic news stories, we searched databases Infomedia and BERTA, which collect articles that appear in the print and online editions of Danish news outlets.[3]

For the manual content analysis, economic news was defined as "information reported by the news media about state of the micro-, meso- and macro-economy of Denmark or other nations." Economic news is defined by the topic it covers rather than by the section of the newspaper in which it is printed or by the journalists writing it (approach similar to Hetsroni et al., 2014 and Soroka, 2006). The macro-level economy includes topics such as the welfare state, imports and exports, interest rates, taxation, and growth. The meso-level economy refers to news about the business section or corporations. The micro-level economy includes topics such as private consumption, personal economic stories, and mortgage rates. A list of search words related to the defining topics was developed to identify economic news articles about the economy (see Box A1). Words that are often used to describe the economy—such as "upturn" and "downturn," "improvements" and "decline"—were left out because they may also appear in other contexts. A sample search with the inclusion of these words resulted in a higher number of articles not related to the economy.

Box A1   Search terms to identify articles about economic news which were used in the manual content analysis

Economy, deficit, debt, national debt, state budget, inflation, employment, unemployment, unemployed, salary, payment, investment, finance, stock market, C20*, stock exchange, tax, financial crisis, house prices, loans, economic growth, consumer, financial profits, exchange rate equivalent, income, deflation, GDP, GNP, imports, exports, trade balance, consumer spending.

Note: *Danish stock market index.

The search terms were used in the population of newspaper and website articles published in this period.[4] The coders made the final manual sampling check, coding only articles about the economy. In a few cases, where a sampled news article was not about the economy, it was replaced with another randomly sampled article from the respective day and media outlet. For each outlet we sampled two economic news items per week. This was done in two steps. First we selected two days from each week. In order to make sure that all weekdays were equally represented in the sample, we started with a randomly selected weekday and then selected each subsequent fourth day. Second, one economic news article or broadcast item was randomly chosen from each outlet on each selected day. Three additional articles per outlet were included for the two weeks leading up to waves 2, 3, and 4 because these recent articles were expected to have a stronger influence than older articles (Lecheler and de Vreese, 2013). In total, 1,554 news items were analysed, which is equal to 8 percent of all economic news stories on the days of investigation (see Tables A3 and A4).

Table A3 Periods included in the manual content analysis

Period	Starting	End
Before 1st survey wave	22 January 2013	18 February 2013
Between waves 1 and 2	5 March 2013	18 May 2013
Between waves 2 and 3	3 June 2013	2 September 2013
Between waves 3 and 4	7 September 2013	26 November 2013

Table A4 Number of news items per outlet

Media outlet	News items (N)
DR	92
TV2	83
Politiken	99
Jyllands-Posten	100
Berlingske	103
BT	98
Ekstra Bladet	89
Børsen	98
DR.dk	103
TV2.dk	94
Politiken.dk	104
JP.dk	100
Berlingske.dk	99
BT.dk	97
EkstraBladet.dk	99
Børsen.dk	96

Four student native speakers of Danish were hired and extensively trained to perform the content analysis. All coders completed four months of intensive training sessions. Two meetings were held each month, for which all coders coded five news items. All precoding was extensively discussed to reach agreement on future coding. A detailed codebook describing all coding rules was distributed to the coders. At the end of the four-month period, inter-coder reliability tests were conducted to ensure the quality of the coding. The coding instructions and results of inter-coder reliability tests are reported in the individual chapters.

Integrating Survey and Content Analysis Data

The combination of survey and content analysis data that was used in Chapters 5 to 9 has become more and more prevalent in communication research. For example, it has been used to identify priming effects (de Vreese, 2004). The method involves linking each user's responses for the days of exposure to each media outlet in each wave with measures of content data for this outlet. By analysing the content of the media outlets to which news consumers are exposed, it is possible to reduce the uncertainty about *which* content they are exposed to. The content analysis is used to measure *how* specific media outlets cover the economy in relation to the relevant content features (negativity, human-interest framing, and ambiguity). The panel survey is used for measuring the *individual level of exposure to each media outlet* for each news consumer as well as the moderating, mediating, and dependent variables (how each of these variables was measured is elaborately described in each chapter). By integrating survey and content data, it is possible to assign each news consumer a score for how much he or she is exposed to the specific content features.

Currently, there is no established standard of how to combine media content and survey data when it comes to weighing news content (Schuck et al., 2016). In order to analyse the effect of exposure to mainstreamed economic news, we combined the self-reported exposure to the 16 mentioned outlets with the presence of the relevant characteristics of economic news in these outlets.

Throughout the book, we follow the argument by Schuck et al. (2016) that explains how to determine media effects when working with these weighted exposure measures. It is of crucial importance that the media effect (the link between exposure to specific content and economic perception) is theoretically supported, whereas the weighted exposure measures do not have to perform empirically better than the unweighted exposure measures.

Time-Series Analysis

In Chapters 2, 4, and 10, we look at the relation between long-term developments in the real-world economy, economic news, and economic perceptions among the audience. We test these relations with a time-series analysis of aggregated Danish media data, national consumer confidence data, and indicators of the Danish economy between August 1996 and December 2012. August 1996 was chosen as a starting point due to the availability of Danish newspapers in the online database Infomedia.

Aggregate time-series analysis has several advantages and disadvantages over cross-sectional analysis and experimental research, which determine the type of research questions that can be answered with this method (Yanovitzky and Van Lear, 2008). The main advantages are that it allows researchers to study communication as a process and make forecasts about the future. It furthermore allows them to test the direction of causality between trends that seem to influence each other. Disadvantages of the aggregated time-series method are that it cannot test or show the mechanisms underlying the relations, and it cannot be used to study the relations at an individual level or to test for differences between groups. Relations that are found at the aggregate level should not be interpreted as showing similar relations at the lower level. Due to the statistical problems that are normally present in time-series data, such as autocorrelation and multicollinearity, time-series analysis normally requires more data transformation and modelling than cross-sectional data. This means that the analysis is necessarily a combination of model building and model testing, rather than only hypothesis testing.

Combined, these characteristics make the method particularly suited to answer research questions that aim to (1) disentangle the mutual influence of seemingly correlated trends, (2) study the time-lag of effects, (3) study how dynamics vary over different time periods, and (4) study how dynamics are influenced by external events. For our study the three main *trends* for which mutual influence can be disentangled are the real state of the economy, consumer perceptions among the general audience, and media coverage of the economy. The actual state of the economy and consumer perceptions are measured with standard economic indicators. These are described in Chapters 2, 4, and 10. To measure media coverage, we conducted automated content analysis, described below.

The two main time-series analyses are used in Chapters 4 and 10.

In Chapter 4 we analyse how the tone and visibility of the economic news reflect economic developments, measured with the Composite Leading Indicators (CLI; see Chapter 4). To test this, the level of the CLI as well as positive change and negative change in CLI are included in an autoregressive distributed lag model where the aggregate tone or visibility of economic news is determined by its own past and the absolute state or change in the economy during the current month. All variables are stationary according to the augmented Dickey–Fuller test and KPSS test. The number of lags of the dependent variable was determined by the AIC, which is used to find the most parsimonious model. In addition, the final models have no autocorrelation and no multicollinearity between the lagged variables.

The tested models can be represented with the following equations:

$$Tone = \alpha_1 + Tone_{t\text{-}1,\,k} + Economic\ Indicators + neg\Delta Economic$$
$$Indicators + pos\Delta Economic\ Indicators + \varepsilon_1 \tag{1}$$
$$Visibility = \alpha_1 + Visibility_{t\text{-}1,\,k} + Economic\ Indicators$$
$$+ neg\Delta Economic\ Indicators + pos\Delta Economic\ Indicators + \varepsilon_1 \tag{2}$$

Alternatively specified models, where the lagged independent variables or several lags of the independent variables were included in the model, lead to the same conclusions. After the models were tested, a Quandt–Andrews test was conducted to see whether a structural break can be identified in the data. Such a structural break indicates a change in the dynamics of the time-series.

In Chapter 10 we analyse whether economic expectations reflect the level of uncertainty in economic coverage. We expect economic expectations to be influenced by the level of uncertainty in the previous month rather than the current month. First of all, because expectations about the future economy are so-called sticky expectations (Doms and Morin, 2004), they have a large degree of stability: It takes time for people to process new information and update their expectations. While this is our expectation about the timing of the effect of uncertainty, we start with a general model and then test the specifications, because imposing restrictions a priori may lead to biased estimates and invalid inferences (De Boef and Keele, 2008). We tested our expectations with an error correction model, which has the advantage that short-term and long-term effects can be distinguished. In addition, we tested our models with autoregressive distributed lag models, which led to the same conclusions. Series stationarity was checked with and confirmed by the augmented Dickey–Fuller test and KPSS test. The general error correction model includes both concurrent changes and lagged levels of the independent variables. We test the following models:

$$\Delta Consumer\ expectations = \alpha_1 + Consumer\ expectations_{t\text{-}1,\,k}$$
$$+ \Delta Economic\ Indicators_{\,t} + Economic\ Indicators_{t\text{-}1}$$
$$+ \Delta Tone_{\,t} + Tone_{t\text{-}1} + \Delta Uncertainty_{t} + Uncertainty_{t\text{-}1} + \varepsilon_1 \tag{3}$$
$$\Delta Consumer\ expectations = \alpha_1 + Consumer\ expectations_{t\text{-}1,\,k}$$
$$+ \Delta Economic\ Indicators_{\,t} + Economic\ Indicators_{t\text{-}1}$$
$$+ \Delta NegativeTone_{t} + NegativeTone_{t\text{-}1} + \Delta PositiveTone_{t\text{-}1,\,k}$$
$$+ PositiveTone_{t\text{-}1} + \Delta Uncertainty_{t} + Uncertainty_{t\text{-}1} \tag{4}$$

Equation 3 tests whether uncertainty in macro-economic news affects consumer expectations after controlling for the influence of consumer expectations in previous months (the lagged dependent variable), the actual economy and tone of economic news. These controls were included because tone and real-world economic developments affect consumer expectations in both lagged levels and concurrent changes (Soroka et al., 2015). Equation 4 is a variation of equation 3, where we control for positive and negative tone separately instead of combined into one tone measure.

When both lagged uncertainty in economic news and concurrent change in uncertainty were included in the time-series, neither variable was significant. When change in uncertainty is excluded from the model, lagged uncertainty has a significant effect. The model has a better fit (AIC) than the model where both change and lagged uncertainty are included. Excluding lagged uncertainty from the model and keeping change in uncertainty improves the model less, and change in uncertainty is not significant. Thus, we conclude that consumer expectations reflect lagged levels of uncertainty in economic news rather than concurrent change in uncertainty, and report the results from the time-series without the concurrent change in uncertainty (see van Dalen, de Vreese, and Albæk, 2016 for further discussion).

Automated Content Analysis

The visibility, tone, and level of uncertainty in Danish macro-economic news were measured with dictionary-based, automated content analysis (see, e.g., Doms and Morin (2004), (Hollanders and Vliegenthart, 2011); Soroka (2006) for a similar approach). The advantage of automated content analysis is that large amounts of data can be analysed, which is necessary given the long time span of the analysis. While human coders are better at classifying individual articles, automated content analysis can classify content characteristics on an aggregate level (Young and Soroka, 2012). We analysed the three most-read Danish broadsheet newspapers (*Politiken, Jyllands-Posten*, and *Berlingske*), which are expected to give a good indication of the overall economic coverage in the mainstream media because they can be considered newspapers of record. Ideally, we would base the time-series analysis on the same 16 outlets which are included in the year-long content analysis. However, due to data availability this was not possible. We assume that the monthly tone and visibility of economic news in the three analysed newspapers are an indication of overall media coverage, because monthly aggregated content characteristics of economic news show strong similarities across different mainstream media outlets (Hollanders and Vliegenthart, 2011). Instead of taking a sample, all articles on Danish macro-economy in the three newspapers were analysed.

First, we developed a search string to identify articles about the Danish macro-economy. These were operationalized as articles that refer directly to the state of the national economy or report on the main indicators and sectors of the Danish economy to describe the state of the national economy. News about the economy is defined by the subject covered rather than by the section of the newspaper in which it is printed or by the journalists writing it. Our longitudinal analysis was limited to the coverage of the *national* economy because it is compared to indicators of the Danish economy. Articles about the European economy, global economy, or US economy are only relevant if the article includes references to consequences for the Danish economy. An article about the local economy or the economy in certain parts of the country is only deemed relevant if it explicitly mentions the relation with Denmark's economy as a whole. This definition of economic news is narrower than the one used in the manual content analysis. This narrower definition was chosen because the aim of the analysis in Chapter 4 is to study the influence of economic news on perceived developments of the national macro-economy.

A literature review of content analyses of economic coverage showed broadly two types of operationalization. First, several studies operationalized news about the economy as stories that contain the term "economy" or terms that refer to the state of the economy (like "recession"; e.g., De Boef and Kellstedt, 2004; Doms and Morin, 2004). Second, several studies operationalized news about the economy as stories that refer to particular economic issues or indicators, such as "inflation" or "unemployment" (Soroka, 2006, 2012). Hetsroni et al. (2014) apply a third type of operationalization and analyse stories that deal with the main sectors of the Israeli economy (among others). This way of operationalizing probably leads to a lot of articles about individual businesses, which fall outside our definition. Therefore, this type of operationalization will be disregarded. In our operationalization of economic news, we combine the first and second types. We include stories that refer directly to the state of the national economy and stories that report on the main indicators and sectors of the economy to describe the state of the economy.

In a first step towards the development of a search string identifying relevant articles, an open search/extensive search string was used to find a broad set of articles that included all relevant articles (but also many irrelevant ones). This search string includes all search terms explicitly mentioned in 13 studies of economic news (Blood and Philips, 1995; De Boef and Kellstedt, 2004; Doms and Morin, 2004; Fan, 1993; Hester and Gibson, 2003; Hollanders and Vliegenthart, 2011; Ju, 2008, 2011; Larcinese et al., 2011; Nadeau et al., 2000; Shah et al., 1999; Soroka, 2012; Wu et al., 2002). Based on several test searches with these search terms, a narrower search string was established through an iterative process (Stryker, Wray, Hornik, and Yanovitzky, 2006). The resulting search string can be found in Box A2.

Box A2   Search string to identify articles about national macro-economic news for the automated content analysis

((econ* OR conjunt*) AND (Danish OR Denmark) in headline, subheading or first paragraph) OR ((econ* OR conjunt*) AND (Danish OR Denmark) in whole article AND (deflation, "price drop," inflation, recession, crisis, depression, downturn, decline, shrink, improvement, upswing, grow*, employment, "consumer spending," "consumer confidence," "housing market," "disposable income," competitiveness, (creditwor*NOT bank) ("balance of trade") AND (deficit, surplus))in heading, subheading or first paragraph) OR (housing* in heading, subheading or first paragraph AND "mortgage statistics" in whole article)

More negative terms (such as "deflation," "recession," "crisis") than positive terms are included in the search string, but it does not have a negativity bias. Most articles are not found by these terms but by the general terms "Denmark" and "economy." In fact, more articles are found by the positive than by the negative terms.

As a first validity check, the yearly number of articles in *Berlingske, Jyllands-Posten*, and *Politiken* identified by this search string was compared to the yearly attention to the economy in Danish radio news between 1996 and 2003. Green-Pedersen and Bjerre Mortensen (2013) coded attention to different topics in the national radio news between 1984 and 2003. Attention to the economy in the Danish national radio news is significantly correlated with the attention to the economy in *Berlingske, Jyllands-Posten*, and *Politiken*.

In the second validation step, the search string was tested for *Jyllands-Posten* and *Politiken* in the period 7 to 13 March 2013. Based on the results of this search and following Stryker et al. (2006), "precision" (percent of found articles that are indeed about the national economy) and "recall" (percent of relevant articles published during this period identified by the search string) were calculated. The search string had a recall of 74 percent and an *initial precision* of 70 percent. We downloaded all articles identified by the search string. Once these articles were downloaded, each headline was checked to exclude irrelevant texts. After that, the final precision was calculated by looking at the first paragraph of 100 downloaded articles published in *Jyllands-Posten*. Six were not relevant, leaving a *final precision* of 94 percent.

The monthly number of articles about economic news in *Berlingske, Jyllands-Posten*, and *Politiken* load on one factor and form a reliable scale (Cronbach's alpha = .79). Based on this, we combined the visibility in the three newspapers in one measure.

The monthly aggregate tone of Danish macro-economic news was measured in a similar way, based on translated dictionaries consisting of 1,789 terms indicating a negative tone in financial news and 293 words indicating a positive tone (Loughran and McDonald, 2011). The number of positive terms is considerably lower than the number of negative terms because it is harder to identify words that have only a positive meaning in a financial context (Loughran and McDonald, 2011, p. 45). In line with De Boef and Kellstedt (2004) and Goidel and Langley (1995), we subtracted the number of positive terms from the number of negative terms to calculate the monthly tone of economic news.[5] In addition, we split the overall tone measure into negative and positive tone. Monthly negative news and monthly positive news were operationalized as the share of negative and positive words respectively, compared to all words in articles about the Danish macro-economy in the three newspapers.

Loughran and McDonald (2011) previously validated the dictionaries. As an additional external validity check, we compared the results of the automated tone coding with hand-coded economic news articles, following the approach by Young and Soroka (2012). Native Danish speakers coded each of these 232 articles as having either (1) a negative evaluation of the general economic climate, (2) a positive evaluation, or (3) no evaluation. Inter-coder reliability between the coders was .73 (Krippendorff's alpha) (Svensson, Albæk, van Dalen, and de Vreese, 2017a). According to the human coders, 74 articles had a negative tone, 116 articles had no evaluation (neutral), and 42 articles had a positive tone. As a test of the validity of the dictionary-based coding, we automatically coded the negativity, positivity, uncertainty, and tone for each of these three groups of articles. The comparison of the hand coding and automated coding supports the validity of the dictionaries (all tests ANOVA with Tukey b post hoc test, $p < .05$, one-sided). Automatically coded negativity is significantly higher in the group of articles that were hand coded as negative than in the other two groups of hand-coded articles. There are significantly more positive terms in the articles that were hand coded as positive than in the other two sets of articles.

Uncertainty in economic news was automatically coded in these articles using a translated uncertainty dictionary developed by Loughran and McDonald (2011) to measure uncertainty in the context of finance. After translation, the uncertainty dictionary consisted of 243 terms—which indicate "uncertainty, with emphasis on the general notion of imprecision rather than exclusively focusing on risk" (Loughran and McDonald, 2011, p. 45)—including "perhaps," "confusing," "possibly," "indeterminable," "may," "maybe," "might," "unforeseen," "rumor," and "speculate." For each month, we analysed how many of these terms were mentioned in macro-economic news. The monthly uncertainty measure used in our study is the average number of uncertainty words per article about the Danish macro-economy in the three newspapers.[6]

Uncertainty is not related to the tone of the articles; there are no significant differences in uncertainty across the three groups of articles. The mean tone of the negative articles is significantly lower than the mean tone of articles that were classified by the coders as neutral or positive. The difference in tone between positive and neutral articles is significant at $p = .06$, which shows that the tone measure can differentiate between negative, neutral, and positive articles at an aggregate level. As is the case for the tone coding with several other word lists (Young and Soroka, 2012, p. 218), the mean tone score for the neutral articles is not 0, but −.67. As a consequence of negative terms being overrepresented compared to positive terms, the mean score for neutral articles is lower than 0. Because tone is included to explain developments in consumer confidence across months, the raw scores are of little importance. Nevertheless, to increase the interpretability of the data, we corrected for the overall low scores by adding .67 to the tone score.

Finally, we looked closely at potential overlap between the dictionary of uncertainty and the dictionary measuring tone—in particular, negativity. At the article level, uncertainty is not significantly correlated with either tone or negativity. The monthly aggregated uncertainty and negativity scores are significantly correlated ($r = .17$, $p < .05$). When monthly uncertainty and negativity for the three outlets are included in a factor analysis, uncertainty in the three newspapers loads on a different factor than negativity in the three newspapers. In the original word lists by Loughran and McDonald (2011), 40 of the terms in the uncertainty dictionary are also in the negativity dictionary. In the translated dictionary, we used 46 terms in the uncertainty dictionary that are also in the negativity dictionary. These terms account for only 5 percent of the words identified as uncertain in the automated content analysis. Comparison of the uncertainty dictionary to the negativity dictionaries AFINN (in Danish, Nielsen, 2011) and the General Inquirer (in English) showed an overlap of 22 and 35 terms, respectively. Similarity is larger with the negativity word list in Lexicoder (Young and Soroka, 2012), where there is overlap for 32 unique terms and 45 variations of these terms. Twenty-seven of the uncertainty words that were also in the Lexicoder word list were classified as belonging to those words that indicate "degree of evidence," according to Roget's Thesaurus. The preceding findings strengthened us in our conclusion that these terms do indeed indicate uncertainty. We conclude from these comparisons that uncertainty is a different construct to negativity, although not fully independent.

Notes

1 Other studies (e.g., the Reuters Institute Digital News Report) ask about news use in the previous week rather than in a typical week. Compared to asking about news use in a typical week, asking about news use in the previous week leads to a higher share of people who report never to use a medium (Chang and Krosnick, 2003). Therefore, we refrain from using these data for comparison.

2 The question wording used in the EES survey was: How often do you read the following newspapers? (*Jyllands-Posten, Politiken, Ekstra Bladet*): Every day/almost every day; several times a week; once a week; once a month; less often; never; do not know. The question wording used in our panel survey was as follows: How many days (if any) do you use the following media in a typical week (*Politiken, Jyllands-Posten, Ekstra Bladet*): None, one day, two days, three days, four days, five days, six days, seven days.

3 Infomedia is a media database that archives all Danish news articles from printed newspapers published by the different media outlets that we focus on in this book. BERTA is another, similar media database that archives all news articles published online by different media outlets. The media database BERTA was developed by Filip Walberg, Centre for Journalism, University of Southern Denmark (see, e.g., http://filip.journet.sdu.dk/berta).

4 The population of articles was obtained by a computer-assisted content analysis using two different electronic databases: Infomedia and BERTA. Infomedia is a database that archives all news articles from printed newspapers published by different media outlets. The specific search in Infomedia is conducted by using search criteria such as search words, date, and media outlet. BERTA is a new archive of all news articles published online by different media outlets. When using different search criteria such as search words, date, and media outlet, BERTA will, like Infomedia, show the population of articles fulfilling these criteria. All the broadcasted news items were requested on DVDs from the Danish State and University Library.

5 The aggregate tone per month = (number of positive terms – number of negative terms)/total number of words × 100. The monthly tone is aggregated across the three newspapers because factor analysis showed that the monthly tone for these three newspapers loads on one factor.

6 The number of words indicating uncertainty/number of articles about economy × 100. The monthly number of words indicating uncertainty in the three newspapers load on one factor.

Appendix Tables

Appendix table 4.1 Explaining the tone and visibility of economic news

	Model 1 Tone		Model 2 Visibility	
	B	SE B	B	SE B
Constant	−0.57	3.33	−47.31	72.41
Σ Tone t-1,3	0.64	0.08***		
Σ Visibility t-1, 4			0.85	0.06***
Composite Leading Indicators (CLI)	0.00	0.03	0.52	0.72
Positive ΔCLI	−0.33	0.41	9.12	9.13
Negative ΔCLI	1.05	0.34**	−18.45	7.52*
Adj. R^2	.39		.53	
AIC	272.13		1,473.48	
HQC	281.39		1,484.05	
SBC	295		1,499.58	
N	194		193	
Breusch-Godfrey	0.76	($p = 0.39$)	0.03	($p = 0.85$)
Ljung Box Q	0.02	($p = 0.89$)	0.01	($p = 0.98$)

Note: Unstandardized beta-coefficients with standard error. ***$p < .001$, **$p < .01$, *$p < .05$ (two-sided t-tests).

Appendix table 6.1 Explaining attention to economic news t2

	B	SE B	β
Constant	1.29	0.16***	
Exposure to negative economic news	0.71	0.18***	.39
Economic interest	0.21	0.04***	.21
Exposure to negative economic news × economic interest	−0.12	0.04**	−.31
Attention t1	0.41	0.03***	.38
Adj. R^2	.24		

Note: $N = 1,666$. ***$p < .001$, **$p < .01$ (two-sided t-tests).

Appendix table 8.1 Explaining attribution of responsibility t2

	B	SE B	Exp(B)
Attribute responsibility to national politicians t1	2.15	0.13***	8.59
Exposure to domesticated economic news	0.02	0.01#	1.02
Government supporter	0.39	0.14**	1.47
Constant	-2.21	0.15***	.110
N	1,666		
-2 log likelihood	1,500.56		
Percentage correctly classified	80.1		
Nagelkerke R^2	.17		

Note: ***$p < .001$, **$p < .01$, #$p < .1$ (two-sided t-tests).

Appendix table 9.1 Explaining economic government evaluations t2

	B	SE B	β
Constant	1.29	0.05***	
Exposure to economic news	0.04	0.05#	.04
Economic interest	0.06	0.02**	.06
Exposure to economic news × economic interest	-0.01	0.02	-.02
Government supporter	0.58	0.05***	.25
Economic government evaluations t1	0.52	0.02***	.55
N	1,286		
Adj. R^2	.50		

Note: Economic interest and exposure to economic news were standardized to avoid multicollinearity ***$p < .001$, **$p < .01$, #$p < .1$ (two-sided t-tests).

Appendix table 10.1 Explaining change in consumer expectations

	Model 1		Model 2	
	B	SE B	B	SE B
Constant	-109.35	24.81**	-100.53	24.39**
Consumer expectations t-1	-0.44	0.06*	-0.43	0.06**
Δ Composite Leading Indicators (CLI)	4.78	1.14**	1.12	0.25**
CLI t-1	1.17	0.25**	4.77	1.14**
ΔTone	1.00	0.39*		
Tone t-1	1.25	0.42**		
Δ Negative news			-1.59	0.53**

(*Continued*)

	Model 1		Model 2	
	B	*SE B*	*B*	*SE B*
Negative news t-1			−1.77	0.59**
Uncertainty t-1	−0.36	0.17*	−0.34	0.17*
Adj. R^2	.27		.28	
AIC	959.27		957.96	
HQC	968.56		967.25	
SBC	982.22		980.91	
N	196		196	
Breusch-Godfrey	1.14	($p = 0.29$)	1.30	($p = 0.26$)
Ljung Box Q	0.45	($p = 0.50$)	0.52	($p = 0.47$)

Note: Unstandardized beta-coefficients with standard error. $**p < .01$, $*p < .05$, $^\#p < .1$ (two-sided t-tests).

Index

Printed in the United States
by Baker & Taylor Publisher Services

Printed in the United States
by Baker & Taylor Publisher Services